Resourcing bishops

Resourcing bishops

The first report of the
Archbishops' Review Group on
bishops' needs and resources

CHURCH HOUSE
PUBLISHING

Church House Publishing
Church House
Great Smith Street
London
SW1P 3NZ

ISBN 0 7151 3854 5

Cover design by Sarah Hopper
Typeset in 10.5 pt Sabon
Printed in England by
Creative Print and Design Group,
Ebbw Vale, Wales

Published 2001 by Church House
Publishing

Contents

Foreword by the Archbishops of Canterbury and York

Bishops are central to the life of the Church of England. We are, after all, a Church that is 'episcopally led'. All the more important, therefore, that arrangements for resourcing these leaders should be adequate to enable them to carry out a ministry that has never been more demanding. It was with a view to trying to ensure that this requirement is met well into the twenty-first century that we asked Professor Anthony Mellows, Emeritus Professor of Law in the University of London, to take an objective look at the issues and to make recommendations about how we might meet the challenge. We were also well aware that the cost of bishops and their houses has been the subject of regular speculation and comment in the media.

Professor Mellows and his colleagues have now submitted their report, the text of which we are publishing so that all may see the true position. Readers will find that the report reveals no financial scandal, no profligate waste; rather it offers a thorough analysis of the current and developing needs of episcopal ministry and makes a number of recommendations as to how present arrangements might be improved. We shall be consulting widely with our brother bishops, their wives and staff, diocesan boards of finance, the Church Commissioners and other interested parties before reaching decisions on which of those recommendations should be taken forward and how.

In commending this report for reflection and debate, we wish to offer two words of thanks. One is to Professor Mellows and his team for their painstaking analysis of the issues and their energy in undertaking the complex task we set them. The other is to our brother bishops, their wives and their dedicated staff. We know at first hand how heavy are the demands on them and how devotedly they serve the Church. If the work of this review serves to educate people about something of the nature of those demands, it will already have done the Church a very useful service.

George Cantuar: David Ebor:
June 2001

Chairman's preface

The Archbishop of Canterbury and the Archbishop of York asked us to carry out our work in two phases, the first relating to the needs and resources of bishops, and the second dealing with the needs and resources of archbishops. This report is on the first phase.

Early in the course of our review, we became aware that there is only a partial understanding of what bishops do and of the present arrangements whereby they are resourced and, in view of this, we have sought to explain at some length the present position as well as to make our recommendations. In doing so, we have assumed that readers of this report will include those who have a general interest in the subject, but who may have no particular background knowledge or relevant professional skills. We hope that this approach may be helpful both in the overall consideration of our recommendations and also in the course of the reviews which we recommend should be conducted of the bishops' working and living accommodation in each diocese.

There were a number of background factors to our review. There was a recognized need for bishops to be properly resourced, so that they could carry out their ministry effectively. But there was increasing concern, both on the part of the Church Commissioners and also of members of the wider Church, that the costs of supporting episcopal ministry seemed to be rising inexorably, at a time when the amount which the Commissioners were able to provide for the support of parochial ministry was falling. These factors need to be seen in the context of the substantial increase in the local funds which have been raised for parochial ministry. But the factors were reflected in, and fed by, increasing public criticism of bishops, much of which was ill-informed. Although our work proceeded in the context of these factors, we were also aware that the archbishops wanted to take the opportunity of the review to be forward-looking, and for it to have a place in constructive planning for the future.

We were determined to understand the present arrangements, but we did not start with any presumption that major alterations would be necessary. Indeed, we were fully prepared, had we thought it right to do so, to make a recommendation that in all material aspects the present arrangements should continue. However, as we considered the resources which bishops need against the background of increasing financial stringency of the Church of England at central and diocesan levels, we concluded that the continuance of the present arrangements unaltered is not a realistic or responsible option.

We have made over a hundred recommendations, but do not regard our work as being in any way complete in itself. We have regarded ourselves as being at the start of a continuing process in which our recommendations will need to be developed and refined in debate, discussion and further consideration. We are also aware that in some respects our work is bound to be regarded as incomplete, as it directly interrelates with other matters which lie outside our terms of reference. Those matters which have been raised with us, and which seem to us to warrant further study, are listed in Appendix F to this report. However, in order to accommodate other points which have been raised with us we have in some respects adopted a liberal interpretation of our terms of reference.

At the outset, we were made aware that the Commissioners had carried out a review of see houses in the recent past, and although we did not concern ourselves with the detailed specification for a see house, we rapidly concluded that the living and working accommodation of both diocesans and suffragans should form an integral part of our review. We have dealt particularly with those aspects in the last part of the report.

We have consulted widely and we are very grateful to all those, both within the Church and outside it, who have willingly helped us. We are also most grateful for two original contributions to the subject which informed us and which we think should be made generally available. These are a paper on the theology of the episcopacy by the Right Reverend Professor Stephen Sykes, formerly Bishop of Ely and now Principal of St John's College, Durham and a paper on the legal role of bishops by Mr Peter Beesley, a senior partner of Messrs Lee Bolton & Lee. Much time and care went into the preparation of those papers, and we reproduce them as Appendices D and E.

We should also like to record our appreciation of the consistently helpful and supportive stance of the Church Commissioners and their staff throughout our work and, in particular, of our secretary, Stuart Deacon, who was seconded to us by the Commissioners and whose diligence and emollience have contributed to no small extent to our work. In addition, we should like to record our thanks to my personal secretary, Debbie Bishop, who throughout the review uncomplainingly laboured on preparing many papers for our work as well as drafts of this report.

We have all regarded it as a privilege to be asked to participate in this review. We have been conscious of our independence and that we are not part of any formal church structure. At the beginning of our work each of us was unknown to most of the others. In prayer and in vigorous but honest debate, we have developed our own cohesion and have reached a common mind.

Our report is unanimous.

I end on a personal note. The work of this review has been demanding. It has involved many meetings and much time and endeavour outside meetings. I am deeply grateful for the unfailing support which I have had throughout this process from every one of my fellow members of the Review Group.

Anthony Mellows

The Review Group
and its terms of reference

The following were appointed by the Archbishops:

as chairman Professor Anthony Mellows, TD, LL D, Emeritus
Professor of Law at King's College in the University
of London

as members Mr Richard Agutter, senior adviser to KPMG,
chartered accountants, and formerly chairman of
KPMG International Corporate Finance. Currently
an alderman and sheriff of the City of London

The Reverend Canon Bob Baker, parish priest, until
December 2000 a church commissioner elected by
the General Synod and a member of the Church
Commissioners' Bishoprics and Cathedrals Committee,
and since December 2000 prolocutor of the province
of Canterbury

The Venerable Richard Inwood, Archdeacon of Halifax

Mr Alan King, chairman of the Bath and Wells
Diocesan Board of Finance since 1990 and chairman
of the Consultative Group of Diocesan Board of
Finance Chairmen and Secretaries since 1999.
Member of the General Synod. Until 1998 managing
editor of the *Bristol Evening Post*

Mr Luke March, corporate governance director of
British Telecommunications until April 2000.
Currently chief executive of the Mortgage Code
Compliance Board

The Right Reverend Peter Nott, Bishop of Norwich
until 1999

Mr Peter Parker, TD, Fellow and sometime vice-president of the Institute of Actuaries. Formerly chairman of Phillips & Drew International Limited

Mrs Lou Scott-Joynt, wife of the Bishop of Winchester, associate member of the Church Commissioners' Bishoprics and Cathedrals Committee as Representative of Bishops' Wives

as secretary   Mr Stuart Deacon, on secondment from the Church Commissioners

The terms of reference of the Group were:

To assess the staff and other resources which are needed now and which are likely to be needed in the next decade in order to provide adequate and efficient administrative and other support for the ministry of bishops (both diocesan and suffragan); to assess the cost of providing such support; to assess the resource implications for the Church Commissioners and the wider Church; and to make recommendations to the Archbishops.

The Group has interpreted these terms of reference as requiring it:

a.   to consider, in its many different forms, the work and role of bishops at the present time;

b.   to consider how that work is likely to evolve by the year 2010;

c.   to consider the resources which bishops need now, and which they will need by that time, in order to carry out their work; and

d.   to consider how those resources are to be funded.

The Group was also asked to consider the needs and resources of the Archbishops, for which separate terms of reference were prescribed. Its findings will be the subject of a second report to be published in due course.

Expressions and abbreviations and their meanings

Expressions

In this report, unless it appears otherwise from the context, we use the following expressions with the following meanings:

area bishop
A suffragan whose primary responsibilities relate to a geographical area within a diocese.

bishop
A bishop, whether archbishop, diocesan, suffragan or assistant bishop, who receives a stipend for acting in that capacity.

Bishops' Resources Group; or Resources Group
The diocesan bishop's small advisory group which we recommend should be formed to advise with regard to resources for all bishops in the diocese. See para. 10.20.

clergy
Although technically the term includes bishops, for the purposes of this report, 'clergy' means all ordained ministers who are not bishops.

Commissioners
The Church Commissioners for England.

Department
The Bishoprics and Cathedrals Department of the Commissioners.

diocesan
A diocesan bishop.

ecclesiology
We use this expression in the special sense of 'the principles which underlie the structure and organization of the Church of England and the roles of its office holders, both ordained and lay, including their respective rights, duties and obligations'. See para. 2.5.1.

Episcopal Committee   A committee of the Commissioners with some members nominated by the Archbishops' Council which we recommend should be established. See para. 10.7.1.

episcopacy; episcopal   Derived from the Greek word for oversight, it denotes the role of a bishop in caring for, guiding, leading and teaching churches and congregations. Episcopacy is not a ministry that is only exercised by bishops, but is something that is shared with others in the Church. However, in this report, in general, we use the expression in the restricted sense of referring to that part of the ministry which is exercised by a bishop.

fiduciary account   An account to be operated by the Diocesan Board of Finance, not for its own money, but for money held by it on trust for the bishops of the diocese. See para. 10.30.4.

hospitality   We use this expression to refer to the ministry of welcome, which is related to that hospitality enjoined on all Christians in the New Testament and which bears little resemblance to its secular use in the term 'corporate hospitality'.

long term, medium term or short term   We regard short term as being up to five years; medium term as being between five years and ten years; and long term as being in excess of ten years.

official   We use this expression in relation to a bishop to refer to his capacity as such, as contrasted with his capacity as a private individual. It is similar in non-church contexts to 'business' or 'duty'.

Ordinal   The form of service by which a person is consecrated and ordained as a bishop.

outsourcing	Making arrangements for the supply on commercial terms of goods or services by a third party.
parish share	The amount payable by a parish to its Diocesan Board of Finance towards the cost of activities within the diocese and central overhead expenditure. Also sometimes called 'parish quota' or 'common purse'.
pro bono	Voluntary or free of charge.
Provincial Episcopal Visitors	Suffragan bishops who provide alternative episcopal oversight under the provision of the Episcopal Ministry Act of Synod 1993. See para. 16.34.1.
see	The office held by a diocesan or suffragan bishop. All sees have a territorial title, but the powers, rights, duties and responsibilities may and usually do extend beyond that territory.
see house	Living and, usually, working accommodation provided for a diocesan and his personal support staff. However, we exclude from the expression the accommodation provided for the Archbishops of Canterbury and York, which will be the subject of a separate report. Although a suffragan has a see, it is only a house provided for a diocesan which is referred to as a see house.
suffragan	Any stipendiary bishop or stipendiary assistant bishop who is not a diocesan. Suffragans are: • area bishops; or • suffragans, with no specific geographical area of responsibility; or • Provincial Episcopal Visitors (see further para. 3.5.2).

suffragan's house   Living and, often, working accommodation
provided for a suffragan.

working costs   We use this expression in the same sense as
that in which it is used by the Commissioners
in their annual report and accounts. The
expression includes the costs of a bishop's
personal support staff; of his and their office
accommodation; and travelling and hospitality
expenses. It is in no way confined to a
bishop's personal expenditure, but to a large
extent covers the cost of conducting various
activities within the diocese.

Abbreviations

We also use the following abbreviations with the following meanings:

AABM   Archbishops' Adviser on Bishops' Ministry

ASB   Alternative Service Book, 1980

BCP   Book of Common Prayer

BCC   The Bishoprics and Cathedrals Committee of the
Commissioners

DBF   Diocesan Board of Finance

IT   Information technology, particularly for the purposes of
this report, the means of electronic communication such
as e-mail

PEV   Provincial Episcopal Visitor: see the definition above

chapter 1

Overview and summary of recommendations

Overview

1.1　Our general findings on the evidence presented to us are that:

a.　bishops are very hardworking – perhaps excessively so;

b.　the pressures on them are increasing;

c.　they do not have lavish lifestyles;

d.　there is no place in which the total cost of the support for episcopal ministry is clearly stated;

e.　the range of the facilities which are currently made available to bishops is, broadly, appropriate to the role as it is currently perceived. Any material reduction in facilities would necessitate a change in what bishops are expected to do. In some respects the resources may need to be improved;

f.　the members of the Commissioners' staff who operate the present arrangements centrally have a substantial collective knowledge base, and seek to respond constructively and supportively;

g.　the present system does not encourage financial crispness in approach, but does encourage excessively overdetailed central financial management;

h.　the expression 'bishops' working costs' can readily give a misleading impression because for the most part they are not bishops' costs in a personal sense, but costs incurred in the day-to-day activities of the Church of England, mainly in the dioceses;

i.　the system produces anomalies and inequities between one bishop and another and between the bishops in one diocese and those in another;

j.　the system does not produce the best value for money;

k.   the system does not encourage bishops to exercise
financial management and control; and

l.   there is inadequate recognition of the principle of
partnership between the central organs of the Church on
the one hand and dioceses on the other hand in the support
of episcopal ministry.

A continuing process

1.2   We have not regarded our review as an endeavour which is
complete in itself, but as part of a continuing process. Consideration
of the issues will be necessary by a number of bodies, such as, as
well as bishops individually, the Archbishops' Council, the Church
Commissioners, the House of Bishops, the General Synod and
Diocesan Boards of Finance. We have intentionally formulated some
of our recommendations with a sufficient width to enable them to
be developed in those discussions. We hope that to the fullest practical
extent a consensus will emerge from those discussions.

1.3   Some of our recommendations could be implemented by
administrative action. Many will require consultation and discussion.
Some would require legislation. It follows that some of our recommendations could be implemented in the short term; some are for the
medium term; and some are for the long term.

The recommendations

1.4   We make 20 keynote recommendations:

1.   The provision of all resources should be measured against
standard principles (Chapter 9).

2.   The Commissioners should have a much reduced role in the
detailed provision and management of resources for the support of
episcopal ministry (paras 10.9; 11.5.1.a; 11.6).

3.   Activities should only be conducted at the centre where there
is a demonstrable need or benefit in doing so (para. 10.8.1).

4.   There should be a new approach to the budgetary allocation of
central funds to be deployed in support of episcopal ministry (para.
10.14).

5.   With certain safeguards, bishops should be given much greater financial control and independence (para. 10.18).

6.   This should be achieved by making a block-grant to the diocesan bishop of each diocese (para. 10.17).

7.   In deciding upon the use of the block-grant, as well as dealing with other resourcing issues, the diocesan bishop should be assisted by a small Resources Group to be appointed by him (para. 10.20).

8.   The amount of central funds to be made available by block-grant should be determined by formula (Chapter 12).

9.   Where there is a reduction of expenditure by the Commissioners as a result of the implementation of any of the proposals, there should be a corresponding increase in the amount distributed to dioceses by Selective Allocations (para. 10.3.2).

10.   Revised accounting treatment should be adopted by the Commissioners and in particular it should be made clear that most of the expenditure currently described as 'bishops' working costs' is not related to the personal ministry of bishops, but to the administration of the Church of England locally and nationally (para. 10.42).

11.   There should be full disclosure of expenditure on working costs and premises, both under the present regime and under the proposed regime for block-granting (para. 13.11). Information about this expenditure should be made available both within the diocese and to all bishops (para. 13.13.d).

12.   There should be a modification to the rules about secrecy in certain aspects of the process for the appointment of new bishops (para. 14.16.2).

13.   There should be widely recognized the incalculable debt of gratitude owed to bishops' wives (para. 17.1).

14.   There should be adopted the general principle that no wife of a bishop should be prevented from pursuing her own career or from following other activities by the demands made on her by her husband's ministry or by the house in which they are required to live (para. 17.6).

15.   There should be a review in each diocese of the living and working accommodation provided for all bishops in that diocese (Chapter 19).

16.   If a see house is found to be no longer appropriate, it should be replaced at the expense of the Commissioners (para. 18.32.2).

17.   Ultimately the Commissioners should transfer without charge the ownership of see houses to DBFs (para. 18.37.3).

18.   There should be special provisions regarding the Church's responsibility for national heritage properties which are currently used as see houses (para. 19.38).

19.   The amount to be paid from central funds for the maintenance and repair of see houses should be redefined and limited (para. 18.32.3).

20.   The ultimate transfer of the ownership of see houses to DBFs should be accompanied by a transfer to them of the obligation to maintain and repair the houses (para. 18.37.4).

1.5   We also make further recommendations. In some instances they develop the keynote recommendations and in other instances they are independent of them. These further recommendations are as follows:

21.   Bishops should be fully involved in the preparation of all budgets which affect them (para. 6.19.a).

22.   Bishops should receive full management accounting information in respect of budgets which affect them (para. 6.19.b).

23.   Where there is an exercise of a discretion in relation to the provision of resources, there should be made clear: the fact that a discretion has been exercised; the result of the exercise of that discretion; the name of the person or persons by whom the discretion was exercised; and the factors which were taken into account (para. 7.8.2).

24.   There should be a fundamental review of the extent to which professional legal assistance is required and the method and cost of its provision (para. 7.14.2).

25. There should be a strong presumption that where future church legislation would impose additional duties on a diocesan, then those duties should be capable of being undertaken on his behalf by some other person nominated by him (para. 7.16.1).

26. A proposal for new legislation which would impose further duties on a bishop should be accompanied by a time and resource assessment (para. 7.16.2).

27. Where it does not happen at the present time, DBFs should be strongly encouraged to provide diocesans with part-time bishops' press or communications officers (para. 7.17.2).

28. It should be clearly recognized that there is a partnership between the Commissioners and DBFs in funding the support of episcopal ministry (para. 10.4).

29. The Bishops' Resources Group should contribute to the preparation of any episcopal strategy plans (para. 10.25).

30. There should continue to be a national committee, called in this report an Episcopal Committee, with specific responsibility for the support of episcopal ministry (para. 10.6.1). It should at least initially be a committee of the Commissioners (para. 11.5.1.b).

31. Stipends, diocesans' living and working accommodation and central services should for the time being continue to be funded by the Commissioners (para. 10.14).

32. The DBF should act as banker in respect of block-granted funds (para. 10.30).

33. Any funds which the DBF provides in support of episcopal ministry should be credited to a fiduciary account (para. 10.33.2).

34. No part of an underspent block-grant should be returned to the Commissioners (para. 10.35).

35. The Commissioners should not be expected to make good any local overspend (para. 10.37).

36.   Accounts should be produced within each diocese of the expenditure of block-granted funds (para. 10.39.1).

37.   The Commissioners' accounts should contain a note showing how block-granted funds have been spent (para. 10.42).

38.   There should be greater use of outsourcing: it should not be confined to cars (para. 11.11.1).

39.   The archbishops should consider appointing senior bishops as episcopal consultants (para. 11.20).

40.   There should be a fresh start to the budgetary process (para. 12.9).

41.   The same formula should be used for the separate purposes of indicating the cost of episcopal support and of determining the allocation of central funds (para. 12.10.1).

42.   The Episcopal Committee should determine the formula amount in relation to the bishops of each diocese (para. 12.17).

43.   Separate discussions should be held with each diocese to identify special circumstances to be taken into account in determining the formula amount (para. 12.18.2).

44.   All special circumstances which are taken into account should be made known (para. 12.18.3).

45.   In the event of any insufficiency of the Commissioners' funds for the support of episcopal ministry, the Selective Allocations approach should be followed in determining DBF contributions (para. 12.21.3).

46.   The bishops in each diocese should receive a statement showing the calculation of their block-grant (para. 12.22).

47.   The calculation of the formula amount should not govern the way in which the block-grant is spent (para. 12.23.2).

48.   There should be no adjustment to the formula amount for an underspend (para. 12.24.2).

49.   The principle of mutual support might be followed between the bishops of one diocese and those of another (para. 12.24.3).

50.   The amount of a block-grant for one year should not be reduced merely because of an underspend in a previous year (para. 12.25).

51.   Disclosure of the expenditure of funds should be in a standard format (para. 13.13).

52.   Such disclosures should be reconciled with the Commissioners' accounts (para. 13.15).

53.   In order to counteract distortions, a rolling ten-year record should also be prepared (para. 13.18).

54.   In the case of new appointments, the period between when a candidate is first approached and when the announcement of his appointment is made should be kept to the minimum (para. 14.16.3).

55.   The induction course for a newly appointed bishop should include training in time and diary management; effective use of personal staff; financial management; and office procedures (para. 14.40).

56.   There should be a coordinated timetable for consecrations and induction courses (para. 14.42).

57.   There should be adequate time between the announcement of the appointment of a new bishop and when he takes up office (para. 14.46).

58.   Immediately following the announcement of the appointment of a new bishop, he should be put in touch with the Resources Group of the diocese in which he will serve (para. 14.47.2).

59.   Removal expenses should be treated separately from resettlement expenses (para. 14.49).

60.   Removal expenses incurred by a bishop on retirement should be reimbursed to him (para. 14.50).

61.   There should be a structured hand-over between an outgoing bishop and his successor (para. 14.52).

62.   On appointment, every new bishop should be informed of any proposals to carry out major works to his house (para. 14.26.2).

63.   Every new bishop and, if he is married, his wife, if she so wishes, should be encouraged to have mentors (para. 14.29.1). The mentors should be from a different diocese from that in which the new bishop will serve (para. 14.29.3).

64.   There should be one designated officer in each province to handle all aspects of the consecration of a newly appointed bishop and the post-consecration reception (para. 14.36.1). Payment for the reception should be made centrally (para. 14.36.2).

65.   All newly appointed bishops should be strongly encouraged to participate in an induction programme, to spend a week in residential preparation for the post, to go on retreat, and to have a holiday (paras 14.37; 14.40).

66.   There should be another designated officer in each province to coordinate all aspects of the appointment process (para. 14.18.2).

67.   All suffragans should have job descriptions (paras 14.20.2; 16.15).

68.   There should be regular appraisals of all suffragans (paras 14.21; 16.10).

69.   All diocesans should have a clear Statement of Expectations (para. 14.22.1).

70.   There should be regular reviews by the archbishops of progress against those statements (para. 14.23.2).

71.   Before being invited to accept an appointment, every new bishop should be told what resources will be made available to him (para. 14.24).

72. Bishops' Resources Groups in a region should liaise to consider the provision of resources on a collective basis (para. 15.3).

73. The possibilities of obtaining *pro bono* support should be actively pursued (para. 15.5).

74. So far as possible, a bishop should have freedom to choose his personal support staff (para. 15.10).

75. A bishop's secretary or secretaries should be employed by the DBF (paras 15.12.1; 15.13.1), but the bishop should continue to have the same involvement as at present in the selection process (para. 15.13.1.c).

76. Where it is necessary for a bishop to have a driver, the Bishops' Resources Group should explore the possibility of contract hire of a car and driver (para. 15.20.4).

77. The Resources Group should consider how the travel needs of all bishops in the diocese might best be met (paras 15.20.4; 15.21.1).

78. There should be published guidelines as to the class of train travel (para. 15.22.2).

79. Certain expenses incurred in travelling to a meeting of a church body outside the diocese should be charged to that body (para. 15.24.2).

80. Reimbursement of expenses incurred in travelling to a meeting of an outside body should generally be sought from that body (para. 15.24.3).

81. The Resources Group should explore the possibilities of obtaining locally IT equipment, training and support conforming to national protocols (para. 15.26.4).

82. The Resources Group should consider how facilities for hospitality might best be provided (para. 15.29).

83.   In the consultations leading to the appointment of a new suffragan, full account should be taken of the longer term needs of the national Church as well as those of the diocese (para. 16.14.2).

84.   The principle of 'need not status' should apply to the provision of resources for both diocesans and suffragans (para. 16.19.1.a).

85.   The Resources Group should be concerned with the provision of resources for all bishops in the diocese (para. 16.19.1.b).

86.   Special financial arrangements should be made to facilitate the interchangeability of the posts of suffragan and archdeacon (para. 16.27.1).

87.   The housekeeping allowance for single diocesans should be phased out, but not so as to prejudice those currently serving (para. 16.32.1).

88.   The Resources Group should take account of any exceptional costs which are imposed on bishops – whether married or single – by virtue of the nature of the accommodation which they are required to occupy (para. 16.32.3).

89.   A separate Resources Group should be established for PEVs (para. 16.40).

90.   The chairman of the PEVs' Resources Group might have a wider role (para. 16.42).

91.   A bishop's wife who is acting directly in support of her husband in the exercise of his ministry should be provided with the appropriate resources to do so (para. 17.13.2).

92.   The resources for a bishop's wife should be arranged by the Bishops' Resources Group (para. 17.13.4).

93.   Certain conditions should be satisfied when a bishop employs his wife (para. 17.14.3).

94.   Except in relation to catering, a decision to employ a bishop's wife should never be taken by the bishop alone (para. 17.15.1).

95.   The circumstances in which a bishop's wife may charge for catering should be clarified (para. 17.16).

96.   Rooms should continue to be provided in a see or suffragan's house for the provision of hospitality if those rooms are also to be used for meetings (para. 18.21.1).

97.   The norm for a see house should be four bedrooms for private use (apart from a bedroom for official guests) (para. 18.24.3).

98.   The Commissioners should reappraise the guidelines for a see house (para. 18.25).

99.   If a suffragan's secretary's office is in the house, the Commissioners should pay the heating, lighting and cleaning costs attributable to it (para. 18.28.2).

100.   The present arrangements with regard to the cost of the maintenance and repairs of see and suffragans' houses should continue for the time being (para. 18.29.2).

101.   Where the cost of maintaining and repairing a see house is greater than it otherwise would be because it is a heritage property, then those costs should be identified separately, and accounted for separately (para. 18.35.1).

102.   For a five-year transitional period the Commissioners should contribute to the cost of maintaining and repairing see houses transferred to DBFs (para. 18.39.1).

103.   All suffragans' houses should have, at the minimum, a room or other space for worship (para. 18.43.4.a).

104.   A chapel should be provided in a suffragan's house only where there is a demonstrable need (para. 18.43.4.b).

105.   There should be a written licence governing the terms of occupation of see and suffragans' houses (para. 18.45.3).

106.   There should be a modification of the Commissioners' obligation to seek the best price which is reasonably obtainable when dealing

with any heritage properties which cease to be used as see houses (para. 19.39).

107. The group to review the living and working accommodation of bishops in a diocese should have an independent chairman, and its members should include the diocesan, the chairman of the DBF and a representative of the Commissioners (para. 19.43).

108. The diocese-by-diocese reviews of accommodation should be initiated by the Commissioners (para. 19.44).

Part I

chapter 2

Theological background

Introduction

2.1   In this chapter we outline the early historical development of the episcopacy, and say something of the theology of the episcopacy and its practice. We also state our position in relation to ecclesiology.

2.2.1   Those whose primary interest is in the practical issues which we have been examining may wonder why this chapter is given such a prominent place, at the beginning of this part of our report. While much of our work has been concerned with practical issues, our starting point has always been prayer and theological reflection. Indeed that prayer and reflection have informed our work at every stage, and we therefore thought it important to share at this stage something of the theological basis for our considerations. As we hope will become clear in the remainder of this report, theology has guided our work and has had direct consequences for almost every aspect of it.

2.2.2   We have read a number of articles and papers on the subject, and have been assisted in our reflection by a variety of reports, not least that of the Archbishops' Group on the Episcopate 'Episcopal Ministry' (1990), generally known as the Cameron Report. We are also very grateful for the time Professor Stephen Sykes spent with us, and we reproduce his valuable paper as Appendix D.

2.2.3   At an early stage we asked one of our members, Bishop Peter Nott, to lead our theological reflection on the episcopate, and the remainder of this chapter is based on the paper he wrote.

History

2.3.1   In the days following Pentecost, the structures of the Early Church were rudimentary. They were concerned with converting unbelievers and founding local congregations. There was also a strong sense that they were living 'in the last days' – that is, they had a vivid expectation that Christ's coming again was imminent and that the world would end. These factors naturally meant there was little imperative for formal structures. The task of forming a permanent organization and introducing systematic instruction remained in the background until this expectation receded and the rapid spread of the faith made it a practical necessity.

2.3.2 At first, the twelve apostles were the sole directors and administrators of the Church. Then, in order to leave themselves free for their chief work of 'prayer and ministry of the Word'[1] they enlisted help, through which the first of the threefold orders of ministry developed. They appointed seven deacons, whose prime function was to relieve the apostles of practical tasks, though it is clear that quite soon the deacons also became involved in preaching. From the beginning there do not seem to have been clear boundaries between forms of ministry.

2.3.3 The second order of ministry to emerge was that of presbyters.[2] They were modelled on the elders of the synagogues. In each local church there was invariably a board or college of elders, who were responsible for the administration and government of the local church, as well as for teaching and the conduct of public worship. The existence of these 'colleges' is significant. For the Early Church, teamwork in ministry was the norm. The concept of an individual ministry was as alien to the young Church as it had been in Judaism.

2.3.4 The development of a distinctive third order of ministry is more difficult to trace. In the New Testament the terms 'bishop' and 'presbyter' are interchangeable, and for the first 50 years at least there was a twofold, not a threefold, ministry. But, although the details of the process are obscure, it is clear that by the middle of the second century the threefold ministry of bishops, presbyters and deacons had become firmly established.[3]

2.3.5 How did the separate office of bishop come into being? Most historians conclude that it developed from the college of presbyters, in which the head, chairman or president of the college became known as the bishop. Others have suggested that bishops were appointed to succeed the apostles. There is little evidence for this, because although some of the twelve apostles may have become the first bishops, the offices are certainly not identical. For example, apostles were very much universal figures of authority, while bishops presided over local areas. The earliest bishopric was in Jerusalem where the apostle James was regarded as a bishop in the later sense, that is, having precedence, but still a member of the body of elders. Even in the fourth and fifth centuries bishops referred to themselves as 'fellow presbyters'.

2.3.6   Another factor in the growth of bishops as a separate order was probably the death of the twelve apostles. As they were martyred one by one, a new focus of unity and authority would have been needed in the local churches, as well as the gathering together of local bishops in councils in order to guard the unity of the whole Church. In fact, this function of the bishop as a sign and focus of unity quickly became central to the meaning of episcopacy.

2.3.7   Ignatius of Antioch, writing at the end of the first century, is the earliest writer who is clear about the distinctive threefold ministry. He held an exalted view of the office, but he gets to the heart of the meaning of episcopacy as a focus of unity when he writes 'avoid divisions, as the beginning of evil. Follow, all of you, the bishop as Jesus Christ followed the Father'.[4] It is worth noting that Ignatius was also responsible for another saying about bishops, which many people cherish, that a bishop is most like God when he is silent.[5] Underlying this saying, which is not entirely tongue-in-cheek, is a reminder that the bishop's ministry is shared with others, and woe betide the bishop who forgets that first and foremost he remains a deacon.

Theology

2.4.1   For Christians and Jews, theological conviction has normally developed through reflecting on historical experience. Hence the development of episcopal ministry has itself pointed to many of its theological characteristics.

2.4.2   The notion of apostolic succession is often misunderstood. It can denote the physical link of the laying on of hands from apostles to bishops in succession through the centuries, but the difficulties of proving such a physical succession are obvious. More importantly, it has come to mean that bishops are the successors to the apostles in terms of teaching the apostolic faith and maintaining apostolic unity. Apostolic succession thus stands for the given nature of episcopacy. The development of episcopacy was not just a practical necessity but providential: it is a gift of God. Indeed, it is that understanding, rather than historical mechanisms, which enables fruitful ecumenical dialogue about episcopacy to take place.

2.4.3   A theology of ordained ministry is rooted in a theology of the total ministry of the Church, of which it is a part. This is one reason why the threefold ministry of the Church always has two distinct purposes. First, it consists of people who perform certain functions in the Church – they have a job to do. Secondly, it exists as a sign to the whole Church of the meaning of ministry. Every baptized man, woman and child is a minister, and through understanding the meaning of the diaconate, priesthood and episcopacy, he or she will come to understand the meaning of his or her own ministry. Episcopacy is not something exercised exclusively by a particular group of ordained people. It is focused and exemplified in the ministry of bishops, but the ministry of leadership, teaching, unity and pastoral oversight is a ministry that is shared with many other people, both lay and ordained.[6]

2.4.4   It follows from the historical development of the threefold ministry that there is a special relationship between the bishop and his fellow clergy. This particular aspect of shared ministry is expressed in a number of ways, both practical and symbolic. For example, at the institution of a new incumbent, the bishop traditionally commissions the priest with the words 'Receive the cure of souls, which is both thine and mine'[7] (now often revised as 'Receive this charge which is both yours and mine').

2.4.5   Consequently, it is imperative that the bishop is committed to teamwork and understands his leadership in these terms. The whole theology of the Church as the Body of Christ implies that the Church's leadership will exemplify and promote this understanding.

2.4.6   All this is closely linked to the bishop's vocation to be a focus and an enabler of unity. It is a vocation that is complex, reflecting the nature of unity itself. For example, the bishop is both a local and a universal minister. It is sometimes mistakenly thought that the apostolic nature of the bishop's ministry means that he is sent to the local church by the universal Church. The truth is that the bishop is rooted in, and belongs to, his diocese; but he also belongs to the universal Church, which he represents to the local church. Keeping the balance between these two is not easy, but it is essential that this tension is maintained if the truth of episcopacy is to be upheld.

2.4.7   Although language about the bishop as the 'icon of Christ'[8] is little known in mainstream Anglican theology, there is no doubt that as a figurehead he is often seen as representing Christ in an authoritative way, and the bishop is certainly the focus of people's expectations and criticisms of the Church. He carries the public image of the Church, and in this sense the word 'icon' is not inappropriate. This is why it is important for bishops, as for all Christian ministers, constantly to remind themselves of the source both of their understanding of their ministry and of the grace that alone enables them to exercise it.

2.4.8   All Christians are called to witness by their lifestyle to the values and priorities of the gospel. But, as the public representatives of the Church, clergy in general and bishops in particular have a special responsibility in this respect. Their witness, for example, to the values of simplicity and hospitality can be of great importance.

2.4.9   The liturgy of the Ordinal, which provides the basis for the meaning of episcopacy, highlights history, theology and practice as together providing a balanced understanding. However, before considering it, we comment on ecclesiology.

Ecclesiology

2.5.1   We have been cautious about the use of the word 'ecclesiology'. In correspondence and conversation it has been used, but in a variety of ways and with no agreed definition.[9] To facilitate the dialogue, we have adopted a definition of our own. Our definition of 'ecclesiology' is: 'The principles which underlie the structure and organization of the Church of England and the roles of its office holders, both ordained and lay, including their respective rights, duties and obligations.'

2.5.2   In considering the provision of resources for bishops, these principles may be said to relate particularly to balance: to the unity that should exist between the Church at the centre and the Church in the diocese.

2.5.3   Our position in relation to ecclesiology, in the sense in which we have defined that expression, is that:

> a.   it is no part of our function to propose any change to the ecclesiology of the Church of England as an end in itself;

> b.   we should endeavour to be aware of ecclesiological consequences which might flow from the implementation of any of our recommendations; and

c. we should reflect with particular care and caution before making any recommendations which, if implemented, might lead to a change in ecclesiology.

Practice

2.6.1 In the service for the ordination (or consecration) of a bishop,[10] the archbishop prefaces his examination of the candidate with the following exhortation:

> A bishop is called to lead in serving and caring for the people of God and to work with them in the oversight of the Church. As a chief pastor he shares with his fellow bishops a special responsibility to maintain and further the unity of the Church, to uphold its discipline, and to guard its faith. He is to promote its mission throughout the world. It is his duty to watch over and pray for all those committed to his charge, and to teach and govern them after the example of the Apostles, speaking in the name of God and interpreting the gospel of Christ. He is to know his people and be known by them. He is to ordain and to send new ministers, guiding those who serve him and enabling them to fulfil their ministry.
>
> He is to baptize and confirm, to preside at the Holy Communion, and to lead the offering of prayer and praise. He is to be merciful, but with firmness, and to minister discipline, but with mercy. He is to have special care for the outcast and needy; and to those who turn to God he is to declare the forgiveness of sins.

2.6.2 One cannot read a job description into the Ordinal, but the liturgy sets the priorities for a bishop's ministry.

2.7 As the leader of the Church's mission, it is the bishop's vocation to enable and encourage that mission through the variety of ways in which his ministry is exercised:

2.7.1 He teaches: through preaching, through writing, in personal interviews, in synods and councils, and through the media. He bears ultimate responsibility as 'guardian of the faith' for maintaining and setting forth the truths of the Christian faith in his diocese and, together with his fellow bishops, in the nation.

2.7.2 He ordains. He is, with his brother bishops, and advised by various people, responsible for selecting, training and commissioning men and women for the work of ministry. Also, under this heading, is much of the day-to-day work of a bishop in advising people about their ministry, and in appointing clergy and lay ministers to parishes and other posts. He is in a real sense the interpreter of the will of God for the Church and its ministers.

2.7.3   In the Church of England (but not in other churches) he confirms. This derives from the historical function of the bishop in the Early Church as the chief celebrant of the Eucharist (the only celebrant in the small areas the first bishops cared for). It is also a practical way in which he can share with his priests in the initiation and nurture of new Christians.

2.7.4   He administers. Good order is part of effective pastoral care and of his vocation to maintain the unity of the Church. Some bishops may become too much involved in administration, but it cannot and ought not to be avoided altogether, for it is part of what care for the Church means. Nevertheless, the burden of administration has undoubtedly become heavier in recent years, and it is essential that ways are found for bishops, as well as receiving adequate resources, to share more of this aspect of their ministry with others.

2.7.5   He meets with his fellow bishops as part of his ministry in the wider Church. A bishop is not just local, but part of an episcopal team, or college, which ministers to the Church and nation as a whole, and which is linked to bishops in other areas in the world. Hence the double concern of those who select bishops – taking into consideration both the needs of the local church and of the Church at large.

2.7.6   He is involved in the secular world. The bishop has natural links with leaders of the community in many spheres: local authority, professional and commercial. It is here that the diocesan has unique opportunities, for the secular world is by nature hierarchical and sees him as the leader of the Church in the area. Whatever one's personal views about such thinking, it is a feature of secular life to be used by the bishop in the interests of mission.

2.7.7   In this context, the ministry of welcome, of creating and maintaining relationships through the giving and receiving of hospitality, is potentially of immense importance. In a sense this aspect of the bishop's ministry is but an extension of the hospitality traditionally offered through the use of the parsonage house. But its sheer scale, and the opportunities it provides as part of the bishop's mission, are very different from those of a parish priest.

2.7.8   The involvement of senior bishops in the House of Lords has been a significant ministry, which is highly valued by many both inside and outside Parliament.

2.7.9   Ministry to the clergy of the diocese has a high priority for both diocesans and suffragans. The clergy of the diocese are licensed under authority to the diocesan, and in human terms they are answerable to him. In turn, he is responsible for their care and discipline, a ministry that is shared especially with suffragans and archdeacons, but also with many other ministers, both ordained and lay.

2.7.10   This pattern of care and responsibility in general serves the Church well, but it begs certain important questions. To whom is the diocesan accountable? The order for the consecration of bishops in the Book of Common Prayer includes an oath of obedience to the archbishop of the province – the oath is now generally taken outside the liturgy[11] – which would seem to answer the question, at least in theory. But how real is that accountability? To whom are archbishops accountable? Conversely, who exercises responsibility for the pastoral care and discipline of diocesans and archbishops? These questions at present seem to have no answer, but the immense and increasing responsibilities borne by the holders of these offices clearly call for the issue to be addressed.

2.7.11   If a bishop is to exercise effective pastoral care and discipline, offer strategic thinking within the diocese and in the wider field, and provide leadership in teaching and mission, then time for prayer, reading, reflection and rest must have a high priority. The difficulties are notorious, but the need is paramount, and it is not merely a personal need, but in the best interests of the whole Church. Related to this, many would say that the bishop's ministry of teaching in prayer should have a prominent place, and that teaching is most effective through the sharing of one's own experience.[12]

Suffragan bishops

2.8.1 The Ordinal recognizes no distinction between types of
bishop. All are called and ordained to the same ministry. They are all
members of the same order of ministry. This needs emphasis, because
sometimes people talk as if a suffragan is a totally different kind of
bishop. There is a parallel in the ministry of priests. There are varieties
of post occupied by priests, but they share the same order of ministry
and the same basic vocation. The differences are essentially differences
of function and responsibility. Similarly, to speak of the differences
between diocesans and suffragans in terms of rank or status could be
said to bear little relationship to a New Testament understanding of
the varieties of ministry within the Body of Christ.[13]

2.8.2 The word 'suffragan' denotes someone who exercises a
vote on another person's behalf: hence the suffragan is someone to
whom the diocesan delegates certain functions. (Contrary to a common
assumption that diocesans have always been national figures, while
suffragans remained local, it is interesting to note that in the Middle
Ages there is evidence that diocesans sent suffragans to international
councils to deputise for them, preferring themselves to remain in their
home dioceses.)

2.8.3 There is, however, a clear difference between diocesans and
suffragans in terms of legal authority. A diocesan (but not a suffragan)
is referred to as 'the Ordinary'. This means that he has original
jurisdiction; that is, it does not depend on delegation by anyone. By
contrast, a suffragan has no jurisdiction of his own, and may perform
only such of the diocesan's functions as are delegated to him.[14]

2.8.4 The legal differentiation naturally involves differences in
function. The position varies from diocese to diocese, but in general
the evidence reveals a clear difference in the weight of responsibility
between that borne by a diocesan and that borne by a suffragan. But
it is not adequate or accurate to describe the ministry of a suffragan as
merely 'an extension of the ministry of the diocesan'. In some dioceses,
suffragans exercise episcopal oversight in defined geographical areas,
and often have a considerable degree of autonomy within those areas.
Their responsibilities within the area are often akin to those of a
diocesan – indeed some area bishops have larger areas, with a greater
population, more clergy and parishes than some dioceses. Where there
is only one suffragan, it is not usually feasible for him to have

responsibility for a geographical area, but he can have a sphere or spheres of responsibility in which he exercises episcopal leadership. Delegation does not imply dependence, but a genuine sharing between diocesans and suffragans.

2.8.5   Some people have maintained that the suffragan is an anomaly because the unity of the Church can only be focused on one bishop. Therefore, the argument goes, if a diocese is too large for one bishop, there ought to be more dioceses rather than the creation of suffragan bishoprics. The practice of the Church of England seems to indicate that this view is no longer held, but it is evident in conversation and correspondence that a minority does still believe it to be true.

2.8.6   However, there is another theological view, which is perhaps more deeply rooted in Scripture. The unity of the Church is complex, not simple. It is clear from the evidence of the New Testament and from developments in the apostolic age that ministry is corporate by definition. Therefore, it can be argued that a corporate episcopate at every level more truly represents the truth about the nature of ministry than the single bishop. Teamwork, it should be noted, does not diminish the function of leadership. On the contrary, it is much more demanding of leadership skills than autocracy. During the course of our review, we were interested to note the emphasis, in his enthronement sermon,[15] of the new Bishop of Ely, Dr Anthony Russell. When speaking of the ministry he shares with the suffragan bishop of Huntingdon, he said, 'Episcopacy in this diocese is a single function performed by two people.'

2.8.7   Just as all orders of ministry exist as signs to the whole Church of the meaning of its ministry, so episcopal teamwork exists as a sign to clergy and laity of the meaning of shared ministry. The importance of this witness to the Church (and to the world) should never be underestimated.

Conclusion

2.9   In any study of the ministry of the Church, history, theology and practice are intertwined and influence each other. We have never assumed that the examination of resources for the episcopate is a 'practical' issue devoid of other considerations. On the contrary, our understanding of the history and theology of the Church and its ministry, as much as pragmatism, has informed our deliberations and our conclusions.

chapter 3

Bishops and the context of their work

Introduction

3.1.1 In Chapter 2, we included an outline of some of the practical aspects of a bishop's ministry, and how they had arisen from historical and theological considerations. Because many of these features of episcopal ministry are rooted in Scripture and the life of the Early Church, they have formed a common thread of episcopal priorities through countless generations. On the other hand, there are aspects of any ministry which are historically conditioned, but which are to be seen in the contemporary context in which the ministry is exercised.

3.1.2 Although certain fundamentals do not change, the ministry of a bishop is always affected by its context. (See also Appendix D, para. 11 in this report.) That is particularly true in our present age because of the number of radical and far-reaching changes in the structures of the Church which have happened in the last 50 years. The purpose of this chapter is to indicate some of the ways in which a modern bishop's ministry relates to, and is profoundly affected by, that context. Accordingly, in this chapter we outline first the structure of the episcopate within the Church of England, then the relationship of a bishop with the main diocesan bodies with which he works, and finally something of what his work involves.

Dioceses

3.2.1 Dioceses are the *basic* unit of church administration within the Church of England.[1]

3.2.2 Originally, a diocese was a local worshipping community of which the bishop was the chief pastor. However, the concept subsequently developed into the present one of a geographical area within which there are a number of worshipping communities or churches. The bishop continues to be the chief pastor.

3.3.1 In the Church of England, there are 44 dioceses. Forty-two of these dioceses are in England.[2] One is in the Isle of Man.[3] The remaining one, the diocese in Europe,[4] is headquartered in England, but its main territorial area is in mainland Europe.

3.3.2 Thirty dioceses form the Province of Canterbury and the remaining 14 dioceses form the Province of York.

Bishops

3.4 Each diocese has a diocesan bishop. Generally, in this report we refer to him as 'the diocesan'.

3.5.1 In most, but not all, dioceses there are, in addition to the diocesan, one or more suffragan bishops.

3.5.2 For our purposes, we divide suffragans into three categories:

a. Area bishops, who have particular responsibilities in respect of a geographical area within the diocese. They may act under either a formal or an informal Area Scheme;

b. suffragans, who do not have particular responsibilities in relation to a geographical area, but who may have particular responsibilities for specific aspects of the life of a diocese; and

c. Provincial Episcopal Visitors or PEVs. Their geographical areas of activity are wider than diocesan boundaries and we describe them in further detail in Chapter 16.[5]

3.6.1 There are also three categories of assistant bishop.

3.6.2 An assistant bishop can be stipendiary and can have a full-time or part-time appointment. At 1 January 2001, there was only one full-time stipendiary assistant bishop in post. The Commissioners treat him for resourcing purposes as a suffragan and we do likewise.

3.6.3 Second, some bishops who were consecrated for service abroad are living in England and are serving as parish priests or in some other non-episcopal role. The diocesan may, but by no means always does, appoint them to be honorary assistant bishops in the diocese. They do not receive any enhanced stipend by virtue of being in episcopal orders[6] and if they incur any expenses in performing an episcopal role on behalf of the diocesan,[7] those expenses are usually reimbursed by the diocesan. Assistant bishops in this category are not treated as suffragans by the Commissioners for resourcing purposes.

3.6.4 Third, the great majority of assistant bishops are those in episcopal orders who have retired from stipendiary posts in England or elsewhere. They are appointed by the diocesan as honorary assistant bishops in the diocese in which they are resident. Like retired clergy, they receive no stipend or other remuneration, but are reimbursed the expenses which they incur.

3.6.5 None of our recommendations are directed towards honorary assistant bishops.

3.7 There are exceptional cases. In one case the same person holds the offices of suffragan bishop and archdeacon. In another, an assistant bishop provides part-time services in exchange for a house. We expect that in constantly changing circumstances, the number of exceptional cases will increase. The proposals which we make in this report are deliberately flexible, and we think that they will accommodate these exceptional cases.

3.8 Our proposals are confined to bishops who are in episcopal posts, that is, they are serving as diocesans or suffragans (including area bishops). We do not consider those who, having served as diocesans or suffragans, are now serving in some other post.[8]

Number and disposition of bishops

3.9.1 As at 1 January 2001, there were established episcopal posts for 113 bishops. These were:

  a. 44 diocesan bishops, including the archbishops of Canterbury and York;

  b. 36 area bishops;

  c. 30 suffragans without special responsibilities for a geographical area; and

  d. 3 Provincial Episcopal Visitors.

3.9.2 Details are given in Appendix C.

3.9.3 It will be seen from that Appendix that the number of bishops within each diocese varies markedly.

Bishops and clergy[9]

3.10.1 During the period from 1975 to 2000 there was a slight increase in the number of bishops, from 107 to 113.

3.10.2 During the same period there was a fall of about 20% in the number of stipendiary clergy.

3.10.3 We have not been able to obtain full statistics about the numbers of non-stipendiary clergy during this period.

3.10.4 The number of clergy pensions has risen during the period.[10] Although there are obvious difficulties of definition, a material proportion of retired clergy continues to be active.

3.10.5 A diocesan, with the assistance of others, ministers to all clergy in the diocese, whether stipendiary or non-stipendiary and whether serving or retired, as well as to readers and others in non-ordained roles. Because of difficulties of definition and the absence of figures we cannot be precise, but it seems to us likely that although the proportion of bishops to serving stipendiary clergy has risen during the period, the proportion of bishops to all clergy has been broadly static.

The constitutional and legal framework

3.11 There may be an impression that a diocesan bishop is the head of a diocese in somewhat the same way as the chairman of the board of directors of a major commercial company is the head of that company; that the diocese of which the diocesan is the head has an integrated management structure; and that as the head of that structure the diocesan is a person of considerable power and influence.

3.12 The reality is very different. There is no integrated management structure within the diocese, but a number of bodies which to a greater or lesser degree are disparate. Furthermore, although the diocesan is a person of influence, the legal powers which he possesses are limited.

3.13 Our understanding of these issues has been much assisted by Mr Peter Beesley,[11] who, at our request, wrote a paper on 'The legal role of bishops'. We reproduce it as Appendix E. This appears to be the first occasion on which the various aspects of the subject have been brought together in this way. We are grateful for the time and care which were involved in preparing this paper, and we commend it for wider reference.

Diocesan structures

3.14.1 In the light of Mr Beesley's paper, we consider next the main bodies within a diocese with which a bishop will work. Apart from parishes, the main bodies in the diocese are:

    a.   the diocesan synod;

    b.   the bishop's council;

    c.   the Diocesan Board of Finance; and

    d.   the bishop's senior staff meeting.

3.14.2 In addition to these bodies, there is a multiplicity of boards, some statutory and others not; some self-standing and others as committees of the diocesan synod or bishop's council.

3.15.1 The *formal* relationships so far as the diocesan is concerned are as follows:

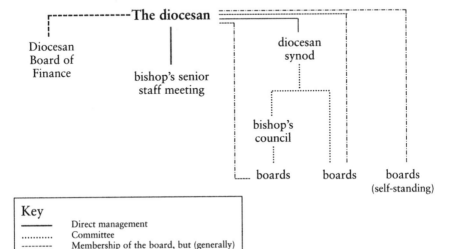

3.15.2 It will be noted that:

a.   the diocesan is the president of the diocesan synod. He is required to take the chair for certain items of business, but he usually shares the chairmanship with the clerical and lay vice-presidents or vice-chairman;

b.   likewise, the diocesan is also the president of the bishop's council, but he is not necessarily the chairman of it;

c.   the bishop's senior staff meeting is a body chaired by the diocesan. It is the only one of these bodies where the business is as the diocesan decides; and

d.   the diocesan is an *ex officio* member and director of the DBF, although he will not normally be its chairman.

3.15.3 Many suffragans are not members of the DBF, but suffragans are always members of all three other bodies.

The diocesan synod

3.16.1 The Church of England is said to be episcopally led and synodically governed.

3.16.2 The concept of a synod, as developed within the Church of England, is that of a council, with separate constituencies or 'houses' of bishops, clergy and laity presided over by the diocesan.[12]

3.16.3 The remit of a diocesan synod is remarkably wide. It includes:

a.   considering doctrinal and other matters referred to it by the General Synod;

b.   considering non-doctrinal matters concerning the Church of England in relation to the diocese and making provision for those matters; and

c.   considering 'any other matters of religious or public interest'.[13]

3.16.4 The diocesan synod must also approve the delegation of powers to suffragans.[14]

3.16.5 Furthermore, the bishop is under a statutory duty 'to consult with the diocesan synod on matters of general concern and importance to the diocese'.[15]

3.16.6 The diocesan is not as a matter of law bound by advice given by, or opinions expressed by, the diocesan synod, but 'where the assent of the bishop is required to a resolution of the diocesan synod, it shall not be lightly nor without grave cause be withheld'.[16]

3.17 The results, in practice, are that the clergy and laity, through their representatives, are involved in the policy decision-making and consultation process, and accordingly, that these matters are not within the exclusive remit of the diocesan, or of all the bishops in the diocese together.

The bishop's council
3.18.1 There is in each diocese a bishop's council.[17] It is both:
    a.   the standing committee of the diocesan synod; and
    b.   a body advisory to the diocesan.

3.18.2 The diocesan is the president, but not necessarily the chairman, of the bishop's council. Its membership is as determined by the diocesan synod[18] and varies widely from one diocese to another.

3.18.3 The bishop's council can discharge all or any of the advisory and consultative functions of the diocesan synod.[19]

3.18.4 In practice, the bishop's council is the main body in which the strategy for the diocese is evolved. It is also concerned with appointments to sector ministry and certain other non-parochial posts.

The bishop's senior staff meeting
3.19.1 A diocesan will have regular meetings with his senior staff.

3.19.2 It is for the diocesan to decide who should attend the meetings, but the core membership will include the suffragans, the archdeacons and the dean[20] of the cathedral. In most cases the diocesan secretary, and in some cases the chairman of the DBF, will also be members. The diocesan may invite others of his choice to attend on a regular or occasional basis.

3.19.3 It is for the diocesan to determine the procedure to be followed at the meeting, and which of those present are to be voting members.

3.19.4 This group is not statutory, and it has no externally prescribed function. It is advisory to the diocesan and deals with such business as he thinks fit. Usually a major part of its business is to consider clergy appointments and other personnel issues.

The Diocesan Board of Finance

3.20.1 There is a Diocesan Board of Finance (DBF) for each diocese.

3.20.2 a. Each DBF is organized as a company limited by guarantee;

b. Each DBF is registered as a separate charity; and

c. Some, but not all, DBFs are registered for VAT purposes.

3.20.3 As limited liability companies, DBFs are governed by the general provisions of company law. The members are usually the same persons as the directors and, as directors, they have the same rights and duties as directors of other companies. The directors of a DBF may form an executive committee, as a committee of the board, to conduct most of its business. As a matter of general company law, the chairman owes his primary obligation to the company and not to the diocesan.

3.21.1 The Articles[21] of the DBF provide for the election of its chairman. This is usually dealt with annually, although in most cases the chairman is eligible for re-election. The chairman is not a salaried officer and provides his services voluntarily.

3.21.2 Unless there is any provision in the Articles to the contrary, the diocesan may be elected to be the chairman of the board, but in practice this is unusual. If the diocesan is so elected, he holds that position in his personal capacity and not in his capacity as bishop.

3.22 In outline, the functions of the DBF are:

a. to act as the central financial arm of the diocese;

b. to provide central services to parishes and others within the diocese; and

c. to own and manage diocesan assets.

3.23   Under the first heading, the DBF:

a.   prepares the annual budget, monitors the financial performance against that budget, and prepares the statutory accounts;

b.   receives contributions from parishes (the contributions usually being known as 'parish shares' or 'parish quotas');

c.   in some cases receives an allocation from central funds (generated by the Church Commissioners and directed to it by combined decisions of the Commissioners and the Archbishops' Council);

d.   pays for its own operations, including the salaries of those employed by it;

e.   funds the stipends and housing of parish and other clergy in the diocese, including archdeacons;

f.   funds the pension contributions of stipendiary parish clergy[22] (a responsibility which is currently being absorbed with transitional assistance from the Commissioners);

g.   provides office facilities for, and pays the working costs of, archdeacons and other sector ministers;

h.   provides houses and, if separate, office accommodation for suffragans; and

i.   makes a contribution towards the administrative costs of the Archbishops' Council and the national costs of training clergy.[23]

3.24   As the provider of central services, the DBF is generally the employer of the officers who provide those services.[24]

3.25   In its capacity as the owner and manager of diocesan assets, the DBF maintains parsonage houses[25] and owns and maintains other clergy houses in the diocese, including the houses of suffragans.

3.26   In practice, the chairman of the DBF, in addition to acting as such, generally acts as an adviser to the diocesan on diocesan financial matters and is usually a key member of the bishop's council.

3.27　The senior salaried officer of the DBF is the diocesan secretary. The details vary from one diocese to another, but broadly, the diocesan secretary is responsible for the management of the activities of the DBF and certain other diocesan bodies, and for the oversight of the staff employed at the diocesan office. The diocesan office is the building or, if there are more buildings than one, the main building in which the DBF conducts its activities.

The structures in practice

3.28　Various practical measures, which differ from one diocese to another, are taken to improve the efficiency and harmonization of these bodies.[26] These measures may include having a substantial similarity of membership of the bishop's council and an executive committee of the DBF, or a substantial similarity of membership of the diocesan synod and the DBF. In many dioceses, the bishop's council takes the initiative in bringing about this harmonization.

Diocesan boards

3.29　In addition to these main structures, there are various diocesan boards dealing with matters such as education, mission and ministry. The diocesan is generally at the minimum a member of these boards.

Responsibilities and powers

3.30.1　This brief outline of the diocesan structures leads to more general consideration of the bishop's responsibilities and powers, particularly those of the diocesan.

3.30.2　As is clearly shown in Mr Beesley's paper, there are responsibilities of different natures: they might be classified as canonical,[27] legal[28] or moral,[29] and there might be an overlap between one category and another.[30]

3.30.3　There is, however, a mismatch between a bishop's responsibilities and his enforceable powers to discharge them.

3.30.4　Some acts which a bishop does are those which he is empowered to do by virtue of being a bishop.[31] Examples are to confirm or to ordain. These acts may be circumscribed by canon law, but in order to do them the bishop does not need any further authority.

3.30.5 For other acts, a bishop needs some external authority, or, before doing so, he needs to go through some external process. As has been stated,[32] this external element will usually involve the diocesan synod or the bishop's council.

3.30.6 For yet other acts, the bishop neither has nor requires canonical or legal authority, but he does them in exercise of moral authority. An example would be to exercise his influence to intervene in the affairs of the Diocesan Board of Finance were something to go seriously wrong.

Observations

3.31.1 Certain points stand out. First, with regard to the diocesan structures, the diocesan has no power of direction over the DBF. It is relevant for the purposes of this report to note that the bishop can ask the DBF for the provision of certain resources and, as will be seen, many DBFs do assist, but he cannot *require* those resources to be provided.

3.31.2 Second, also with regard to the diocesan structures, with the possible exception of the bishop's senior staff meeting, the diocesan has no executive control over any of these bodies. Wide consultation is valuable, but the process necessarily affects the time which the bishop must devote to their affairs.

3.31.3 Third, it has been suggested to us that the distinction between the acts which a bishop is empowered to do by virtue of being a bishop and those for which he needs some further authority might be followed in the way in which resources are provided or funded.[33] It will be seen that we have rejected that approach, partly because much of what a bishop actually does falls outside either category.

3.31.4 More generally, the mismatch between responsibilities and powers means that to exercise effective leadership, the bishop has to act by persuasion, encouragement, exhortation and example. This system has its merits, but it is time consuming. It requires a collaborative style of episcopal leadership. Furthermore, episcopal ministry is a relational process in which bishops share the task of episcopacy with others.[34]

Working hours

3.32.1 Finally, we note the very long working weeks[35] of bishops.

3.32.2 At our request, most bishops (and their wives) completed long questionnaires for us, and many also completed detailed time-sheets. From these it appears that although the position varies from bishop to bishop, a not unusual pattern is that:

> a.   a bishop attempts to take off one day out of seven, but often commitments intrude, so that, on average, bishops work for about six and a half days out of seven;
>
> b.   the average day[36] starts at about 7.30 a.m.[37] and finishes at about 10 p.m.;[38] so that
>
> c.   the working week is of the order of 70 to 100 hours; and
>
> d.   working at this level is not exceptional, but the norm.

3.32.3 Bishops and almost all clergy, as well as working very long hours, are subject to pressures. In the case of bishops, the particular pressures are that much of the work carries a high degree of responsibility and is undertaken under the spotlight of public scrutiny and a considerable degree of media interest.

chapter 4

The financial context

The cost of episcopal ministry

4.1.1 In order to put our review into a financial context, we sought to establish both the total cost of episcopal ministry in the Church of England at the present time, and that part of the cost which is applied in the provision of resources for bishops.

4.1.2 The information does not appear to have been previously collated and published.

4.2 Although it is not widely referred to in this way, there is a partnership between the Commissioners and DBFs in funding episcopal ministry.

4.3 The present arrangements are that:

4.3.1 The Commissioners pay for:

a. the stipends (and associated pension contributions) of all bishops serving in episcopal posts;

b. all or part of the cost of pensions of retired bishops;

c. certain central services which are provided for all bishops;

d. the personal staff and other working costs of bishops;

e. legal costs incurred by bishops in the discharge of their official duties; and

f. the cost of providing working and living accommodation for diocesans.

4.3.2 Diocesan Boards of Finance (DBFs) pay for:

a. the cost of providing working and living accommodation for suffragans; and

b. the cost of providing accommodation for some bishops' chaplains; and

4.3.3 DBFs may, by local arrangement, make additional contributions. Examples are the payment for a bishop's press or communications officer, who is usually part-time, or payment of part of the salary of a lay assistant, or the provision of IT support, where the costs of these resources exceed the amounts which the Commissioners are prepared to meet under their current practice.

4.4 For this part of our enquiry we have considered:

a. the duties of the Commissioners to apply funds in support of episcopal ministry;

b. the way in which these duties are currently being exercised; and

c. the financial support which is being provided by DBFs.

The Commissioners' obligations: the background

4.5 We refer to three background factors to the Commissioners' obligations in relation to the funding of episcopal ministry. First, during the last two centuries the sources of the funding of episcopal ministry have progressively changed from being derived from assets owned by bishops (in their official capacity) to general funds of the Commissioners over which the bishops have no rights of ownership.

4.6 A simple summary of the history of this development is as follows:

4.6.1 Until the beginning of the nineteenth century bishops were the legal and beneficial owners of the episcopal estates, and funded their ministry from money derived from those estates;

4.6.2 In 1836, the income from the episcopal estates of the more wealthy sees was subjected to a levy for distribution to the poorer sees.[1] This was intended to lead to an average income for each see, but the ownership of the episcopal estates was unaffected;

4.6.3 By a combination of legislation passed in 1840 and 1850, the predecessors of the Commissioners[2] established a common fund which was derived partly from income from the episcopal estates and partly from certain cathedral estates which were redistributed at that time.[3] The episcopal estates remained vested in the bishops. They retained an income from them, of a fixed amount which was determined by Order in Council, and the excess was paid into the common fund;

4.6.4   In 1860 the ownership of the episcopal estates was transferred to the Commissioners, subject, in effect, to a legal charge on the income of these estates to secure the payment of the fixed amount;[4]

4.6.5   In 1943 the charge on the income was abolished;[5] so that:

4.6.6   Since 1943 the support of episcopal ministry by the Commissioners has depended on the Commissioners' performance of certain duties, and the exercise of certain discretions. Neither the amounts required for the performance of those duties nor those for the exercise of discretions have been secured on any specific part of the Commissioners' funds.

4.7.1   The second background factor relates to the Commissioners' obligations in respect of what are frequently referred to as areas of need and opportunity.

4.7.2   In 1840 the then Commissioners[6] were required, from the common fund, to make 'additional provision . . . for the cure of souls in parishes where such assistance is most required, in such manner as shall . . . be deemed most conducive to the efficiency of the Established Church'.[7]

4.7.3   This obligation was reinforced in 1998. The Commissioners are now required[8] in relation to the management of their assets 'to have particular regard to' the requirements of the 1840 Act 'relating to the making of additional provision for the cure of souls in parishes where such assistance is most required'.

4.8   The third background factor is that the Commissioners are under a duty to fund pensions for service prior to 1998.[9]

4.9   The Commissioners have told us that they estimate that their present funds are, very approximately, derived from three main sources:

    a.   about 24% from the former episcopal estates;[10]

    b.   about 30% from the former cathedral estates;[11] and

c. the remaining 46% from the assets of Queen Anne's Bounty,[12] the former Clergy Pension Fund, and certain parochial endowments.[13]

The Commissioners' present obligations

4.10.1 The Commissioners have:

a. duties (which have to be discharged before any discretionary payments can be made); and

b. discretions, which may be:

i. as to matters to which, as stated in paragraph 4.7.3, they are 'to have particular regard'; and

ii. as to other matters.

4.10.2 When considering the exercise of their discretion, the Commissioners must always keep to the forefront of their minds the matters to which they are to have particular regard, but they must also take account of the other matters.

4.11 The present position is as follows:

4.11.1 *Stipends of diocesans* The Commissioners have an obligation to pay the stipends of *diocesans*, but it is for them to decide what amount is 'appropriate'.

4.11.2 *Stipends of suffragans* The Commissioners have a discretion to pay the stipends of suffragans, and if they decide to do so, they have a discretion as to the amount.

4.11.3 *See houses* The Commissioners have an obligation to provide a 'suitable' residence, but it is for them to decide what is 'suitable'.

4.11.4 *Office expenses* The Commissioners have a discretion to pay 'office expenses' of diocesans and suffragans to the extent that they are 'necessary'.[14] The Commissioners must, therefore, decide, first, what expenses are necessary, and second, whether to pay all or some of them.

4.11.5 *Travelling and other expenses* Travelling and other expenses, apart from office expenses, are not provided for in the legislation, but on historical grounds they are considered together with stipends.

4.11.6 *Discretions generally* In considering the exercise of their discretions, the Commissioners have regard to the statutory duties placed on bishops. In the exercise of all discretions, the Commissioners must act reasonably.

4.12 In the exercise of their discretions, the Commissioners need to balance on the one hand the payment of the stipends of suffragans and bishops' office expenses, and on the other hand the other discretionary purposes, particularly those in the category of needs and opportunities.

Commissioners' financial support of episcopal ministry

4.13.1 The latest statutory accounts of the Commissioners available to us have been those for the year which ended on 31 December 1999. Those accounts were not prepared for the purpose of bringing together the total cost to the Commissioners of supporting episcopal ministry, and they do not do so. We have, therefore, made our own analysis, and, in doing so, we have considered:

> a. stipend and pension costs;
> b. accommodation costs;
> c. working costs; and
> d. central overhead costs.

4.13.2 We recognize that there are exceptional items in almost any year, and that care needs to be taken in extrapolating figures of one year to another. We also recognize that there can be particular difficulties in apportioning various items of overhead expenditure. However, we have no reason to think that the figures for 1999 to which we refer do not give an adequate indication of the general position.

Stipend and pension costs

4.14 Stipend and associated costs are not within our remit, and we do not comment on them in any detail. We merely note that in 1999 the total cost of bishops' (both diocesans' and suffragans') stipends was £3.5 million. This includes pension contributions of £461,347.

4.15.1 With regard to pensions, until the end of 1997 pensions for retired bishops, in the same way as pensions for retired clergy, were paid by the Commissioners from their current income.

4.15.2 As has been noted, the Commissioners continue to be liable for the payment of pensions to retired bishops and their widows, in the same way as for pensions to all retired clergy and their widows, so far as the pensions are attributable to service prior to 1998.

4.16.1 The Pensions Measure 1997 introduced a new funded scheme with effect from 1 January 1998. It applies to bishops and other clergy.

4.16.2 Contributions are paid into a separate fund operated by the Church of England Pensions Board. Contributions are the responsibility of the body which pays the stipend. For most clergy, that is the DBF out of monies provided by parishes. For bishops they are paid by the Commissioners.[15]

4.16.3 The members of the scheme do not pay contributions.

4.16.4 The pension contributions paid for bishops in a year cover the cost of the pension accruing during that year's service. When a clergyman is made bishop, he immediately becomes entitled to a higher rate of pension for all the previous years of his ministry. In common with the practice in defined benefit contributory schemes generally, the cost of that enhancement is met from general contributions to the scheme and is not identified separately for attribution to the costs of bishops.

4.17.1 On retirement, a bishop receives a lump sum of the same amount as other clergy. This is equivalent to three times the amount of the basic clergy pension. He also receives a pension which is calculated as a multiple of the basic clergy pension.[16]

4.17.2 The Church of England Pensions Board does not maintain records which indicate how much of the total pension payment[17] is attributable to pensioners' service as bishops.

4.18 Accordingly, excluding that part of pensions paid to retired bishops and their widows in respect of pre-1998 service as bishops, we adopt the Commissioners' figure of £3.5 million for the cost of stipend and in-service pension contributions.

Accommodation: recurrent costs

4.19 The Commissioners' accounts show recurrent expenditure in 1999 on 'bishops' housing' of £3.3 million.

4.20.1 We were supplied with the following breakdown of this figure:

	Expenditure in relation to diocesans[18] £	Expenditure in relation to suffragans £	Other expenditure £
Maintenance and repairs	1,309,465		
Depreciation	179,993		
Gardeners' pay and pensions contributions	724,887		
Council tax	368,045		
External agents' fees	142,313		
Lambeth Palace expenditure			96,067
Block property insurance			150,662
Lambeth Palace Library			381,536
Miscellaneous		28,700	
Net rental income from see houses	(83,992)		
	2,640,711	28,700	628,265
Grand Total			£3,297,676

4.20.2 We will comment on the Lambeth Palace items in our second report.

4.21 There are four reasons in particular why we think that the description 'bishops' housing' needs explanation.

4.22.1 First, the figure of £3,297,676, rounded up in the accounts to £3.3 million, applies, with minor exceptions, only to the housing of diocesans.

4.22.2 Second, the description accords with the legislation by referring to the provision of a suitable 'residence'. In earlier times by far the predominant use of a bishop's house was indeed as his residence, with only ancillary use as a place of work. However, the house is now substantially a place of work.

4.22.3 As we describe later (para. 5.11), most see houses comprise:

a. working accommodation for the bishop himself;

b. office accommodation for his staff;

c. accommodation for meetings and receptions;

d. a chapel; and

e. private living accommodation.

4.22.4 We fully realize that this does not affect the amount of expenditure from church funds, but in our view the more appropriate description is 'working and living accommodation'.

4.22.5 It will be seen (para. 5.20) that for income tax purposes it is necessary to draw a distinction between the private residential use and other uses of see houses. By applying these principles, we calculate that not less than 62.5% and, in some instances, much more, is attributable to what we consider to be working use.

4.23 Third, the figure in the accounts for bishops' housing is for recurrent expenditure only, and does not cover expenditure on major improvements or other capital expenditure. To that extent, it does not represent the total cost. We refer to capital values below (para. 4.42).

4.24.1 In the fourth place, houses are managed by agents (with some agents managing more than one house). Out of 43 see houses (excluding Canterbury), 34 were managed by external agents, that is, members of outside professional firms. The Commissioners plan that by June 2001 the remaining 9 houses will also be managed by external agents leaving the Commissioners to continue to manage directly Lambeth Palace and the Old Palace at Canterbury.

4.24.2 The figure for bishops' housing includes only the fees paid to external agents. The cost of members of the Commissioners' own staff comes within central administration costs (see para. 4.30).

4.25 In assessing the cost of the provision of working and living accommodation for diocesans, accepting that the capital expenditure is excluded and the cost of the Commissioners' staff is accounted for separately, we adopt the Commissioners' figure of £3.3 million.

Working costs

4.26 The Commissioners' 1999 accounts show[19] as bishops' working costs, all of a recurrent nature:

Staff salaries, fees and pensions	£5.1 million
Other working costs	£3.4 million
	£8.5 million

4.27 We were provided with the following analysis:

	Expenditure in relation to diocesans[20] £	Expenditure in relation to suffragans £	Other expenditure £
Office costs			
Staff salaries and pension contributions	2,916,311	853,199	
Office expenses	561,118	310,918	
Office equipment	100,419	68,530	
Office furnishings[21]	nil	32,088	
Sub-total	3,577,848	1,264,735	
Travel and hospitality			
Travel	250,431	190,967	
Motor cars	234,361	186,614	
Drivers' pay	310,906	nil	
Hospitality	251,751	114,986	
Sub-total	1,047,449	492,567	
Accommodation			
Heating, lighting and cleaning	167,564	nil	
House and garden items	111,620	15,093	
Sub-total	279,184	15,093	
Other			
Consecration expenses, robes, resettlement and removal expenses	38,311	97,497	
Miscellaneous and exceptional items	224,217	122,580	
Sub-total	262,528	220,077	

	Expenditure in relation to diocesans £	Expenditure in relation to suffragans £	Other expenditure £
Salaries, pension contributions, and travelling expenses of Archbishops' Appointments Secretary, Clergy Appointments Adviser, Archbishops' Advisers on Bishops' Ministry			296,931
Bishops' legal officers' and other fees			784,923
Overseas travel			155,531
Other, including accommodation at meetings of the House of Bishops and General Synod; media training; car insurance; biennial medicals; office equipment insurance			130,920
	5,167,009	1,992,472	1,368,305
Grand Total			£8,527,786

Comment

4.28   We do not doubt the figures with which we have been supplied, but we are concerned with the description of these items as 'bishops' working costs'. This description seems to us to give a misleading impression. The great majority of these items are, in our view, not 'bishops' working costs' as that expression would commonly be understood, but costs incurred in the day-to-day activities of the Church of England, mainly in the dioceses. However, for the purpose of reconciliation with the Commissioners' accounts we adopt the figure of £8.5 million for costs under this heading.

Administration costs

4.29 There are two relevant areas of central administration costs which are attributable to episcopal ministry.

4.30.1 The Commissioners' accounts have a category of expenditure described as 'Commissioners' administration of national church functions'.

4.30.2 A sub-category[22] is 'Commissioners' expenditure and clergy payroll', with a total expenditure in that sub-category of £2 million.

4.30.3 We have been told that of that sum of £2 million, £1.090 million is related to the central administration costs of providing services for bishops.

4.30.4 The breakdown which we have been given is as follows:

	£
Administration of diocesans' housing	
(in-house agents' costs)	279,000
(other staff costs)	403,000
Administration of diocesans' working costs	188,000
Administration of Provincial Episcopal Visitors' housing (see para. 16.37.2)	20,000
Administration of suffragans' working costs	134,000
Administration of bishops' car scheme	61,000
Other	5,000
	1,090,000

4.31.1 The Commissioners have told us that other general overhead expenditure attributable to services provided to bishops in 1999 amounted to £90,000.

4.31.2 We therefore regard the total overhead expenditure for that year as being £1,180,000.

Commissioners' recurrent expenditure: summary

4.32 It follows that, in our view, on 1999 figures, the present recurrent expenditure by the Commissioners in relation to episcopal ministry, including – in our view importantly – *the cost of day-to-day activities mainly in the diocese* – is:

	£
Stipend and pension contributions (para. 4.19)	
(not including pensions to retired bishops)	3,500,000
Accommodation costs (para. 4.25)	3,300,000
Working costs (para. 4.28)	8,500,000
Central administration costs (para. 30.4)	1,180,000
Total	16,480,000
	or, say, 16,500,000

DBF payments

4.33   DBFs pay for:

a.   the living and working accommodation of suffragans (other than Provincial Episcopal Visitors);

b.   a contribution to the accommodation costs of PEVs;[23]

c.   in some cases the living accommodation of diocesans' chaplains;

d.   where the diocesan does not have a chaplain, in some cases a contribution to the salary costs of his lay assistant; and

e.   in the case of suffragans and in some cases the chaplains of diocesans, council tax and water charges.

4.34   In addition, as a result of arrangements made locally, some dioceses provide supplementary support for the bishops in the diocese, particularly the diocesan. Most frequently this takes the form of assistance with staff costs.

4.35   According to returns made to us by Diocesan Secretaries, the total cost to DBFs of meeting the costs in these two categories in 1999 was about £675,000.

Aggregate recurrent costs

4.36   The aggregate recurrent costs are therefore:

	£
From central funds (para. 4.32)	16,500,000
From local funds (para. 4.35)	675,000
Total	17,175,000

4.37   We refer later to the trends, but before doing so we consider capital assets which are deployed.

See and official houses: capital values

4.38.1   We recognize that it can be difficult to the point of being misleading to attempt to value those see houses which are heritage properties, and that, generally, in ordinary circumstances there may be no point in doing so where there is no prospect of sale.

4.38.2   We note the Commissioners' stated approach[24] of valuing for the purposes of their accounts:

> a.   13 see houses, which are heritage properties and which are unlikely to be sold, at £1 each; and
>
> b.   other see houses by reference to the relevant council tax band.

4.39.1   On this basis the value of the estate of see houses at 31 December 1999 is carried in the Commissioners' accounts at £23.1 million.[25]

4.39.2.   A desktop valuation which was carried out at our request indicates that the market value of these properties is unlikely to be less than £40 million.

4.40.1   Diocesan secretaries have furnished us with estimates of the cost of official houses provided by their DBFs for suffragans.

4.40.2   The aggregate of those values is in the region of £25 million.

4.41.1   Accordingly, we have regarded the total capital value of see and suffragans' houses as being not less than £65 million; and we recognize that in evaluating the economic cost of the support of episcopal ministry, account should be taken of the loss of income which could be derived from these assets.

4.41.2   We understand that actuarial advice currently being sought by the Commissioners is likely to indicate that if a fund is to be retained indefinitely and its value is to be preserved in real terms, distributions could be made at the rate of about 2.3% p.a. If that is applied to the capital value of see and suffragans' houses, £65 million, there would be a notional annual cost of about £1.5 million.

Capital expenditure

4.42 In 1999, the Commissioners spent somewhat in excess of £350,000 on capital improvements to see houses, although that figure is not separately identified in the accounts.[26] We understand that from 2000 the Commissioners propose to disclose the expenditure as a separate item.

The recent trend

4.43.1 The Commissioners append to their accounts a helpful ten-year financial record. We understand the concern which has been expressed that whereas over the decade expenditure by the Commissioners in the support of parish ministry has decreased by nearly 70%,[27] expenditure on bishops' working costs has increased by more than 50%.[28] But this is to be seen in the context of the increasing parochial support to which we refer in the next paragraph.

4.43.2 The relevant figures, and those of the broader financial context, in the following table are in respect of the last ten years. The figures in column (6) are supplied by the Church of England Statistics Unit and all the other figures are taken from the Commissioners' published accounts:

£ million

Year	Total of Commissioners' financial support for the Church	Commissioners' funds applied for pensions	Commissioners' funds applied for 'bishops' working costs'	Expenditure on clergy stipends and pension contributions	
				Provided by the Commissioners	Provided by dioceses
(1)	(2)	(3)	(4)	(5)	(6)
1990	142.3	53.0	5.3	65.5	68.7
1991	148.5	58.3	6.0	66.1	79.9
1992	150.7	63.9	6.3	61.9	92.0
1993	151.7	69.4	6.7	57.2	98.8
1994	153.4	73.9	7.0	51.1	102.3
1995	143.0	76.9	7.4	37.2	113.7
1996	136.9	79.6	7.6	27.9	124.1
1997	130.1	82.1	8.1	19.5	135.1
1998	158.9	108.2	8.8	20.0	140.5
1999	156.1	104.2	8.5	20.6	144.1

Notes: (a) The figures in column (3) for 1998 and 1999 include transitional support to dioceses for pension contributions.

(b) The figures in column (6) represent, very approximately, 40% of the total recurrent expenditure by dioceses.[29]

4.44   The figures show that:

4.44.1 A notable financial trend in recent years is that dioceses have taken an increasing responsibility for the cost of supporting parish ministry. The total support, when both central and local funds (as shown in columns (5) and (6)) are taken into account, has been slightly increasing, but the proportion of that provided by the Commissioners has been decreasing; and

4.44.2 Of the total amount which the Commissioners have made available for the purposes of the Church, by far the greater part has been expended on pensions. It is that, far more than the increase in bishops' working costs, which has resulted in the decrease of the Commissioners' funds applied in support of parish ministry.

The financial future

4.45   It is not for us to determine how the funds available to the Church, both centrally and locally, should be spent. On the other hand, it would be unrealistic to make recommendations about the resources which should be provided for bishops in the future without taking into account the financial context.

4.46.1 Any overall view of the funds of the Church of England needs to look at the three levels of:

    a.   the centre, namely the funds generated by the Commissioners;

    b.   the DBFs; and

    c.   the parishes.

4.46.2 At the risk of oversimplification:

    a.   there will be increasing pressure on central funds;

    b.   there will be increasing pressure on diocesan funds;[30] and

    c.   there will be widespread divergencies with regard to parochial funding.

4.46.3 For our purposes, there may well be a total sufficiency of funds, but to a material extent not accessible under the present system for the support of episcopal ministry.

4.47.1 The financial pressures on some parishes will be at least as great as at other levels. It is common for parishes to be running down slender reserves in order to pay their shares or quotas to the DBF.

4.47.2 However, there are substantial surpluses in other parishes. The latest year for which figures have so far been collated is 1998. Taking all parishes together, in that year there was a surplus of £41 million, or 11% of expenditure.[31]

4.47.3 Furthermore, the recent extensions of tax reliefs on gifts to charities,[32] particularly the widening of the Gift Aid scheme rules, should result in further funds accruing to parishes.

4.47.4 There are signs that churchgoers in many areas are willing to give to projects, particularly those in which there is direct local involvement or control, but are unwilling to provide funds for what they regard as diocesan or central imposts.

4.48 Events clearly could change this, but as a working hypothesis, we regard it as unrealistic to assume that apart, perhaps, from inflationary adjustments, there will be any increase in the central funds available for episcopal ministry and that it is more likely that the amount of these funds could reduce.

4.49 From that fact alone it follows that, in our view, the present system cannot continue indefinitely and, accordingly, in later chapters we recommend that a number of changes should be made in the present arrangements. We anticipate that some of those changes might lead to greater local contributions.

chapter 5

The present resources

Introduction

5.1   In this chapter, we consider the resources which are currently provided for bishops. We are concerned both with services or facilities which are provided in kind, and with funds which are provided so that services or facilities can be acquired. The majority of resources are provided by, or are paid for by, the Commissioners, but, as we note later in this chapter, some, such as living and working accommodation for suffragans, are provided by DBFs.

5.2   The present arrangements for the provision of resources by the Commissioners involve:

>   a.   in some cases the Commissioners both paying for the resources and themselves providing them;

>   b.   in other cases the Commissioners paying for these resources;

>   c.   in many cases where the Commissioners provide funds, making their provision subject to overall budgetary limits; and

>   d.   in some cases where there is local expenditure, the Commissioners requiring specific authorization.

5.3.1   This chapter is concerned with the main resources which are, *in general*, available. This does not, however, mean that they are applicable to all bishops.

5.3.2   In the first place, some bishops do not use all the resources to which they are entitled. In the second place, the Commissioners have a discretion about the provision of resources under which non-standard resources may be provided or funded in a particular case.

5.4   We consider the present budgetary system in Chapter 6.

5.5   There are a number of differences in the nature or scale of resources between those provided for a diocesan and those provided for a suffragan. We have noted the main differences where they apply.

5.6   In many cases, payment for resources is made from either a central account, which is maintained by the Commissioners, or from a local account, which is maintained by the bishop. The Commissioners conduct central accounts for working costs and separate central accounts for housing costs. In the following sections we have noted the relevant account.

Taking up office; and retirement

5.7.1   The main provisions which are made on appointment, on changes of appointment, or on retirement are as follows:

Nature of provision	Diocesan bishops	Suffragan bishops	Account from which paid or other remarks
a. On appointment			
Pre-consecration office and travel expenses	Yes	Yes	Central
Expenses of consecration service	Yes	Yes	Central
Legal fees on election and confirmation	Yes	Not applicable	Central
Legal fees on consecration	Yes	Yes	Central
Post-consecration reception, hire of venue, and refreshments for official guests	Yes (up to £15 a head)	Yes (up to £15 a head)	Central
Enthronement:			
Legal fees	Yes	Not applicable	Central
Other fees	Yes	Not applicable	Paid by diocese
Grant for robes	Yes (£2,500)	Yes (£2,500)	Central
Cope and mitre	Yes	Yes	Central
Removal expenses and re-settlement expenses (for adaptation of personal furnishings, etc.), with a combined limit for both removal and resettlement expenses of	Yes £8,000	Yes £8,000	Central

Nature of provision	Diocesan bishops	Suffragan bishops	Account from which paid or other remarks
Within that overall limit:			
a. removal expenses	as incurred	as incurred	
b. resettlement expenses	100% on first £3,000 of expenditure; 75% on next £3,000 of expenditure; 50% on expenditure over £6,001	100% on first £2,500 of expenditure; 75% on next £2,500 of expenditure; 50% on expenditure over £5,001	
b. On translation			
Removal and resettlement expenses	Yes (as on appointment)	Yes (as on appointment)	Central
Legal fees	Yes (as on appointment)	Yes (as on appointment)	Central
c. On retirement			
Removal expenses	none	none	

5.7.2 Bishops are able to claim partial reimbursement of removal and resettlement expenses where the aggregate exceeds £8,000, but the excess would be taxable[1].

Living and working accommodation

5.8.1 The nature of living and working accommodation varies widely, and we consider this in greater detail in Chapter 18.

5.8.2 In the most common case, where the bishop both lives and works in the same building, the accommodation can be divided between:

a. what is generally described as 'official' and which in a commercial context would be described as 'business'. In this report, we use the expression 'official'; and

b. private.

5.9.1   The official accommodation can be subdivided between:

    a.   study and offices;

    b.   chapel; and

    c.   rooms for meetings and the provision of official hospitality.

5.9.2   In particular cases a room may be used for more than one of these purposes.

5.10   The current standards of living and working accommodation in a see house were agreed between the House of Bishops and the Commissioners in 1975 and reaffirmed in 1995. The corresponding standards in respect of suffragans' houses were agreed in 1977.

5.11   The main elements are as follows:

	Diocesan bishops	Suffragan bishops
Official study and offices		
Study for the bishop	Yes	Yes
Offices for secretaries	Yes, for two secretaries	Yes, for one secretary
Office for chaplain	Yes	Yes
Waiting area	Yes	Not expressly stated
Chapel		
Chapel or oratory	Yes	No
Rooms for meetings and official hospitality		
Dining room	Yes (to seat 10 or 12)	Yes (number of seats not specified)
Drawing room	Yes	Yes
Meeting room	No separate room but the dining room or drawing room or, where they are interconnecting, both together, to provide space for a meeting or party of 30 people	Not specified

	Diocesan bishops	Suffragan bishops
Kitchen	Yes	Yes
Overnight visitors		
Official guest bedroom	Yes, 1	No
Private		
Bedrooms	5	4 to 5
Sitting room	1	Not specified
Bathrooms	2	1 or 2

5.12   In 23 cases a gardener or driver lives in. In those cases a flat may be provided in the house or a nearby cottage may be provided.

5.13.1   See houses, for diocesans, are provided by the Commissioners.

5.13.2   Suffragans' houses are provided by DBFs.

Staff

5.14.1   Bishops are provided with the following staff at the expense of the Commissioners:

	Diocesan bishops	Suffragan bishops	Account from which paid or other remarks
Chaplain or lay assistant	Yes	See para. 5.14.2	Central
Senior secretary	Yes	Yes	Central
Assistant secretary	Yes, part-time	No, save in very exceptional cases	Central
Press (or communications) officer (particularly for dealings with the media)	See para. 5.14.3	No	Central (if provided)
Driver	Yes, in most cases part-time	See para. 5.14.4	Central

	Diocesan bishops	Suffragan bishops	Account from which paid or other remarks
Gardener	Yes, in most cases part-time	Part-time (see para. 5.14.5)	See para. 5.14.6
Cleaner	No, but see below in respect of heating, lighting and cleaning	No	Local
Housekeeper	For unmarried bishops or widowers only: 50% of the actual cost, up to a maximum of £1,500 p.a.	No	Local

5.14.2   The Commissioners pay for each suffragan to have one member of staff, although not necessarily full-time. Usually that member of staff is the bishop's secretary. If, however, the suffragan can manage with a part-time secretary, the Commissioners will pay for him to have a part-time chaplain.[2]

5.14.3   In general, the Commissioners do not pay for a bishop's press or communications officer, but the majority of DBFs provide, at their expense, the services of such an officer. If, however, a diocesan chooses to have a part-time chaplain, the Commissioners will also pay the salary, pension contributions and working costs of a part-time press or communications officer. At the present time this occurs in about six cases.

5.14.4   The Commissioners do not pay for a suffragan to employ a driver. However, where there is special need for particular journeys, a driver may be engaged for those journeys, and the cost charged to the local account.

5.14.5 In relation to all suffragans appointed since 1998, the Commissioners pay 50% of the cost of a gardener, up to a maximum of £1,500 p.a. For suffragans appointed before that time, the Commissioners continue with the previous arrangement of paying the total cost of the gardener, with no upper limit.

5.14.6 Gardeners' pay for diocesans is paid from a central housing costs account. Gardeners' pay for suffragans is paid from the local account.

5.15.1 Where there is a part-time driver and a part-time gardener, the same person may perform both roles.

5.15.2 Bishops' wives sometimes act as volunteer drivers or gardeners and, indeed, as volunteer cleaners.

5.16 Removal costs and resettlement grants on the change of appointment of chaplains, as in the case of other clergy, are also payable.

Accommodation costs

5.17 The repair and maintenance of see houses are undertaken on behalf of the Commissioners and are paid for by them. The repair and maintenance of suffragans' houses are undertaken and paid for by DBFs. Further details are given in Chapter 18.

5.18.1 In addition to the costs of repairs and maintenance, the following accommodation and garden costs are paid:

	Diocesan bishops	Suffragan bishops	Account from which paid or other remarks
Basic furniture and furnishings for official rooms (see para. 5.18.2)	Yes	Yes	Central (housing costs) (diocesans) Local (suffragans)
Equipment for official rooms	Yes	Yes	Central (diocesans) Local (suffragans)
Specified items of kitchen equipment	Yes	Yes	Central

	Diocesan bishops	Suffragan bishops	Account from which paid or other remarks
Heating, lighting and cleaning	Part (see para. 5.19)	No	Local
Council tax on house and water charges for bishop	Yes	Yes	Central (housing costs) (diocesans) DBF (suffragans)
Council tax on house and water charges for chaplain	Yes	Generally not applicable	DBF (diocesans)
Council tax on house and water charges for live-in staff	Yes	Generally not applicable	Central (housing costs)
Garden:			
Seeds and fertilizers	Yes	No	Local
Provision and repair of garden tools and equipment	Yes	Yes	Central and local
Greenhouse heating	Yes (up to £200)	No	Local
Safety equipment and protective clothing	Yes	No	Local

5.18.2 a. The official rooms in the case of a see house are the office, study, drawing room, dining room, kitchen, chapel, official guest bedroom, and the hall, stairs or corridors leading to them.

b. The official rooms in the case of a suffragan's house are the office and study, and the hall, stairs or corridors leading to them.

5.19.1 The Commissioners pay the following part of the heating, lighting and cleaning costs of a see house:

a.   if the total floor area of the house is less than 6,000 square feet, the Commissioners pay 50% of the cost, and the bishop pays the other 50%; but

b.   if the total floor area exceeds 6,000 square feet, the bishop pays that part of the cost which is attributable to 3,000 square feet and the Commissioners pay the balance.

5.19.2   The Commissioners do not pay any part of the heating, lighting and cleaning costs incurred by a suffragan

Income tax relief on heating, lighting and cleaning costs

5.20.1   The net cost to the bishop of the amount which he pays for the heating, lighting and cleaning of the house depends on the amount of the income tax relief which he receives.

5.20.2   The background is that parochial clergy are entitled to income tax relief on that part of the cost of heating, lighting and cleaning their houses which is attributable to official, as contrasted with private, use. The Inland Revenue grant relief on 25% of the cost without enquiry,[3] but it is open to the individual to seek to negotiate a higher proportion according to his particular circumstances. With one important exception in the case of see houses, the same principle applies in relation to bishops' houses.

5.20.3   In the case of see houses:

a.   the cost of heating, lighting and cleaning the exclusively working part of the house is paid by the Commissioners as an expense of office (in the same way as the Commissioners would pay these expenses if the bishop's office were in separate premises);

b.   the bishop pays the remainder of the cost; but

c.   the bishop is entitled to income tax relief on 25% of the amount which he pays, or on such larger proportion as he agrees with the Inland Revenue.

5.20.4   The position in relation to a suffragan's house is different. The bishop pays the whole of the cost. If his office is not in the house, he is in the same general position as a member of the parochial clergy and can claim relief on 25% of the amount which he pays, or such higher proportion as he negotiates with the Inland Revenue. If his office is in the house, in principle he can base his claim on the full cost relating to the office space and up to 25% of the remainder.

Other provisions

5.21   The other main provisions are:

	Diocesan bishops	Suffragan bishops	Account from which paid or other remarks
5.21.1 Office costs			
Office and study equipment, including computers and equipment maintenance	Yes (up to 4 computers)	Yes (up to 2 computers)	Central and local
Postage, telephone and fax charges	Yes	Yes	Local
Standard publications	Yes	Yes	Local
Stationery and printing	Yes	Yes	Yes
5.21.2 Travelling			
Car	Yes	Yes	Central
Driver's uniform	Yes	Not applicable	Local
Travelling expenses when on official business	Yes	Yes	Local
Senior Citizen's railcard	Yes	Yes	Local
Hotel expenses and meals when on official business (or subsistence allowance)	Yes	Yes	Local
Overseas travel (where undertaken at request of Archbishop of Canterbury)	Yes	Yes	Separate central account

	Diocesan bishops	Suffragan bishops	Account from which paid or other remarks
Petrol and oil when on official business	Yes (or mileage allowance)	Yes (or mileage allowance)	Petrol and oil: central; mileage allowance: local

5.21.3 Provision of hospitality

	Diocesan bishops	Suffragan bishops	Account from which paid or other remarks
Major events costing more than £400 (see para. 5.22)	Yes (subject to prior specific approval)	Yes (subject to prior specific approval)	Local
Events costing £400 or less, where caterers are engaged	Yes (as incurred)	Yes (as incurred)	Local
Events costing less than £400, where caterers are not engaged	Yes (as incurred or according to tariff: see para. 5.23)	Yes (as incurred or according to tariff: see para. 5.23)	Local
Overnight official visitors	Yes (as incurred or according to tariff)	Yes (as incurred or according to tariff)	Local

5.21.4 Clergy selection and appointment costs

	Diocesan bishops	Suffragan bishops	Account from which paid or other remarks
Candidates' travel and subsistence expenses	Yes	Yes	Local
Ordination expenses	Yes	Yes	Local

5.21.5 Legal fees

	Diocesan bishops	Suffragan bishops	Account from which paid or other remarks
Bishops' registrars' retainers and other legal fees	Yes	Yes	Central

	Diocesan bishops	Suffragan bishops	Account from which paid or other remarks
5.21.6 Chapel			
Furnishings	Yes	Yes	Central (housing costs)
Requisites	Yes	Yes	Local
5.21.7 Training			
Conference fees	Yes	Yes	Local
Training courses	Yes	Yes	Central and local
Expenses on study leave	Yes	Yes	Local
5.21.8 Insurance			
On see house	Yes	Not applicable	Premium for block policy paid by Commissioners from separate account
On suffragan's house	Not applicable	Yes	DBF
On furnishings and equipment owned by Commissioners	Yes	Yes	Commissioners' block policy
On furnishings and equipment owned by the bishop	No	No	Not applicable
On public liability for official guests and visitors	Yes	No, but see para. 5.20.9	Commissioners' block policy
On employer's liability and personal accident for staff	Yes	No	Commissioners' block policy

5.21.9 Suffragans may be covered for public liability under their contents insurance policy, or under a diocesan block policy. Because the position varies, it is prudent for each suffragan to check the position as it applies to him.

5.22.1 Most bishops use cars which are provided under a fleet lease scheme operated by the Church Commissioners with Avis.

5.22.2 The Commissioners draw up a list of recommended cars, and set a price limit for cars not on that list. The bishop chooses a car either from that list or within the price limit. Avis purchase the car from one of their preferred dealers and lease it to the Commissioners. The Commissioners authorize the bishop to use it (but do not enter into a written licence with the bishop). The chosen car is delivered directly to the bishop and is replaced after four years. The Commissioners pay up-front the rental for the four-year period in the year in which the car is required.

5.22.3 In general, the list is the same for both diocesans and suffragans. However, there is a supplementary list, for diocesans only, if they wish to have a slightly larger car because they have a driver and are thus enabled to work in the back of the car.

5.23 The £400 limit in respect of the provision of hospitality is subject to review from time to time. It is imposed partly for audit purposes in the context of the arrangement agreed with the Inland Revenue, and partly for authorization purposes.

5.24.1 The arrangements for charging the provision of hospitality where caterers are not engaged are confusing to a number of bishops and their wives.

5.24.2 There can be charged to the local account either the actual cost incurred; or, if the bishop prefers, he can charge according to a tariff. The tariff is reviewed annually and at present[4] it is as follows:

For food and drink:	£
breakfast	2.45
coffee	0.65
lunch	4.00
afternoon tea	1.60

| supper | 4.00 |
| dinner | 5.70 |

In respect of overnight official visitors
(to cover laundry and incidental
expenses, in addition to meals):   £

| For the first night | 7.25 |
| For each subsequent night | 2.50 |

5.24.3   There are no tariff figures for wine or other refreshments, which are, therefore, charged at cost.

5.24.4   The tariff figures are only guidelines: the bishop is authorized to formulate his own tariff where this is more appropriate to local costs.

5.24.5   The tariff is intended to be a guide to cover the cost of the food, including a modest element of recompense for its preparation.

5.24.6   In the majority of cases where the bishop's wife prepares the food, she does so without remuneration. If, however, she so wishes, she is entitled to make a reasonable charge for catering, in addition to the cost of the food. However, all of this is subject to the bishop's overall local budgetary amount[5] being sufficient. We make further observations on payments to bishops' wives in a later chapter.[6]

Observations
5.25   After making, in Chapter 6, observations on budgetary management, we comment on the nature and scale of the present resources in Chapter 7.

chapter 6

Budgetary management

Introduction

6.1   In this chapter, we consider some aspects of the present budgetary system so far as it affects bishops, and we make recommendations for change.

6.2   We deal first with working costs and then with premises expenses. It will be recalled (para. 4.28) that we ourselves do not regard most working costs as being working costs *of bishops* as such.

Working costs: budgets

6.3   In relation to working costs, it is necessary to consider separately:

    a.   local budgets; and

    b.   central budgets

    together with their associated accounts.

6.4   The Commissioners allocated an amount to each bishop for local operational expenses. This amount is often referred to as a 'local budget'. It is, so far as the Commissioners are concerned, an item of budgeted expenditure.

6.5.1   The bishop is involved in the process by which the local budgetary allowance is determined, particularly by indicating any anticipated changes of circumstance which will affect local spending requirements in the following year. The bishop has the opportunity of commenting on the proposed amount, but it is determined by the Commissioners and not formally agreed with the bishop.

6.5.2   The amounts in question vary considerably, but £33,000 for a diocesan and £11,000 for a suffragan are not untypical.

6.5.3   The bishop is the budget holder in respect of the allocated amount. It is for him if he so wishes – there is no obligation on him to do so – to prepare a budget for the way in which it is to be spent. There is a list of the types of expenditure which can be paid for from that amount,[1] but provided that he keeps within that list, the bishop can decide how the money is spent.

6.5.4 The bishop conducts a separate bank account, known as his local account, through which this amount is carried. The Commissioners credit the account quarterly with the allocated amount.

6.5.5 The bishop sends to the Commissioners a quarterly return of how the money has actually been spent.

6.6.1 Much the larger part of the expenditure budget relates to items, particularly salaries of bishops' staff, which the Commissioners themselves pay, either directly or by reimbursement to dioceses. These costs are paid from the central account. The Commissioners prepare the central account budget themselves, using information submitted by bishops about their staff and office requirements, but without agreeing with each individual bishop that part of the budget which concerns him.

6.6.2 The Commissioners send to each bishop a quarterly return of expenditure from the central account so far as it relates to him.

6.7 As has been seen, the bishop is involved in the process by which the amount to be allocated to him for local spending is determined. He is not, however, involved in the remainder of the working costs budgetary process for his see, including that part of it which deals with the expenditure which the Commissioners make and charge to the central account.

6.8.1 Bishops are able to make special requests, either before a year begins or, if unexpected circumstances arise, during a year.

6.8.2 The staff of the Department manage these requests according to their assessment of priorities, but within the overall working costs budget and subject to the priorities set by the Bishoprics and Cathedrals Committee. The Committee also monitors the way in which the staff exercise their discretions, as well as financial performance against budget. This system has often involved the staff declining or deferring requests, and from the information available to us, it seems that the staff are successful in keeping the total expenditure within the working costs budget.

6.8.3   This discretion does, however, lead to the perception on the part of some bishops that there is inequitable treatment between one bishop and another, and that the bishop who is the most insistent is likely to obtain the greatest resources. We comment on that in a later chapter.[2]

Working costs: expenditure analyses

6.9   From the returns prepared by the bishop of expenditure charged to his local account and from their own records of expenditure charged by the Commissioners to the central account, a quarterly analysis is prepared.

6.10   The chart on pages 70–71 is an example of the type of analysis prepared for a diocesan. The figures in this example are solely for the purposes of illustration: they are not taken from any actual case and are not intended to indicate a typical case.

6.11   It will be seen that this analysis shows:

a.   separately and in aggregate actual expenditure under various headings; and

b.   in respect of the local account only, the total budgetary amount for the year and the unspent balance at the end of each quarter.

6.12.1   It will also be seen that the analysis:

a.   does not show how the figures have been calculated, and so does not enable the bishop easily to reconcile the local account figures with his own records (although the local account figures are prepared from his returns);

b.   does not take account of seasonal or timing differences; and

c.   so far as it relates to the local account is on a cash basis, and so does not make any provision for accruals (the central account figures do); and

d.   does not show any income that is derived from lettings.

Expenditure analysis up to the quarter ending 31 December 2000

Bishop of Loamster

Local account

Quarter ending	Heating lighting, cleaning	House and garden	Gardener's pay	Ordination expenses	Patronage costs	Secretaries' pay
31/03/99	1,837	1,392	0	0	0	0
30/06/99	1,092	670	0	278	170	0
30/09/99	675	1,774	0	629	0	0
31/12/99	1,470	209	0	0	0	0
Local Totals	5,074	4,045	0	907	170	0

Central account

Quarter ending						Chaplain/ secretaries
31/03/99						22,032
30/06/99						18,544
30/09/99						20,192
31/12/99						28,317
Central Totals						89,085
Overall Totals	5,074	4,045	0	907	170	89,085

Office expenses	Driver's pay	Travel	Hospitality	Misc.	Total	Budget	Balance
1,628	0	1,217	1,389	77	7,540	27,500	19,960
1,270	0	629	813	36	4,958		15,002
1,953	0	1,137	1,387	86	7,641		7,361
2,132	0	1,857	1,522	54	7,244		117
6,983	0	4,840	5,111	253	27,383		

Office expenses	Driver's pay	Travel	Hospitality	Misc.	Total
738	2,928	0	0	602	26,300
0	4,192	0	0	0	22,736
0	1,444	0	0	435	22,071
172	3,897	0	0	0	32,386
910	12,461	0	0	1,037	103,493
7,893	12,461	4,840	5,111	1,290	103,876

6.12.2 Although the Commissioners estimate the salaries for the staff of each bishop when compiling the central budget and take into account bishops' requests for equipment and other items, no separate central budget is prepared for each bishop. Accordingly, the analysis does not show any budgetary amount of unspent balances on the central account.

6.12.3 The analysis also does not show any income from lettings. This falls within the costs of bishops' housing, which are outside the scope of the analysis which is confined to bishops' working costs.

The present system: expenditure on see houses

6.13.1 The basic position in respect of expenditure on see houses is that during one year a programme of maintenance and repair for the following year and, where applicable, capital improvements, is discussed between the bishop and the agent (whether in-house or external);[3] and

6.13.2 When the programme, reduced if necessary, has been agreed[4] and costed, it is incorporated in the housing costs budget for that house, and a copy is provided to the bishop.

6.14 With effect from 1 January 1999, the Commissioners have instituted a system of quinquennial inspections, and the carrying out of a rolling programme of maintenance and repairs based on those inspections.

6.15 Although the maintenance, repair and improvements programme is discussed with the bishop, he is not otherwise involved in the preparation of the budget, nor is he provided with regular information about the actual expenditure which is being incurred.

The present system: expenditure on suffragans' houses

6.16 The position with regard to expenditure on official houses varies from diocese to diocese. To a greater or lesser extent, programmes are agreed between the bishop and diocesan surveyor. However, it seems to be rare for the bishop to be involved in any budgetary process.

The system generally

6.17   We have shown that:

a.   a bishop is only a budget-holder, and therefore a budget-manager, in relation to his local account;

b.   in all other respects the budget managers are staff of the Department; and

c.   a bishop is not presented with information which enables him to take a more active role.

6.18   This arrangement has found favour with some bishops: with the exception of local accounts, it has meant that they have not had to be concerned with budgetary management. But it has caused frustration on the part of others. The weight of evidence presented to us is that bishops consider that to a much greater extent the balance should shift so that they (or their staff) become the managers of those accounts which directly affect them. We support that approach.

Recommendation

6.19   We make further proposals for the devolution of budgetary control to bishops (in Chapter 10), but as an immediate measure we **recommend** that bishops:

a.   should be fully involved in the preparation of *all* budgets which directly affect them (central account, local account and premises), so that they understand and support them; and

b.   should receive full management accounting information in respect of all of those budgets.

6.20   We also **recommend** that there should be a sharing of budgetary information between bishops, and we make specific proposals in that respect.[5]

chapter 7

Aspects of the present regime

Information

7.1   In this chapter, we comment on two general aspects of the present regime and then on more specific aspects.

Nature of resources

7.2.1   In Chapter 5, we outlined the resources which are at present provided for bishops.

7.2.2   We comment later (para. 16.18) on the differences between the resources provided for diocesans and those provided for suffragans.

7.3   Most of these resources can be summarized as amounting to the provision of:

    a.   somewhere to live;

    b.   somewhere to work;

    c.   staff to assist in that work;

    d.   somewhere for the staff to work;

    e.   the means to travel for official purposes;

    f.   the means with which to provide official hospitality;

    g.   the means with which to communicate;

    h.   the means with which to be trained;

    i.   the equipment to do the work; and

    j.   the legal, medical and other professional support necessary to do the work.

7.4   We observe at this stage that:

    a.   we regard the range of these resources as necessary;

    b.   with the possible addition of:

    i. press or communications officers; and

    ii. mentoring and continuing training.

We do not consider that there are other resources of a nature which in ordinary cases ought to be provided;

    c. where there are cash limits or tariffs, we do not regard any of them as excessive, and, indeed, we regard some of them as being distinctly modest; but

    d. we make proposals which we think will lead to a better provision of many of these resources.

The culture: financial nannying?

7.5   Any description of the present culture is bound at least to some extent to be subjective, but certain aspects have stood out.

7.6.1   The first is the sense of financial dependence of bishops on the Commissioners in respect of working costs. According to the evidence presented to us, this is not what the majority of bishops want. We referred to this in the previous chapter, and at this stage we only observe that:

    a. despite the highly responsible role which they are asked to perform in other respects, bishops have budgetary control over a sum which, even in the case of a diocesan, might be only in the order of £30,000 a year and in respect of hospitality, conferences and training courses their spending authority is limited to £400; and

    b. quite apart from spending authority, bishops are not given the information which they require in order to exercise budgetary control except to the most minor extent.

7.6.2   If the present system can be described as financial nannying, the recommendation which we made at the end of the last chapter was, in essence, that there should be a change of approach designed to confer much greater discretion on bishops, and to enable them to take greater financial responsibility. The recommendation is designed to bring to an end the system of excessively detailed control exercised by the Commissioners, and the way in which it denies bishops both the opportunity and the responsibility to manage their own resources.

The culture: discretionary expenditure

7.7.1 The second cultural aspect relates to the exercise of discretion both in respect of working costs and in respect of expenditure on premises by the staff of the Department.

7.7.2 As we have shown in Chapter 5, the standard scales of provision are formulated and are clearly stated. But beyond those scales there is a discretion. The staff of the Department endeavour to meet special requests where the staff consider them reasonable and within the budgetary constraints.

7.7.3 There is a widespread perception that those bishops who are the most clamorous in their requests are the most successful in having their wishes met. There is probably some truth in this, although in a number of cases where special requests have been met, this has been for entirely proper reasons, and the requests would have been met irrespective of clamour. Nevertheless, the present system leads to the *perception* of inequity, whether or not it is soundly based.

7.8.1 The third cultural aspect, which is closely related to the previous one, is that there is a lack of general understanding on the part of many bishops about the method by which decisions are taken by the Commissioners and members of their staff and the factors which are taken into account. Anomalies are perceived to exist, and there is a lack of clarity about what is, or is not, a reasonable expectation.

7.8.2 In order to deal with this and the previous point, we **recommend** that to the fullest practical extent where there is a discretion in relation to the provision of resources, there should be made clear:

a. that discretion has been exercised;

b. the result of its exercise;

c. the person or persons by whom the decision has been taken; and

d. the factors which have been taken into account.

The culture: the Commissioners and the bishops

7.9 The fourth cultural aspect is the relationship between the Commissioners and, more particularly, the staff of the Department on the one hand and the bishops on the other.

7.10.1 The majority[1] of bishops have expressed appreciation of the support which they receive from the Commissioners and the staff of the Department. There is widespread recognition of the wish of the staff to be supportive, and of the substantial knowledge base that there is within the Department.

7.10.2 However, there is some evidence that members of the staff of the Department, particularly the more junior members, can – in our view very understandably – have difficulty in putting themselves in the position of bishops, and in gauging and adopting the appropriate responses. We emphasize that this is not a comment on the capabilities of any of the members of the Department, but on the organizational structure and the relationships which flow from it.

7.10.3 We think that the difficulty is partly due to the physical distance between the offices of the Commissioners and those of the bishop, and the lack of local knowledge which that can engender. We also think that it is in further part due to the present system which involves dealings between bishops and the staff of the Department over relatively small amounts of money.

The culture: micro-management

7.11.1 The fifth cultural aspect relates to central micro-management, that is, management in detail from the centre.

7.11.2 A number of examples have been put to us, usually in relation to the supply of office equipment or furniture, with the common theme that:

    a.   arrangements have been made by the Department with a supplier;

    b.   bishops have been encouraged to purchase items (within a stipulated range) from a supplier; but

    c.   the more worldly-wise have made local purchases at a much reduced cost.

7.11.3 In the system which we propose in Chapter 10, we hope that these weaknesses will be rectified.

Legal fees

7.12.1 We now comment on two more detailed aspects of the present system. The first relates to the legal expenses which are being incurred by the bishops and by the Church more widely.

7.12.2 The position varies, but the basic pattern is that:

a. a lawyer acts both as the diocesan bishop's legal officer and as the diocesan registrar; and

b. a separate retainer is paid for acting in each of these capacities.

7.12.3 In addition to diocesan registrars, there are provincial registrars for the two provinces.

7.13.1 The amount of the retainer and the scope of the work which it covers is regulated.[2]

7.13.2 In the year 2001, total retainers payable[3] to bishops' legal officers and diocesan and provincial registrars will exceed £1.75 million.[4]

7.14.1 This subject lies outside our remit, and we have not investigated it. We are certainly not suggesting that there is overcharging, and, indeed, it is clear that the lawyers charge less than their usual hourly rates.[5] Nevertheless, the total cost to the Church of legal fees is such that we think the issue needs to be re-examined.

7.14.2 Accordingly, we **recommend** that there should be a fundamental review of the extent to which in modern circumstances professional legal assistance is required and the method by which it should be supplied. It may be that some things which are done now with lawyers could be done in a different way without them; and it may be that such legal services as are essential might be provided by lawyers retained on a regional rather than a diocesan basis.

Legislative demands on bishops

7.15.1 The second point relates to the burdens imposed on bishops by both Church and State legislation.[6] There is a widespread perception that this burden is increasing.[7]

7.15.2   In relation to church legislation, in part this is owing to numerous provisions to the effect that 'the bishop', namely the diocesan, shall do a specified act. It does not seem to us that all of such acts need to be done by the bishop personally.

7.15.3   Furthermore, we think that all proposals for new legislation which would impose obligations on bishops should be accompanied by resource assessments.

7.16   Accordingly, we **recommend** that in relation to any further legislation which would impose duties on bishops:

7.16.1   There should be a strong presumption that this legislation should provide that those duties are to be performed by the bishop 'or by such other competent person as he shall nominate'; and

7.16.2   That legislation should be accompanied by an assessment of the time and resource implications for bishops (and indeed for others).

Press or communications officers

7.17.1   There is no standard provision for diocesans to have press or communications officers for dealing with the press and other media, although some DBFs make available the diocesan communications officer to act on a part-time basis as the bishop's press officer, and in some other cases the Commissioners fund a part-time appointment within the bishop's overall office staffing allowance.[8]

7.17.2   We welcome that approach, and **recommend** that there should be general encouragement of DBFs to provide this facility.

Part II

chapter 8

Future needs

Introduction

8.1   We have referred in Chapter 3 to the context in which bishops work and we have indicated[1] our view that, in the present circumstances, the scale of the resources provided for bishops is broadly right. However, our terms of reference have also required us to consider how the work and, therefore, the needs of bishops will change during the first decade of the twenty-first century. In this chapter we summarize the predictions and concerns about the future which bishops have expressed to us and then consider the resourcing implications.

8.2   In looking to the future, it is necessary to take into account the possibility that there will be women bishops. We refer to that later,[2] but we observe at this stage that nothing in this chapter would be invalidated if there were women bishops.

The fundamentals

8.3   There is no suggestion that the fundamental role and work[3] of a bishop will change radically during the decade and, accordingly, we do not propose any fundamental change in the scale of the resources[4] which should be provided.

Predictions

8.4   In this section we summarize the predictions for the future which bishops have shared with us so far as they relate to resources. In doing so we observe that:

> a.   different bishops make different predictions or put the emphasis in different ways and, accordingly, it does not follow that every bishop would share all of these predictions;
>
> b.   in our summary we have not sought to categorize the predictions in any order of importance;
>
> c.   the summary does not purport in any way to be comprehensive;
>
> d.   the factors are not new; and

e. we hope that statements in this short form will be adequate for present purposes.

8.5   *Bishops will continue to have a valued role in the community*
Bishops will continue to be regarded as leaders whose standing relates to that of senior leaders in the community. They will continue to be asked to chair local, regional and national bodies. They will be invited to contribute to the development of regional identities and structures and they will continue to be spokesmen for those in their area,[5] particularly the needy and disadvantaged.

8.6   *Opportunities for the bishop will abound but respect for the office will decline*
Although the pattern will be mixed, and will differ from one diocese to another, the general trend will be for respect for the *office* of the bishop to decline. However, the opportunities for the bishop as an individual will be at least as great as they are at the present time, but will become increasingly dependent on his personal qualities, and the calibre of his pronouncements. The bishop will be listened to because of the depth and well-founded research of his statements. The bishop will continue to have the opportunity to call to conscience both those in his diocese and those outside it.

8.7   *Bishops' dealings with the media will have increasing immediacy*
A bishop will continue to be a public figure and it may be a sign that he is taking advantage of his opportunities that he will attract media attention.[6] It is likely that he will be expected to have at least as much contact with the press, radio and television as at present, and it may be more. He will be expected to make informed comments at short notice, and he will therefore need to be a highly effective communicator.

8.8   *The demands of leading the diocese will increase*
Many dioceses are large and complex. It is not for the diocesan to run the administration of them, but it is for him, together with his suffragans, to provide inspirational leadership of them. The demands of doing so are likely to increase. Just as society is changing, so the decade will be one of change within the Church. As Professor Sykes has put it to us, 'A bishop's responsibility for oversight of his diocese . . . is bound to entail an understanding of good governance'.[7] There will be change in the pattern and complexity of ministry; changes in numbers of

worshippers and occasions of worship; changes in the balance between stipendiary and non-stipendiary clergy; pastoral changes; and, perhaps, greater movement towards inter-diocesan co-operation, if not regionalization. Through all of this the bishops will need to lead the diocese to provide stability for it and to be a focus of unity.

8.9 *The demands of leading the diocese will be exacerbated by financial pressures*
In addition to the other changes just noted, the financial circumstances of the Church may cause changes of a nature not so far contemplated.[8]

8.10 *Accessibility to the clergy*
There will continue to be an increasing expectation on the part of clergy of accessibility to the bishop. Many clergy who have been in secular employment before ordination will have had experience of a recurrent relationship with their line manager. We do not use that expression to describe the relationship of a bishop and his clergy, but something of that expectation will influence the relationship. Furthermore, many of the clergy who are now serving will have been accustomed to working as part of a team, and that experience will also influence their relationship with the bishop.

8.11 *Accessibility to the laity*
The increasing expectation on the part of clergy of accessibility to the bishop will be paralleled with increasing expectation of accessibility on the part of the laity and the general public. It will be accompanied by a reduction in deference to the office of bishop. A layperson who writes to the bishop will not be content with any answer merely because it comes from the bishop, but is likely to persist in expecting a reasoned response. This is particularly so in a litigious culture where the layperson has a complaint or grievance.

8.12 *The House of Lords*
At present, the two archbishops and the Bishops of London, Durham and Winchester are *ex officio* members of the House of Lords. In addition, the 21 most senior bishops, by length of service as diocesans, are also members. It may be that, during the decade, the number of bishops who are members of that House will reduce. If there is such a reduction, it will result in a greater workload on those who continue.[9]

Anxieties

8.13.1 Bishops have told us of some of their anxieties. Three stand out to us.

8.13.2 First, increasing administrative burdens;

8.13.3 Second, and partly as a result of the first, the danger that bishops will become increasingly introverted – increasingly concerned with church business and less with the community, while recognizing that episcopal ministry is God's gift to the world, not only to the Church;[10] and

8.13.4. Third, the need to reappraise the role of bishops: where does the balance lie between *leading* the Church and *running* the Church?

Communication and information technology

8.14 The predictions which we have summarized are those of the bishops; we add a factor of our own. There must also be taken into account electronic communication. We do not predict exactly what developments in the field will occur during the decade with which we are concerned, but it must be anticipated that there will be many. It will not be unusual for a bishop to have his own website.

8.15 Such means of communication *by* the bishop can become a powerful instrument in his hands. Simultaneous electronic communication by a bishop with everyone in his diocese is but one example.

8.16 For our purposes, however, we are more concerned with handling electronic communication *to* the bishop. It will be increasingly easy for communications to be sent to the bishop, and for originators to wish to enter into e-mail dialogue with the bishop or, at least, his office. We anticipate that during the decade there will be a substantial increase in the communications traffic to the bishop's office: it will need to be handled.

Future needs

8.17 Against this background, what will be the future needs of bishops?

8.18.1 First, and overwhelmingly, time: more time to reflect, more time to pray, more time to study and more time to teach.[11]

8.18.2 In one sense this has nothing to do with resources, but in another sense it has a great deal to do with them. As there can be no increase in the total amount of time, it is only by rigorously restructuring administrative and some other burdens, and by enabling increased delegation, that bishops will have the time for prayer and reflection which we consider *crucial* for them to have. We believe that it is increasingly essential for bishops to possess the ability, including personal organizational ability, to structure and arrange their duties so as to make full use of the skills and abilities of all those with whom they work. In order for bishops to avoid becoming increasingly absorbed by bureaucracy they must be empowered to be skilled managers of their own work and the work of their subordinates and colleagues. Only in this context will they be able to develop their full spiritual gifts and potential in ministry.[12]

8.19.1 The second need is that bishops seek more training and we commend the steps being taken by the Archbishops' Adviser on Bishops' Ministry to enable this to be provided.

8.19.2 The subjects in which various bishops have told us that they would welcome training include:

    a.   mission strategy and practice;

    b.   theology, especially applied theology;

    c.   management of change;

    d.   uses of information technology;

    e.   conflict management;

    f.   stress management;

    g.   media presentation;

    h.   prioritizing and learning the ability to say 'no';

    i.   leadership, especially team leadership; and

    j.   multi-cultural, social and broad contemporary issues.

8.20.1 Third, there are needs in relation to a bishop's personal staff.

8.20.2 There will be an increasing emphasis on the calibre of staff, permitting more formal delegation;

8.20.3 There is an increasing need for the training of staff; and

8.20.4 There is also an increasing need for support in research.

The sober picture

8.21 The picture is stark. We see increasing tension between on the one hand the need both to maintain resources at their present level and to increase them to meet future needs and on the other hand the increasing pressures on the central and diocesan funds of the Church which provide them. In all of these cases, the needs are not those of bishops for their own sakes, but so that they can minister to all people. The recommendations which we make in the remaining chapters of this report are set against this background.

chapter 9

Resources: the principles

Approach

9.1 Before making proposals for a different regime, we have attempted to identify the principles which in our opinion should govern the future provision of bishops' resources.

9.2 We set forth in this chapter 15 principles. Many of them can be, and are, shortly expressed, in some cases without any elaboration.

9.3 We recognize that in a particular case one principle can conflict with another, and that it is unrealistic to expect that all principles will be satisfied in relation to each resource. Nevertheless, we hope that it will be helpful for there to be a reference base against which specific proposals, whether made now or in the future, can be measured. We **recommend** that the provision of all resources, both now and in the future, should be measured against these principles.

The principles

9.4 The principles are as follows. They are not put forward in any specific order of priority or importance.

9.5 No. 1: Necessity

A bishop should have the resources which are necessary to enable him to carry out his roles and responsibilities. This applies to the nature and extent of the resources, both human and physical, and indicates that both kinds of resources should be of appropriate quality for the task. The principle implies that the roles and responsibilities of each bishop are sufficiently defined.

9.6 No. 2: Objective determination of necessity

The resources which are necessary should be objectively determined and should be reflected in published national guidelines.

9.7 No. 3: Individual gifts and skills

So far as practicable, resources should be provided in such a way as will facilitate bishops' exercising their ministry according to their individual gifts and skills. This will usually, if not always, involve a bishop having some freedom of choice in the use of resources.

9.8   No. 4: Married bishops

The nature and scale of resources provided for a bishop should be sufficient to enable him to do his job irrespective of whether or not he is married. We state later that we recognize the great support given to bishops by their wives (whether or not their wives have external employment). However, we think it wrong that there should be any assumption that wives will provide support of any particular nature, and therefore we think that the resources which are provided should be sufficient without taking into account support from wives.

9.9   No. 5: Need not status

Resources should be provided according to need, not status. One diocesan can have needs differing from those of another. Furthermore, while in general the weight of responsibility borne by a diocesan is greater than that borne by a suffragan, it does not follow that a diocesan, *ipso facto*, should have a resource of a nature or scale different from that provided for a suffragan.

9.10   No. 6: Cost-effectiveness

Resources should be provided in a cost-effective manner. A resource of appropriate quality should be made available in the least expensive practical manner provided that any increased efforts in obtaining it from one source do not outweigh the increased cost in obtaining it from another.

9.11   No. 7: Simplicity in operation

Resources should be provided in the manner which leads to the greatest simplicity in operation.

9.12   No. 8: Categorization

For budgeting and accounting purposes, there should be a distinction between (a) office costs, (b) other administrative and operational costs, (c) individual working costs and (d) premises expenses. More detailed categorization will be appropriate in particular circumstances. Under *office costs*, we include:

a.   staff salaries and employment expenses;

b.   office expenses; and

c.   office equipment.

Under *other administrative and operational costs*, we include the costs of the appointment and deployment of clergy, ordination expenses, legal fees and training costs.

Under *individual working costs*, we include expenditure on:

a. official travelling; and

b. the provision of official hospitality.

Under *premises expenses*, we include expenses relating to gardeners, and we consider that statements about premises expenses should distinguish between:

a. recurrent costs; and

b. capital expenditure.

9.13   No. 9: Accountability
Bishops should be accountable for the expenditure of funds to the body which provides them. This will be primarily to the Commissioners, but, where applicable, also to the DBF.

9.14   No. 10: Transparency
There should be transparency about the use of funds. Information about the expenditure of funds should be made known to those with a proper interest in receiving it. In relation to a particular bishop, this would include all other bishops and his DBF.

9.15   No. 11: Involvement in expenditure statements
A bishop should be involved in the preparation of any statement to be made to others about the expenditure of funds made available to him, so that to the fullest practical extent he can be satisfied as to its accuracy.

9.16   No. 12: Subsidiarity
Decisions as to the amount and expenditure of financial resources should be taken at the nearest practicable level to that at which the expenditure is incurred.

9.17   No. 13: Openness
To the fullest practical extent, there should be openness about the nature and scale of resources provided, and the principles by which they are determined.

9.18   No. 14: Equity

The nature and scale of resources provided to one bishop should be the same as those provided to other bishops in comparable circumstances.

9.19   No. 15: Discretion

Where there is any discretionary element in the provision of resources, there should be made known:

> a.   *the parameters within which the decision is taken;*
>
> b.   *the method by which the decision is taken; and*
>
> c.   *the person or persons by whom the decision is taken.*

chapter 10

A new regime

Introduction

10.1 In this chapter, we put forward proposals for a new regime which includes:

a. the principle of partnership in the funding of episcopal ministry;

b. a redefined role for the Commissioners;

c. the block-granting of central funds for the bishops in a diocese; and

d. local decision-making in respect of those block-granted funds.

10.2 Apart from demonstrating the partnership, the main objectives of these and associated proposals are:

a. to give bishops a greater degree of responsible financial independence, flexibility and empowerment;

b. to reduce central overhead costs; and

c. to increase the quality of resources at no additional cost to the Church.

Applications of the Commissioners' funds

10.3.1 Before outlining our specific proposals we make a general one. The implementation of some of our proposals would result in a reduction of expenditure by the Commissioners, partly as a result of the saving of overhead expenditure.

10.3.2 We recommend that all sums saved by the Commissioners from the implementation of our proposals should be applied in increasing the amount available for distribution to dioceses by Selective Allocations.

Partnership

10.4.1 Although it is not usually expressed in this way, there is at present a partnership between the Commissioners and the dioceses in supporting episcopal ministry. Much the greater part of the total cost is borne by the Commissioners, but the contribution by the dioceses is by no means insignificant.

10.4.2 The dioceses meet the costs incurred in providing: living and working accommodation for suffragans; in some cases living accommodation for chaplains; in some cases part of the salaries of lay assistants; and in many cases supplementary support for diocesans.

10.4.3 At present, we regard about 94% of the total cost of supporting episcopal ministry as being contributed by the Commissioners and 6% by dioceses.[1]

10.5 We think that in this context the partnership concept is right and we **recommend** that it should be clearly recognized. We explore it in greater detail (para. 10.27) after considering the future central structure and the role of the Commissioners.

The Episcopal Committee

10.6.1 The present Bishoprics and Cathedrals Committee is:

    a.   a committee of the board of governors of the Church Commissioners; but

    b.   a body whose members include those nominated by the Archbishops' Council.[2]

10.6.2 The Committee acts for the board in matters relating to episcopal and cathedral support, though the governors retain ultimate responsibility for these matters.

10.7.1 We propose a revised role for the Commissioners, but we **recommend** that there should continue to be a central body with specific responsibility for the support of episcopal ministry.

10.7.2 We consider that, as in the case of the existing committee, such a body:

    a.   should be a committee of the Commissioners; and

b.   should have members appointed or nominated by both the Commissioners and the Archbishops' Council.

10.7.3   In contrast with the existing committee, we consider that the future body should also have DBF representation. This might be achieved by having one or more members nominated by the Consultative Group of Diocesan Board of Finance Chairmen and Secretaries.

10.7.4   As in the case of the present Bishoprics and Cathedrals Committee, we consider that the new body should report formally and primarily to the Commissioners and informally to the Archbishops' Council.

10.7.5   We make no comment on whether this body should also be concerned with cathedrals. The predecessor of the Bishoprics and Cathedrals Committee was only concerned with bishops. The present committee itself came into existence on 1 January 1999 and no evidence has been given to us on whether it is in practice an advantage or disadvantage to have responsibility for episcopal and cathedrals matters combined.

10.7.6   The body which we propose might be formed from the existing committee, or might be a new, but very similar, committee. In either case, some continuity of experience is desirable. However, in order to demonstrate that the new body will have a different role from the existing committee, we refer to it in this report as the Episcopal Committee. (This is not to prejudge whether or not the new body should be responsible also for cathedral matters, in which event the working title may need to be adjusted accordingly.)

10.7.7   As will be seen (para. 11.6), an important role of the Episcopal Committee would be to prescribe minimum resource standards for all bishops.

The future role of the Commissioners

10.8.1   We recommend that there should only be carried on at the centre:

a.   those activities which it is necessary to carry on at the centre in order to provide common minimum standards;

b.   those activities which it is necessary to carry on at the centre because they relate to matters which are wider than those affecting only one diocese. The setting of nationwide IT protocols is an example; and

c.   those activities for which value is demonstrably added as a result of their being carried on at the centre rather than locally.

10.8.2   The corollary is that we consider that all activities which do not satisfy one or more of these tests should be conducted away from the centre. This might be within the diocese, but it might be on a regional basis.

10.9   We recommend that the primary role of the Commissioners in relation to bishops should be to manage investments and to generate from them spendable funds, which can be deployed in the support of episcopal ministry.

10.10   We describe in the following chapter the activities which we think should be carried on at the centre. We next consider here the application of the Commissioners' funds.

The central provision of funds: the starting point

10.11   We have referred (para. 4.43.2) to the Commissioners' funds which over the last decade have been applied in the support of episcopal ministry and in the operation of the Church of England in the dioceses.

10.12   We have found nothing improper in the use of funds for these purposes. Indeed, to some extent it has been the result of: upgrading staff; bringing their working accommodation up to the level necessary to comply with health and safety at work legislation; and introducing computers and IT equipment – to a standard which is not over-elaborate.

10.13   Nevertheless, where expenditure budgets are constructed on a bottom-up basis, there will almost certainly be pressure for a greater spending allocation. Furthermore, the discrepancies between budgets (see para. 12.4.2) suggest that some savings can be made.

10.14   We recognize that any satisfactory budgetary approach will be a two-way process, between funder and spender. However, we recommend that there should be a change of emphasis, and that after any necessary amendment to legislation, the starting point should be a central decision, perhaps taken jointly by the Commissioners and the Archbishops' Council, as to the total amount which should be allocated from central funds for the support of episcopal ministry and diocesan activities.

Central funds and block-granting

10.15 In outline, we recommend that:

10.15.1 As we have just stated, there should be determined the total amount from central sources which is to be applied for the support of episcopal ministry and diocesan activities;

10.15.2 From that amount, there should be set aside, and retained at the centre, the cost of:

  a. bishops' stipends;

  b. providing accommodation for diocesans;

  c. providing central services for all bishops;

  d. meeting the costs of national episcopal ministry; and

  e. establishing a contingency reserve; and

10.15.3 The balance should be devolved for the bishops in each diocese by way of block-grant.

Allocation between dioceses

10.16 We outline in Chapter 12 how we propose that the amounts of the block-grants should be calculated.

The bishops and the block-granted funds

10.17 We recommend that the devolved funds should be block-granted to the diocesan of each diocese, for the support of all bishops in that diocese (not to each bishop in each diocese).

10.18 We recommend that the spending decisions over those funds should be taken by the diocesan, in close consultation with the other bishops in the diocese and with the assistance of a small group appointed by him.

10.19 We make these recommendations:

a.   to encourage the needs of all bishops in a diocese to be considered together;

b.   because we consider that the bishops in a diocese are in the best position to decide how the available funds are to be spent. For example, if a bishop considers that his gifts lie primarily in visiting and teaching, and that he requires more funding for these purposes, then if he is able to reduce other costs, he should have the budget flexibility to redeploy the amount saved;

c.   because we consider that in many cases the most cost-effective arrangements, including obtaining *pro bono* support, can be made using local knowledge or contacts; and

d.   because we believe that the time of the bishop and his staff, as well as staff employed by the Commissioners, can be saved by taking decisions locally.

The Bishops' Resources Group

10.20   We recommend that each diocesan should appoint a Bishops' Resources Group.

10.21.1 In addition to the diocesan, the Bishops' Resources Group would comprise:

a.   all suffragans in the diocese; and

b.   not less than two other members ('the appointed members') appointed by the diocesan.

10.21.2 As well as having the power to appoint the appointed members, the diocesan would have the power to remove them.

10.21.3 A newly appointed diocesan would be required to review the membership of the Group within one year of taking up his appointment. Existing appointed members would be eligible for reappointment, but there should be no presumption that they would in fact be reappointed. We regard it as important that the appointed members should be persons of the diocesan's genuine choice and with whom he can have a constructive relationship.

10.22 It would be the responsibility of the diocesan to provide himself and the other bishops in the diocese with the necessary resources, up to the standard prescribed by the Episcopal Committee. This would be wholly or mainly from the block-granted funds.

10.23 Apart from the diocesan, all members of the Bishops' Resources Group would be advisory to the diocesan. They would have executive authority only if that was specifically conferred by the diocesan.

10.24.1 The main function of the Group as a whole would be to advise the diocesan with regard to the provision of resources.

10.24.2 The Group would have regard to the diocesan, regional and national implications of resourcing.

10.24.3 Any bishop in the diocese would be able to refer any resourcing issue to the Group.

10.24.4 The diocesan would be able to authorize any member or members of the Group to act on his behalf in the procurement of resources. This might particularly be so where:

> a. terms are to be negotiated for the supply of services or other facilities (whether from within the diocese or, for example, under regional arrangements);

> b. local negotiations are to be conducted with the DBF for supplementary provision; or

> c. endeavours are to be made to elicit *pro bono* support.

10.25 We attach importance to much financial planning being on a medium-term, as well as a short-term, basis. Accordingly, we envisage that the Group would draw up and maintain a five-year rolling programme (which we call an Episcopal Resources Plan) to take account of future financial requirements. It would, for example, deal with the replacement of major equipment or with expenditure to mark a special anniversary within the diocese.

10.26 Some bishops have told us that, apart from diocesan strategy plans, they have, or are contemplating introducing, episcopal strategy plans, setting out what they, as bishops, hope to achieve within the diocese, and how they will do so. Resourcing is only a small part of such plans, but so far as it is within our remit, we commend that approach, and **recommend** that the Resources Group should contribute fully to the resourcing elements of such plans.

Respective responsibilities of the Commissioners and DBFs

10.27.1 As we have stated (para. 10.4), we think that there should be a clearly recognized principle that there is a partnership between the Commissioners and the DBF in supporting the bishops in the diocese.

10.27.2 Because a bishop has, to a greater or lesser extent, a role both within the diocese and outside it, some have suggested that the costs which are incurred by bishops in exercising a diocesan role should be met from diocesan funds, and the costs which are incurred in exercising a wider role should be met from central funds.

10.28.1 We have considered that suggestion carefully but we do not recommend it.

10.28.2 In the first place, the financial pressures to which dioceses are becoming increasingly subject make it unrealistic to contemplate that in the near future they should bear a materially increased share in the costs of episcopal ministry.

10.28.3 In the second place, there is room for endless debate as to what constitutes a diocesan role and what a wider role, and indeed, they often overlap. Detailed analysis of each item of expenditure, and of the use of time (if stipends and premises expenses are to be brought into the calculation), would add to the burdens of bishops and their staff, as well as the staff of the DBF, significantly. Any such attribution would, therefore, in practice need to be on a very broad and unsatisfactory basis.

10.28.4 In the third place, and more fundamentally, the principle of partnership between the Commissioners and the DBF is the reflection of the theological truth that a bishop's ministry is a unity, whether it is exercised within a diocese or outside it.

10.29 Accordingly, we regard the proposed block-grant as being the Commissioners' partnership contribution to the cost of supporting the bishop's unified and indivisible ministry.

Banking arrangements

10.30.1 Block-granted money could be paid to the diocesan for him to handle in the same way as at the present time he handles his local account.

10.30.2 However, we **recommend** that the DBF should act as the banker of these funds.

10.30.3 We make this recommendation because:

a.   the amount of money would be much larger than the present payments into the local account, and the number of payments from it would be much greater, and we do not wish to impose this administrative burden on the bishop;

b.   the involvement of the DBF in this way will strengthen the notion of partnership;

c.   the handling of the funds by the DBF rather than the bishop will give the bishop some measure of protection;

d.   the block-grant is for the benefit of all bishops in the diocese, not only the diocesan; and

e.   the DBF will have more experience of and a greater opportunity for maximizing the interest to be earned on such funds between when they are received and when they are expended.

10.30.4 It follows from our recommendation that the DBF should act as banker that:

a.   the Commissioners would pay the block-grants to the DBF;

b.   the DBF would credit those amounts to a separate, fiduciary, account in its books (it would be a fiduciary account because the DBF would hold the money standing to the credit of it on trust for the diocesan and not as part of its own funds); and

c.   the DBF would make payments from the account when, but only when, authorized by or on behalf of the diocesan to do so.

10.31 Interest earned on the block-granted funds between the date of receipt and the date of expenditure would be credited to the fiduciary account.

Funding 'working costs'

10.32.1 At present, much the greater part of the 'working costs'[3] incurred both by diocesans and by suffragans is paid for by the Commissioners. We support their action in so doing.

10.32.2 However:

a.   these costs are only paid by the Commissioners on a discretionary basis;[4] and accordingly

b.   particularly in times of increased financial stringency, there is no *certainty* that they will continue to be paid, or that they will continue to be paid in full.

10.33.1 If the Commissioners were unable to fund working costs at about their present level, but no other alteration was made to the present circumstances, then there would need to be any or all of:

a.   an increased contribution from diocesan sources;

b.   procurement of support from other local sources; or

c.   a redefinition of the role of bishops.

10.33.2 Exactly the same position would arise if the block-grants were insufficient to meet the subvention to the extent envisaged. That would not be the result of the introduction of the block-granting system, but a consequence of the limitation of central funds.

10.34.1 While the Commissioners are able to continue funding at the present level, the recommendations which we have made would not cause any increased expenditure other than the modest cost to the DBF of managing the fiduciary account, and so they should cause no significant increase in the cost which is at present being borne by DBFs.

10.34.2 If, however, DBFs came to make additional contributions in cash, as a matter of procedure we **recommend** that they should do so by making the necessary transfer in their books to the fiduciary account. If the DBF provides services in kind, that procedure would not be necessary, but the cost of these services would be reflected in the DBF's accounts.

Underspends

10.35 We turn now to further aspects of the block-grant proposal. The first is that it is possible, but in view of the increasing pressure on central funds and so on the amount of the block-grant, in practice unlikely in ordinary circumstances, that the amount of the block-grant would not be fully expended in a year for its intended purpose.

10.36.1 We recommend that, in that event:

> a.   the diocesan should be able to retain all or part of the amount underspent, to be applied towards the cost of future expenditure which falls within the Episcopal Resources Plan (see para. 10.26); and

> b.   the diocesan should apply any residual balance towards areas of need and opportunity (see paras 4.7.2 and 4.7.3).

10.36.2 It follows that our proposal is that:

> a.   a balance of a block-grant should only be carried forward to a following year in order to meet specific planned expenditure; and

> b.   no part of the grant should be refundable to the Commissioners.

10.36.3 Although this is considered in Chapter 12, we make clear at this stage that if, by financial prudence, there is an underspend in one year, that in itself should not affect the amount of the block-grant for the following year.

Overspends

10.37 At present, if a bishop overspends on his local account, he is usually able to obtain an advance from the Commissioners. This advance is recovered from his local account allocation for the following quarter. If the overspend cannot be recovered in later quarters, the bishop may request that his budget be increased to cover it. This will be settled by negotiation between the bishop and the Commissioners.

10.38   We do not propose a similar facility under the new regime. We recommend that in the event of an overspend, it should be necessary for the diocesan (or, more likely, his Resources Group on his behalf) to make local arrangements to cover it.

Consequential issues

10.39   We refer:

a.   in Chapter 12 to the method of allocating block-granted funds between the bishops in each diocese and the method of accounting for them;

b.   in Chapter 13 to the supply and dissemination of information about the way in which block-granted funds have been used; and

c.   in Chapter 15 to the use of block-granted funds to provide facilities and services.

Auditing

10.40.1 We recommend that:

a.   the diocesan, no doubt through his Resources Group, should be responsible for producing an account of the movements over the fiduciary account and, in the case of expenditure, itemizing the expenditure under the standard headings to which we refer in Chapter 13; and

b.   the account should be certified both to the Commissioners and to the DBF by local auditors who in most, if not all, cases would be the DBF's auditors, but who, if necessary, would be approved by the Commissioners' auditors.

10.40.2 We hope that this certification would be sufficient to enable, without further enquiry, an auditor's opinion to be given on the accounts both of the Commissioners and of the DBF. We also hope that this certification would be sufficient to enable the Commissioners to demonstrate to the Inland Revenue that block-granted funds have been expended wholly, exclusively and necessarily for official purposes.

The Commissioners' accounts

10.41.1 In Chapter 13, we describe how we recommend that information should be given and disseminated about the use of the block-granted funds.

10.41.2 We have stated previously (para. 4.28) that we regard the entry in the Commissioners' statutory accounts of 'bishops' working costs' as being unhelpful because it implies that these costs are in some way personal to the bishops rather than being, as we regard it, largely for essential activities both in the diocese and more widely.

10.42 The Commissioners' accounts are matters for them and their auditors, but we **recommend** certain changes. Our suggestions are that:

a.   the existing description in the consolidated statement of financial activities[5] of 'parish ministry support' is changed to 'ministry support';

b.   the funds which would be expended at the centre on the support of episcopal ministry and the block-grants should be included under that heading; and

c.   in an explanatory note,[6] the amount of the block-grants should be shown in a line described as 'grants for the support of episcopal ministry'.

10.43 We also **recommend**, however, that an explanatory note should be added, indicating in broad terms how the block-grants had been spent. The Commissioners (commendably) seek to finalize their accounts within three months from the end of the year to which they relate. If it is not practical within this period to show how that year's grants have been spent, the note could give details of how those for the previous year had been spent.

The DBF's accounts

10.44.1 Because the DBF would not be entitled to the block-granted funds for its own purposes, those funds would not appear in the main body of the DBF's accounts;

10.44.2 DBF contributions to the fiduciary account would appear as part of its expenditure, and that part of the block-grant which is used to purchase services from the DBF would form part of the DBF's income; and

10.44.3 As the DBF would be the trustee of the fiduciary account, there would be a note setting out in outline the position in respect of the block-grant.

chapter 11

Central activities

Introduction

11.1   In this chapter, we consider the activities which should be conducted at the centre when the block-granting system is in operation.

11.2   For this purpose, we assume that the present payroll arrangements for the payment of stipends and pensions will continue in force.

11.3   We deal with the central activities in relation to see houses in Chapter 18.

The principles

11.4   We have stated previously (para. 10.8) that we consider:

a.   the centre should deal with:

i.   those activities which it is necessary to carry on at the centre in order to provide common minimum standards;

ii.   those activities which it is necessary to carry on at the centre because they relate to matters which are wider than those affecting a single diocese; and

iii.   those activities for which value is demonstrably added as a result of their being carried on at the centre rather than locally; and

b.   all other matters should be devolved.

Central activities generally

11.5.1   We recommend that:

a.   the main function of the Commissioners in relation to the support of episcopal ministry should be the management of investments and the generation of spendable funds from which resources can be provided; and

b. the body which we have termed the 'Episcopal Committee' (which might be the existing Bishoprics and Cathedrals Committee with some difference in membership)[1] should be a committee of the Commissioners.

11.5.2 If our recommendation for a reduction in the scope of the Commissioners' activities is accepted, it may be that, in due course, the Episcopal Committee should become a committee of the Archbishops' Council, but with some members nominated by the Commissioners. If that does happen, we envisage that it would only do so in the medium or long term.

11.6 We **recommend** that the Commissioners, through the Episcopal Committee, should:

a. set the minimum standards and scales of resources for all bishops;

b. operate the block-granting system which we have recommended,[2] including the calculation of the formula amount;[3] calculating and paying the block-grants; and collecting and disseminating information about the use of those funds;[4]

c. outsource the provision of certain facilities,[5] that is, make arrangements with third parties to provide those facilities on commercial terms; and

d. deal with the Inland Revenue in relation to the general provisions relating to the income taxation of bishops including the preparation and submission of those returns normally required from an employer (but not the individual personal tax returns of bishops).

11.7 In addition, at least for a transitional period, the Commissioners would need to have reserve powers which they could exercise in the event of a failure in the block-granting system.

11.8 We also envisage that whether certain further central activities are conducted by the Commissioners or by some other body, they should be funded by the Commissioners. Examples of these activities are:

a. the provision of the services of officers such as the Archbishops' Appointments Secretary and the Archbishops' Adviser on Bishops' Ministry;

b. the provision or arrangement of induction and other training; and

c. the identification of an officer for each province to deal with consecration and associated arrangements.[6]

Resourcing standards

11.9.1 A crucial function of the Episcopal Committee would be to set out minimum standards and scales of resources for all bishops. In doing so, the committee would be acting in a similar way to that in which guidelines for standards of accommodation in see and suffragans' houses were formulated.[7]

11.9.2 We recognize that, just as the accommodation standards in relation to suffragans' houses are matters of guideline only, the committee would have no powers of direction over matters outside the Commissioners' control.[8] There would, however, be the strongest moral obligation attached to those standards, and we would expect them to be observed.[9]

Outsourcing

11.10 In January 1999 the Commissioners introduced a system of outsourcing the provision of cars, by arrangement with Avis.[10] We commend that approach. The system has not yet been fully implemented and the Commissioners still own some cars. This accounts for some of the present administrative costs.[11]

11.11.1 We recommend a wider approach to outsourcing, both in the interests of efficiency and in the interests of cost-saving.

11.11.2 At some times, it might be advantageous to provide certain facilities centrally by outsourcing and at other times to acquire them locally.

11.11.3 Accordingly, we consider that the Commissioners should have specialist staff who would be responsible for outsourcing generally, and not just in relation to cars.

11.12.1 We consider that, except where it is necessary to provide facilities centrally,[12] the bishops in a diocese should be free to decide whether to take advantage of facilities which are outsourced or whether to acquire them locally. There should always be a strong presumption that facilities should be acquired in the most cost-effective manner, while recognizing that in exceptional circumstances it may be material to a bishop's ministry for a different course to be adopted.[13]

11.12.2 We recognize that where there are outsourcing arrangements, the benefit of using those arrangements is likely to be related to the number of bishops who use them. Nevertheless we consider that the bishops should have the freedom to decide, and that market forces will indicate the most cost-effective course.

Training
11.13 We turn now to two other types of need which have been raised with us. The first relates to in-service training. (We deal with induction training in Chapter 14.)

11.14.1 The provision of in-service training is important and we commend the Archbishops' Adviser on Bishops' Ministry for increasingly facilitating it.[14] It is not for us to make detailed recommendations about the nature of this training.

11.14.2 We observe that generally within the professions, it is now a condition of the authority to practise that the individual undergoes continuing training, and that although we are cautious about applying secular models to the Church, it does seem to us that in this respect the same consideration should apply to bishops, and indeed to all clergy.[15]

Episcopal consultancy
11.15.1 We have considered whether to recommend the appointment of an episcopal consultant.

11.15.2 In outline, the suggestion was made to us that a bishop should be appointed in each province to act as a consultant to other bishops in that province. The consultant would be available: to review with bishops their working practices; where possible, to help in resolving difficulties; to encourage and, if requested, to help in arranging appraisals of bishops; to encourage training; and to spread good or helpful practice. The consultant would be in addition to, and would not replace, the Archbishops' Adviser on Bishops' Ministry.[16]

11.16 Various factors underlie that suggestion. One is that there is at present no organized system for spreading best practice among bishops. We think there should be.

11.17.1 The second factor relates to accountability for ministry. All bishops are directly accountable to God for the exercise of their ministry; human accountability is more diverse.

11.17.2 All bishops owe allegiance to their archbishop, but in practice that is regarded as being canonical allegiance only.

11.17.3 Suffragans are more directly accountable to their diocesan, and most will have agreed a role description with their diocesan.

11.17.4 Many bishops take the initiative to appoint consultants, often in specific fields.

11.17.5 There is, however, no established system in which bishops, particularly diocesans, are by regular discussion called to account in a constructive (and non-oppressive) manner.

11.18.1 The third factor behind the suggestion was derived from the pressure of the work load.

11.18.2 Should there be a structural system in which from time to time a bishop has to stand back from those pressures and discuss the exercise of his ministry with another?

11.19.1 Some bishops have told us that they would welcome such an arrangement. We ourselves see merit in it and, indeed, we think that it could be a means of providing pastoral care for bishops and support for them in their ministry.

11.19.2 The suggestion of having episcopal consultants would, however, in effect involve the appointment of two additional bishops, and in a time of increasing financial stringency, we have concluded that, on that ground, we cannot recommend it.

11.20 We do, however, **recommend** that the archbishops should consider appointing a small group of senior or recently retired bishops[17] to act as mentors to those of their younger colleagues who desire it.

chapter 12

Allocation of central funds

Introduction

12.1   In Chapter 10 we recommended that part of the Commissioners' funds which are to be applied in the support of episcopal ministry should be retained at the centre and that the remainder of such funds should be devolved by way of block-grant to the diocesan of each diocese.

12.2   The recommendation applies only to working costs.[1]

Objectives

12.3   Our recommendations are designed to produce a system which:

    a.   is clear;

    b.   treats bishops equitably; and

    c.   contributes to accountability, transparency and financial control.

Allocation between dioceses

12.4.1   There are a number of clearly stated guidelines as to the nature and scale of resources which are furnished to bishops. As we have shown, these include matters such as the numbers of personal support staff for which the Commissioners will pay[2] and the expenditure which can be charged to local accounts.[3] We refer in Chapter 18 to differences in the cost of maintaining see houses but, subject to that, one would expect that the costs of supporting each diocesan would be broadly the same, and that the costs of supporting each suffragan would also be broadly the same. The actual position is very different.

12.4.2   The Commissioners have provided us with figures in respect of 1999.[4] In addition to the lowest, average and highest figures, we also give the 5th lowest and 5th highest to reduce distortions at the extremes. The figures are:

£	Diocesans	Suffragans
Lowest	45,539	8,896
5th lowest	68,213	13,905
Average	91,662	29,545
5th highest	114,908	49,050
Highest	128,613	53,249

12.5.1 Furthermore, there are great variations within each heading of expenditure on working costs. To some extent the variations reflect general cost levels in different parts of the country.

12.5.2 To some extent they reflect temporary circumstances, such as vacancies in post.

12.5.3 To some extent they reflect special needs which have been recognized by the Commissioners.

12.5.4 To some extent they reflect different styles of ministry, and different expectations of bishops.

12.5.5 To some extent they appear to be historic, in that the usual starting point for the calculation of the budgetary provision for one year is the corresponding figure for the previous year.

12.6 There are numerous other reasons for the variations. They include:

a. the size of the see house, which affects the amount of the Commissioners' contribution to the cost of heating, lighting and cleaning;[5]

b. differences in personal support staff salaries, particularly where bishops do not call upon their full entitlement;

c. office costs, because in some cases these include rent payable or a proportion of diocesan office costs attributable to bishops;

d. the size and nature of the garden, which can affect the gardener's pay;[6] and

e. the distance from London, as that will affect travel costs.

12.7   There is, therefore, a multiplicity of reasons for these variations, but they are not made known either to the bishops generally – a
point to which we revert in the next chapter – or to the members of
the Church at large.

12.8   We regard this aspect of the present system as inequitable,
unhelpful and unsatisfactory.

Allocation by formula

12.9   We therefore **recommend** that:

> a.   the existing method of allocating funds for working costs
> should be abolished;
>
> b.   there should be a completely new start to the budgetary
> process; and
>
> c.   the allocation should be by formula.

12.10.1 We **recommend** that the same formula should be used for two
separate purposes, namely:

> a.   to give an objective assessment of the cost of providing
> the requisite support (irrespective of whether the funds are
> provided by the Commissioners or by the DBF); and
>
> b.   to provide the basis on which the funds which are
> available from the Commissioners are actually allocated
> between the bishops in each diocese.

12.10.2 We refer to the amount which is the product of the objective
assessment in relation to all bishops in a diocese as being 'the formula
amount'.

12.11.1 We describe the formula in the next section, but before doing
so we highlight two aspects of the proposal.

12.11.2 First, under the present system, working costs are budgeted
and accounted for separately in relation to each bishop. Under our
proposal, funds are allocated for all bishops in a diocese, as a group.

12.11.3 Second, although one of the purposes of the formula would
be to determine the allocation of central funds between the bishops in

each diocese, it would in no way prescribe how those funds are to
be spent: expenditure would be a matter solely for the diocesan in
consultation with his Resources Group.

The formula

12.12   Allocation by formula will be successful only if the detail is
worked out in full discussions between those affected. We therefore
only suggest an outline for the formula, as a basis for those discussions, and we recognize that there is much to be done in evolving the
detail of it.

12.13   Some of our suggestions involve reference to the figures for
a base year. We have in mind that such figures will be the average of
those for three years ending with the penultimate year before the year
in which the formula is first applied. Accordingly, the sequence
becomes:

    a.   year 1 :   base year (taking 3-year average figures)

    b.   year 2 :   year in which the formula amounts for the
                            implementation year are calculated

    c.   year 3 :   implementation year

12.14   We suggest that the formula should be based on the number
of posts for bishops in the diocese, irrespective of whether there are
temporary vacancies.

12.15.1 We suggest that the formula should be made up of six
elements:

    a.   staff costs;

    b.   office costs;

    c.   travel costs;

    d.   hospitality costs;

    e.   legal fees; and

    f.   other authorized costs.

12.15.2 We suggest that the staff costs should be calculated by reference to two full-time and one part-time members of staff for each
diocesan and one full-time member of staff for each suffragan. In the

case of a diocesan, the cost of one of the full-time members would be calculated at the national stipend rate. The salary of the other full-time post would be calculated at the prevailing local rates for senior secretaries, and the part-time post at prevailing local rates for more junior secretaries. There would be no allowance under this heading for the cost of a driver, because the costs of a driver are dealt with under travel, nor for the cost of a gardener, because the costs of a diocesan's gardener, if necessary, are dealt with as a housing expense.

12.15.3 Initially, the non-staff office costs would be calculated by taking the total of actual office costs incurred by all bishops in the base year; and then reallocating them between each diocese taking into account regional differences in cost levels.

12.15.4 We regard travel costs as including the cost of: public transport; a driver if one is employed; the costs of the use of an official car if one is provided; and a mileage allowance if a private car is used on official business. In the case of travel costs, we propose that, at the outset, there should be taken the aggregate of the travel costs incurred by all bishops in the base year, with that amount being reallocated between dioceses having regard to the total geographical area of the diocese, and its shape, with some weighting according to the distance from London.[7]

12.15.5 We suggest that hospitality costs should be calculated by taking the total of the hospitality costs actually incurred by all bishops in the base year, and reallocating this total among each diocese according as to 50% to the number of clergy in the diocese and as to 50% to the size of the total population (not church membership) of the diocese.

12.15.6 Legal fees would, at the outset, be the amount of the retainer to be paid to the diocesan's legal officer.

12.15.7 Other authorized costs would include those to be incurred by the bishops in relation to the selection and appointment of clergy in the diocese and in relation to ordinations. They would include the costs of the training of the bishops (the costs of the training of staff being included in the calculation of staff costs). They would also include one-off costs, such as removal and resettlement expenses of bishops and of chaplains. Every item of authorized costs in excess of a very small amount would be itemized. The total of these authorized costs would be calculated by reference to the total incurred in the base year.

12.16   We anticipate that the operation of the formula would be progressively refined during the first few years of the operation of the arrangements; and that it would be periodically reviewed thereafter.

Role of the Episcopal Committee

12.17   We proposed (para. 10.6) the formation of an Episcopal Committee as initially a committee of the Commissioners (the main funding body) to be the prescriber of minimum standards of resources. We **recommend** that this body should determine the formula amount in respect of the bishops in each diocese.

Special cases

12.18.1 We propose that provision should be made for special cases. For example, the travel and hospitality criteria in relation to the bishops in the Diocese of Europe will be different from those of other dioceses.

12.18.2 We **recommend** that there should be separate discussions with each diocese, so that all special circumstances affecting them can be identified.

12.18.3 In accordance with our general approach to special cases, we recommend that these should be identified, and that there should be made known the differences which have been made to the general formula to take account of them.

12.19   We suggest in a later chapter how the formula approach might be applied to PEVs.[8]

Differences between formula amounts and block-grants

12.20.1 If, in its final form, the formula is confined to working costs (as that expression is currently understood), and there is adequacy of the Commissioners' funds, then the formula amount will be the same as the amount of the block-grant.

12.20.2 If, however, the Commissioners' funds are not sufficient to meet the present working costs, so that the balance would fall to be paid by DBFs, the formula amount would be greater than the amount of the block-grant.

12.20.3 We do not envisage any circumstances in which the formula amount would be less than the amount of the block-grant.

12.21.1 We have considered further the consequences which would ensue if the Commissioners' funds are not sufficient to pay the contributions in full.

12.21.2 Our starting point is that there should be a proportionate reduction in the amount of the block-grants. The result would be that each DBF would, in principle, make the same percentage increase in its contribution to the cost of episcopal ministry.

12.21.3 However, we also **recommend** that, by analogy with the Selective Allocations[9] system, the better-off dioceses should make a greater increase in their contribution and the less affluent a lesser increase.

Statements of formula amounts

12.22.1 We recommend that the bishops in each diocese should receive a statement in each year showing:

    a.   the formula amount in respect of their diocese;

    b.   how it has been calculated; and, if different

    c.   the amount of the block-grant; and, by comparison with the formula amount

    d.   how the amount of the block-grant has been calculated.

12.22.2 We do not think that it would be helpful for the statement to include an indication of the contribution payable by the DBF. The *minimum* amount to be contributed from local sources would be the difference between the formula amount and the amount of the block-grant. However:

    a.   if other sources of local support are available, the local contribution might not come wholly from the DBF; and

    b.   as a result of local discussions between the Resources Group and the DBF, more than the minimum amount might be provided locally.

Use of funds

12.23.1 Our suggestion is that the factors in the formula are related to the *theoretical* cost of providing certain types of services and support, such as staff salaries and travelling costs.

12.23.2 It is no part of the proposal that the funds provided, either by means of the block-grant or from the DBF, should be spent in any particular way. Accordingly, we **recommend** that when the formula amount has been determined, and the money has been placed under the control of the diocesan, it should be for him, in consultation with his Resources Group, to decide how it is to be spent.

Effects of Underspends and Overspends

12.24.1 We hope that the block-grant system will enable some resources to be obtained less expensively than at present, and that it will enable different or improved resources to be obtained. We wish to encourage financial efficiency and we do not wish to discourage local endeavours to raise funds.

12.24.2 It would be inconsistent both with that intention and with the concept of allocation by block-grant for the fact of any underspend in one year to result in an adjustment to the formula amount or the amount of the block-grant in a subsequent year. Accordingly, we **recommend** that no such adjustment should be made.

12.24.3 We can envisage the possibility that, particularly as a result of local endeavours, the bishops in one diocese might be materially better resourced than those in another. We do not propose any adjustment to the formula amount on this ground, but we are aware of the work being done elsewhere on the principle of mutual support and we **recommend** that that approach should be adopted by bishops where the circumstances permit.

12.25 Although we do not consider that underspends by the bishops in one diocese should lead to any adjustment in the formula amount, nevertheless if there were to be repeated underspends by the bishops in a number of dioceses, that might indicate a ground for an adjustment to the formula.

12.26 The corollary to the recommendation that an underspend should not lead to an adjustment is that an overspend in one year should not be a ground for an increase in the formula amount or block-grant amount in a following year.

chapter 13

Transparency and disclosure

Introduction

13.1　In this chapter, we make proposals for the disclosure and use of information about working costs[1] and expenditure on bishops' houses.

13.2　Our consultations have revealed that the majority of bishops wish for a greater degree of disclosure. We make our recommendations on this subject, though we are aware that a group comprising members of the House of Bishops and of the Commissioners has also been established more recently to consider this issue.

The present position

13.3.1　At present, there is full disclosure in respect of stipends.

13.3.2　There are published:[2]

a.　the amount of the stipend of every bishop;[3] and

b.　the amount of the non-contributory pension contributions;[4]

c.　and the amount of employer's national insurance pension contributions are annually prescribed by Government.[5]

13.4.1　The total amounts expended on working costs and premises by the Commissioners are reflected in their accounts, but we have commented in Chapter 4 on the difficulty in interpreting them in some respects.

13.4.2　Expenditure incurred on working costs and premises by DBFs is reflected, but not necessarily identified in detail, in their accounts. There is no system for collating and making known centrally the aggregate expense incurred by DBFs on these matters.

Disadvantages of the present system

13.5.1 It is sometimes said that non-disclosure protects personal financial information, particularly salary levels of individual members of staff. This is particularly so in the case of a suffragan's secretary, who may be the only person working for him. It is also said that exceptional personal circumstances can arise in which disclosure would be inappropriate. It is further said that a large amount of time can be spent in answering pernickety questions on matters of detail. More generally, it is said that the circumstances vary so greatly that disclosure of figures without an accompanying, and perhaps lengthy, narrative can be misleading.

13.5.2 We accept the substance of all of these points, but we nevertheless consider that the advantages of disclosure outweigh the disadvantages.

13.6 We consider that:

13.6.1 For so long as there is non-disclosure there will inevitably be speculation;

13.6.2 If recent experience is a guide, much of that speculation will be wrong and it will hinder bishops in the exercise of their ministry;

13.6.3 There is nothing to hide; and

13.6.4 Those who contribute or have contributed, including present members of the Church, should be able to ascertain how their money has been spent.

13.7 Furthermore, several bishops have told us that it would be helpful for them to know how other bishops spend the funds made available to them. That is not so that the practices of others can be unthinkingly followed, but so that there can emerge a common understanding of the norm.

13.8 There is a further positive advantage in disclosure in relation to bishops. In the course of our work it has become clear to us that there is a widespread lack of understanding of what bishops do. We anticipate that disclosure of, and discussion of, the costs of their ministry will have a beneficial effect of making that work better known.

The consequences of change

13.9   So far as we have been able to judge, the experience of introducing disclosure, or increased disclosure, in other spheres has attracted attention for the first two or three years, but in the absence of anything untoward, little attention thereafter. This seems to be the general experience in relation to the enhanced disclosure requirements which have been introduced by statute in respect of the accounts of companies and of charities.

General consideration

13.10   We are in favour of full disclosure, but before describing our proposal, we wish to state as clearly as we can that our approach is not in the slightest prompted by any suggestion of impropriety in the operation of the present arrangement.

Proposal: the present arrangements

13.11   We recommend a policy of maximum disclosure and we hope that those concerned will be bold in adopting it.

13.12   In the next section of this chapter we comment on disclosure if the block-grant system which we have proposed is brought into effect. In this section we deal with disclosure while the existing arrangements continue.

13.13.1 We recommend that:

a   standard reporting format should be adopted;

b.   the DBF should furnish the Commissioners with details of the expenditure which it incurs in the support of episcopal ministry;

c.   information in the standard format should be produced by the Commissioners for each diocese, in respect of all bishops in the diocese; and

d.   those details should be made available both to the Bishop's Resources Group and, for their information, to the DBF.

13.13.2 We also **recommend** that:

    a.   the information in respect of all bishops in the diocese should be collated by the Commissioners by region, to form regional summaries; and

    b.   copies of all regional summaries should be made available to all bishops.

13.14 There is much room for debate about the degree of detail which is appropriate,[6] but our suggestion, as a basis for that discussion, is that it should be as shown in the example on pages 124–6.

13.15 We **recommend** that the totals A and B from all regional summaries should be reconciled by appropriate notes with the Commissioners' published accounts.

Proposal: the future arrangements

13.16 Under a block-grant regime, we envisage a similar process. Accordingly, we **recommend** that:

    a.   expenditure which is passed through the fiduciary account[7] should be analysed into these standard headings; and

    b.   the analyses should form the basis for the summaries which we propose.

13.17 The general appearance of the format would be similar, but its preparation would be made easier by the analyses of the fiduciary account.

Rolling records

13.18.1 One of the difficulties with any form of disclosure of this nature is that there will almost certainly be exceptional cases, and those exceptional cases can distort the general picture.

13.18.2 Accordingly, we **recommend** that when, in the light of experience, the format is refined, there should be published a rolling ten-year record so that the average position will emerge.

Summary of central region

2002 figures

Serial (1)	Description (2)	Diocese [A] (3)	Diocese [B] (4)	Diocese [C] (5)	Diocese [D] (6)	Diocese [E] (7)
	Number of bishops in diocese					
	COMMISSIONERS' FUNDING					
	Office and support staff costs					
	Chaplain's/lay assistant's pay and pension contributions					
	Secretaries' pay and pension contributions					
	Office expenses					
	Office equipment					
	Office furnishings					
	Administrative and operational costs					
	Ordination expenses					
	Patronage expenses					
	Training					
	Legal fees					
	Removal and resettlement expenses					
	Other					

Serial (1)	Description (2)	Diocese [A] (3)	Diocese [B] (4)	Diocese [C] (5)	Diocese [D] (6)	Diocese [E] (7)
	Individual working costs					
	Cars					
	Driver's pay and pension provision					
	Other travel					
	Subsistence					
	Hospitality					
	Premises					
	Heating, lighting, cleaning					
	Maintenance and repairs					
	Insurance					
	Council tax and water charges					
	Gardener's pay and pension provision					
	Garden expenses					
	Agent's fees					
	Other recurrent expenses					
	Less: Income receivable	( )	( )	( )	( )	( )
	TOTAL A					
	Add: Capital expenditure					
	TOTAL B					

Serial (1)	Description (2)	Diocese [A] (3)	Diocese [B] (4)	Diocese [C] (5)	Diocese [D] (6)	Diocese [E] (7)
	DBF FUNDING					
	Office and support staff costs					
	Support staff					
	Office equipment					
	Other					
	Administrative and operational costs					
	Any					
	Individual working costs					
	Any					
	Premises					
	Maintenance and repairs					
	Insurance					
	Council tax and water charges					
	Garden					
	Other recurrent expenses					
	TOTAL C					
	Add: Capital expenditure					
	TOTAL D					
	GRAND TOTAL (B + D)					

Costing

13.19 This is one of the few recommendations which we make which would cost more than under the present arrangements. However, until there is agreement on the amount of detail which is appropriate, the amount of that cost cannot be reliably estimated, but we anticipate that it would involve the services of one member of staff for one-third of his or her time.

chapter 14

Taking up office

Introduction

14.1   In this chapter, we consider the needs and resourcing requirements of newly appointed bishops. We are concerned here with the
period from when an individual is first asked whether he would be
willing to accept a bishopric until the end of his first year in office.

14.2   Many bishops have told us that this was the most difficult
period in their whole ministry, both before and after consecration as
a bishop – a view frequently and strongly endorsed by their wives.

The appointment of a diocesan

14.3   It may be helpful for us first to describe in brief outline the
procedure for the appointment of a diocesan. We do not aim to give
a comprehensive account of the whole process, but only one which is
sufficient for the consideration of the issues which fall within our
remit.[1]

14.4.1   A diocesan is appointed by the Sovereign acting on advice
from the Prime Minister following a submission from the Crown
Appointments Commission. The process begins with the Church,
requires a submission to the Sovereign, and ends with the Church.

14.4.2   Part of the process by which an appointment is made is under
review as we write this report and may change, but at present it
involves:

> a.   *the Crown Appointments Commission.*[2] The Commission
> is chaired by the Archbishop of the Province in which the
> vacancy has arisen. It comprises *ex officio* and elected
> members, including four elected representatives of the diocese;

> b.   *the Diocesan Vacancy in See Committee.* Each diocese
> has such a committee, but it only meets when required.
> The Committee draws up a Statement of Needs and elects
> representatives to serve on the Crown Appointments
> Commission; and

c. *the Prime Minister's Secretary for Appointments and the Archbishops' Appointments Secretary* who consult widely within the diocese concerned and the Church at large. The Archbishops' Appointments Secretary also provides background information about potential candidates from his or her extensive contacts within the Church and elsewhere.

14.4.3 The Crown Appointments Commission is informed in its work by two key documents: the Statement of Needs from the diocese (which usually also contains a detailed description of the diocese) and a joint Memorandum from the two Secretaries which reflects the results of their consultations. It also has biographies of all the candidates.

14.4.4 When the Commission has made its decision, the archbishop who took the chair at the meeting writes to the Prime Minister with the names of the two candidates which the Commission wishes to put forward. If the Commission so wishes, the archbishop puts forward those names in the Commission's order of preference.

14.4.5 The Prime Minister does not initiate the process, and does not introduce any names of his own. He can select his preferred candidate from the names submitted to him from the Commission, but there is no convention that he must follow any order of preference expressed by the Commission.[3] Alternatively, the Prime Minister, usually after consultation with the relevant archbishop, can ask for other names to be submitted to him.

14.4.6 The ultimate decision is that of the Sovereign. However, after the Prime Minister has made his selection, but before the submission is made to the Sovereign, the preferred candidate is approached, in conditions of strict confidentiality and invited, together with his wife, if he is married, to meet the Prime Minister's Appointments Secretary. The candidate is asked to indicate whether, in the event of the Sovereign so deciding, he would be willing to accept the appointment. He is shown extracts from the Appointments Secretaries' Memorandum and the Statement of Needs prepared by the diocese. He is also shown a document prepared from information supplied by the Commissioners' Bishoprics and Cathedrals Department describing the see house and giving certain other information of relevance to a new bishop.

14.4.7   If the candidate indicates his willingness to accept, he is then asked to undergo a medical examination. Provided that the result is satisfactory, thereafter the Prime Minister makes his recommendation to the Sovereign, as constitutional monarch. If the Sovereign agrees to the recommendation, the Sovereign will nominate the chosen candidate for election.

14.4.8   When the Sovereign's will is known, the Prime Minister's Appointments Secretary agrees with the diocesan-designate and others the date on which the announcement is to be made. It is made from 10 Downing Street, and there is a simultaneous announcement and press conference in the diocese.

14.5   Some weeks elapse between when the preferred candidate indicates his willingness to accept, and when the public announcement is made. On receipt of the Prime Minister's letter, the candidate, if married, is permitted to discuss the approach with his wife. After meeting the Prime Minister's Appointments Secretary he can discuss the approach with his diocesan as well as with his spiritual adviser or one close personal friend. A few days before the announcement is made the candidate is also permitted to let members of his immediate family know. He will also have seen the relevant archbishop. However, unless he has special dispensation, until the announcement is made the bishop-designate is not permitted to inform anyone else whomsoever of his prospective appointment.

14.6.1   When the announcement has been made, the Sovereign has no further decision-taking[4] role in the process but will receive the new bishop's homage.

14.6.2   The subsequent procedure is outlined in Appendix E. It includes:

    a.   the election of the bishop-designate by the dean and chapter of the cathedral church of the diocese;

    b.   the confirmation of the election by the vicar-general of the province;

    c.   the consecration of the new bishop, if he is not already in bishop's orders;

d.   the paying by the new bishop of homage to the Sovereign; and

e.   the enthronement of the new bishop in the cathedral church of the diocese.

14.7   Shortly after a candidate has seen the Prime Minister's Appointments Secretary, the candidate meets with the archbishop of the province in which he will serve. The archbishop will offer the candidate advice and give him an assurance of support. The archbishop may encourage the candidate to continue to develop existing interests or to develop new ones. Whatever is said at that meeting is not incorporated into any formal document.

The appointment of a suffragan

14.8.1   The position is different where there is a vacancy in a suffragan see. The initiative for filling that vacancy lies with the diocesan.

14.8.2   The currently recommended procedure[5] is that:

a.   the diocesan consults[6] as to the emphasis of the work which is to be sought during the next episcopate, and the kind of priest best able to carry it out;

b.   in the light of those consultations, the diocesan prepares a draft job description;

c.   the diocesan forms a small group of his choice to assist him in considering names of potential candidates and confers with the Archbishops' Appointments Secretary;

d.   prior to any approach to any candidate, the diocesan consults with his archbishop[7] so that the archbishop becomes fully involved in the process;

e.   the diocesan approaches one or more candidates on a confidential basis, but does not usually conduct any formal interviewing programme;

f.   the diocesan decides upon his preferred candidate and asks him whether, if invited, he would be willing to accept the appointment;

g.   if the candidate indicates his willingness to accept, the diocesan advises the archbishop and the candidate meets with the Archbishops' Appointments Secretary;

h.   a medical examination of the preferred candidate is conducted;

i.   the archbishop petitions the Sovereign, through the Prime Minister, for the filling of the vacancy and submits two names. The first is that of the preferred candidate. The second is that of someone who has not been invited, but whom the diocesan would be happy to see appointed if for some reason the preferred candidate is unable to take up the appointment. In the case of a suffragan, the convention is that the Prime Minister will advise the Sovereign to assent to the appointment of the first name on the petition;

j.   if the Sovereign agrees, the Prime Minister's Appointments Secretary informs the diocesan and the bishop-designate that the Sovereign assents to the appointment; and

k.   the Prime Minister's Appointments Secretary agrees with the bishop-designate and the diocesan the date on which the appointment will be announced from 10 Downing Street, and on which also a local announcement will be made and a press conference held.

14.8.3   If the bishop-designate is not already in bishop's orders, the Sovereign directs the archbishop of the province to consecrate him.

14.9   There is no election or confirmation process for a suffragan; a suffragan does not pay homage to the Sovereign; and a suffragan is not enthroned.

14.10   Although consecrated, a suffragan cannot exercise episcopal functions until powers have been delegated to him by the diocesan. This delegation requires the consent of the diocesan synod.[8]

Secrecy
14.11   A notable aspect of this process relates to the conditions of secrecy during the period from when the candidate is first approached to when the announcement is made.

14.12   The candidate, particularly if he is not already in bishops' orders, may well feel daunted by the responsibilities and challenges of his new role: yet during the secrecy period he is precluded from discussing his concerns and is expected to carry on with the duties of his existing office as if they would be continuing in the ordinary way. This includes making appointments which he knows he will not be able to keep.

14.13   Very often the new bishop will be moving from a different part of the country. Frequently it will be necessary for him and his wife to make arrangements for their children's schooling in an unfamiliar area. Yet, without special permission, during the secrecy period he may not refer to his new position in discussion with schools.

14.14.1 Housing presents another difficulty. The candidate and his wife may try, without being observed, to view the house from the outside, but they cannot make themselves known to the serving bishop, if there is one, and they cannot view the house from the inside.

14.14.2 Furthermore, if the candidate is to become a suffragan, and there are special housing needs, he cannot during this period discuss them with the diocesan surveyor.

14.15   It has not surprised us that bishops have described the secrecy period as the longest period in their lives.

14.16.1 We appreciate the sensitivity in any system of Crown appointments, and we do not make comments on that system as such. It is, however, clear that in many respects the appointment process would be much less stressful if the conditions for secrecy were relaxed. We are not persuaded that some relaxation would be inconsistent with the observance of proper proprieties.

14.16.2 We recognize the need for secrecy until the point at which the preferred candidate is approached. We **recommend**, however, that serious consideration should be given to making the period from when the candidate is approached to when the announcement is made as being one of *confidentiality*, not of *secrecy*. In our view, during this period the candidate should be able, if he so wishes:

    a.   to meet the serving bishop, if there is one;

    b.   to see the house; and

    c.   to discuss schooling.

14.16.3 We also **recommend** that the period of confidentiality should be kept to the very shortest that is practicable.

The wife of the new bishop

14.17   We refer in Chapter 17 to some of the issues concerning bishops' wives, but we note here that when a candidate is approached, his decision will have a fundamental effect not only on him, but also on his wife and his children. Acceptance of the invitation will often involve his wife giving up, or, at the minimum, interrupting, her own career. Furthermore, if the candidate is a parish priest, acceptance of the invitation may well involve him and his family moving from a community in a parish which provides mutual support to a position which can be isolated and lonely. These considerations may not only cause stress to the candidate's wife, but may well increase the burden on the candidate. Clergy often face similar issues when invited to take up new appointments, but their spouses may not experience the same degree of isolation as that of the wife of a new bishop.

Coordination

14.18.1 In view of these and other factors, it might be expected that one person would be responsible for coordinating:

    a.   the preparation of a job description for the post;

    b.   the furnishing of information about the resources which will be available;

    c.   the provision of those resources and of any others that are necessary to enable the job to be done;

    d.   the provision of a suitable house, including dealing with associated issues such as any requisite refurbishment or redecoration;

    e.   the introduction of mentors; and

    f.   the consecration and reception process.

14.18.2 There is no such person: we **recommend** that there should be in each province. We do not propose new posts, but that the responsibilities should be absorbed within the existing establishment.

The Archbishops' Adviser for Bishops' Ministry

14.19.1 We refer here to the Archbishops' Adviser for Bishops' Ministry (AABM), an important resource for bishops-designate and for serving bishops, particularly those who are newly appointed.

14.19.2 The AABM has confidential discussions with the bishop-designate and his wife, as well as arranging an induction programme for the bishop-designate as a bishop.[9] However, the AABM's responsibilities are much wider than supporting in these ways new bishops[10] and he is not in a position to provide the coordination which we recommend.

Job description: Suffragans

14.20.1 We comment now on some of the aspects for which we think coordination is required.

14.20.2 First, we unreservedly support the recommendation that every suffragan should have a clearly defined job description, setting out his duties and responsibilities; what is expected of him; and how his diocesan will support him. Where there is an area scheme, in part the terms of that scheme will cover the scope of his responsibilities. However, we **recommend** that there should be such a description in all instances. Some of the unhappier cases which we have seen are those where there is little shared understanding by diocesan and suffragan of what each can expect from the other.

14.21 We **recommend** in Chapter 16 that there should be regular appraisals, and if appropriate, modifications to the job description as the suffragan's ministry develops.

Expectations of diocesans

14.22.1 Because, in practice, diocesans, unlike suffragans, do not have a clear relationship of accountability to anyone,[11] we do not propose that they should have job descriptions. However, we do think it important that they should have a clear understanding of what is expected of them, and a means by which they can measure themselves against those expectations. This should be made clear when they are approached. Accordingly, we **recommend** that a diocesan should have a Statement of Expectations.

14.22.2 As a result of a fairly recent change of practice,[12] extracts from the Appointments Secretaries' Memorandum[13] are given to a candidate when he is approached. The appropriate parts of that are a helpful starting point in preparing the statement.

14.22.3 Furthermore, where the archbishop has indicated his wish that the new diocesan should develop interests in certain fields, that should also be included.

14.23.1. We envisage that the statement should be provided by the archbishop of the province; if the archbishop thought fit, considered by the Archbishops' Council; and discussed with the new bishop during the appointment process.

14.23.2 Notwithstanding the pressure on the time of both, we think it highly desirable that the statement should be reviewed from time to time in structured discussion between the archbishop and the diocesan.

Statement of resources

14.24.1 We recommend that, at the time when a candidate is invited to accept appointment, it should be made clear to him what resources will be made available to him, and that he should be given an outline of the financial circumstances of the diocese.

14.24.2 This is particularly so in the case of the appointment of diocesans. To us it has the sense of unreality for extracts from the Appointments Secretaries' Memorandum to set out, among other things, the aspirations of those in the diocese without indicating the resources of the diocese which will be available to the new bishop to enable him to meet them.

Housing

14.25.1 In relation to see houses, the Commissioners adopt the sensible policy of seeking to carry out necessary works to the house during an interregnum.[14] We have no doubt that, in general, this policy is right, but we have been given evidence of significant difficulties in its application in some cases.

14.25.2 The causes of these difficulties appear to be:

    a.   in some cases the short period of the interregnum, so that the requisite works cannot be carried out in time;

b.   insufficient coordination between the planning for the appointment of the new bishop and preparation of the property (although in some cases the interregnum may occur at short notice); and

c.   in some cases unexpected difficulties arising in relation to the property.

14.26.1 In the first place, this reinforces our recommendation for all aspects of the appointment process to be coordinated.

14.26.2 We recommend that at a very early stage in the appointment process, the incoming bishop should be fully informed about any on-going works which will be carried out; and about any major works which are intended to be carried out within the foreseeable future. This is even more important if there are any plans, however tentative, to replace the existing house.

14.27.1 Some of the problems have been caused by the fact that a serving bishop approaching retirement has decided not to carry out routine maintenance work, including re-decoration, in order to minimize the inconvenience to himself and his family. This has had the effect of increasing the amount of work to be done in an interregnum.

14.27.2 However, the programme of quinquennial inspections recently[15] introduced by the Commissioners is intended to provide a rolling programme of maintenance work, and when this is fully under-way it should ensure that every see house is generally in good order in the future. We consider that bishops should not have the power to delay these works.

14.28.1 Because DBFs own suffragans' houses, the practice with regard to them varies.

14.28.2 Where there are deficiencies in operation, they appear to be due to the fact that because the provision of suffragans' houses is not part of the mainstream work of the diocesan surveyor, work on these houses has not been planned sufficiently in advance or given sufficient priority in the context of the appointment of the new bishop.

14.28.3 We think that the diocesan, through his Resources Group, when formed, should also have a direct interest in ensuring that each newly appointed suffragan is satisfactorily housed.

Mentoring

14.29.1 We **recommend** that each newly appointed bishop and, if he is married, his wife, should be helped to find another bishop and, if appropriate, his wife to act as mentors.

14.29.2 At present, this happens fairly frequently on an ad hoc basis and the AABM is always willing, if asked, to help effect introductions. However, we think that it would be helpful for all newly appointed bishops to have mentors.

14.29.3 We **recommend** that, in general, the mentor-bishop should be serving in a different diocese, partly so that, in the case of a suffragan, there will be no confusion in his relationship with his diocesan. In the ideal case, the mentor-bishop should have been in post for a few years, so that he and his wife have experience of the operation of the system, but are not too far removed from their own experience on appointment.

Consecration and reception

14.30 We have shown[16] that, unless he is already in bishop's orders, every new diocesan and every new suffragan will be consecrated. It is the practice for there to be a reception immediately following the service of consecration.

14.31 We have reviewed:

    a. the arrangements for the consecration and the reception; and

    b. the costs.

14.32.1 The Commissioners pay the 'official' costs of consecration, namely:

    a. the net cost of the consecration service (that is, the charge levied by the cathedral, less money given at the collection);

    b. the use of premises for the post-service reception;

    c. the cost of entertaining the official guests at the reception; and

d.   the cost of entertaining a small number of family and personal guests of the new bishop.

14.32.2 The official guests include the other serving bishops of the province, and their wives, representatives of the Commissioners and civic representatives of the diocese in which the new bishop will serve.

14.32.3 At least in the past one of the causes of dissatisfaction with the process has been that some newly consecrated bishops have been asked to pay personally the cost of entertaining some of the guests whom he has not personally invited.

14.33.1 The arrangements for the reception in the northern province differ from those in the southern.

14.33.2 In the northern province there are two receptions. The Archbishop of York holds one, for the participating bishops and their wives, together with civic and other official guests. The Commissioners pay the cost, as an expense of the archbishop's office.

14.33.3 The new bishop has his own reception for his family and personal guests. The Commissioners pay the cost of entertaining up to 20 guests, at a maximum charge of £15 a head, inclusive of VAT. The new bishop must pay for any additional guests whom he wishes to invite.

14.33.4 In the southern province there is only one reception, for both the official guests and the new bishop's personal guests. As in the case of the northern province, the new bishop must pay personally for his personal guests in excess of a specified number.

14.34.1 We have been informed by the Commissioners that the average cost to the Commissioners of each consecration and reception in 1999 was about £2,250.

14.34.2 We commend the various measures which are being taken or considered to reduce the costs. These include holding the service in the afternoon, where little more than a cup of tea may be provided for guests; and generally continuing the practice of consecrating more than one bishop in the same service.

14.34.3 We regard as modest the number, up to 20, of the personal guests who can attend the reception at the expense of the Commissioners.

14.35 So far as the new bishop is concerned, many of the problems have in the past arisen, particularly in the southern province, because several people have been involved in the arrangements and the issue of invitations for the service and reception; and because of uncertainty as to the financial arrangements.[17] Almost all new bishops will wish to invite many more than 20 personal guests: quite apart from members of their family and personal friends, they will wish to include those from, for example, parishes in which they have served.

14.36.1 We recommend that:

    a.   in each province there should be one designated officer whose responsibility should be to make all arrangements for the service and reception;[18]

    b.   that officer should inform the bishop-designate in advance of the cost of inviting each personal guest in excess of the stipulated number;

    c.   the number of personal guests for whom the Commissioners pay should be increased, even if the number of official guests has to be reduced; and

    d.   so far as the arrangements for the reception are concerned, the bishop-designate should have to do little more than furnish a list of the names and addresses of the personal guests whom he wishes to invite.

14.36.2 We also **recommend** that all official costs should be paid directly from central funds, and we have not, therefore, made any provision for consecration costs in the calculation of the formula amounts for the purposes of block-granting.[19]

Preparation and induction
14.37 We recommend that newly appointed bishops should follow the strong encouragement which is given to them:

    a.   to spend a week of preparation in residence;

b.   to participate in an induction programme; and

c.   to go on retreat.

14.38.1 The period in residence, usually in a theological college, is intended to give the bishop-designate the opportunity to read and to discuss with those around him issues which he will encounter in his future role.

14.38.2 Where the bishop-designate so requests, the AABM arranges a specific programme, if necessary in confidence. For example, a bishop-designate might seek special briefing on racism or interfaith issues.

14.38.3 We commend the provision of these periods in residence and have no specific recommendations to make in relation to them.

14.39.1 The induction course is in two parts. The first part is in the autumn, usually in September, and the second part in the following spring.

14.39.2 The present style of induction course requires participation by a minimum of about six people: say at least three new bishops and three facilitators. Much of the value is said to be derived from the discussions with and the interchanges between the participants.

14.40.1 We think it important that every bishop-designate should attend an induction course. We **recommend** that it should include – but not be restricted to – training in time and diary management; the most effective use of personal staff; financial management; and office procedures.

14.40.2 We think it highly desirable that at least the initial part of such a course should be held *before* the bishop-designate takes up his appointment.

14.41   The disadvantage of the present arrangements is that if a new bishop is appointed at the beginning of a calendar year, he could wait for nine months before attending the first part of the induction course. If, before his appointment, he had made immovable commitments so that he could not attend that course, he would have to wait for 21 months before attending another.

14.42   We recommend that:

a.   the archbishops should consider reviewing the timetable for consecrations in each of the northern and southern provinces, so that they occur at approximately regular intervals, with, where appropriate, two or three bishops being consecrated on the same occasion;[20] and

b.   induction courses should be arranged as part of that timetable, so that, save in exceptional circumstances, a bishop-designate should be able to attend the first part of the course *before* he takes up his appointment.

14.43   As all the bishops in a province are encouraged to attend consecrations, the consecration of two or three bishops on the same occasion would save expense on post-consecration receptions, but, more importantly, would involve bishops in less time and also fewer travelling expenses.

Timing

14.44   A number of factors affect the period between when the appointment of a new diocesan is announced and when he takes up his appointment[21]. In some instances that period can be unsatisfactorily short.

14.45   In almost all cases a candidate for appointment as a diocesan or a suffragan will be heavily engaged in the post in which he is currently serving.

14.46   We recognize that circumstances can arise where urgent action is necessary, but we **recommend** that the period of time between announcement and taking up office should be long enough:

a.   to enable the bishop-designate to hand over the duties of his present office in an orderly manner;

b.   to enable him to prepare for his new role, both in making the practical arrangements and in participating in:

i.   the period in residence;[22] and

ii.   an induction programme;

c.   to enable any necessary works to be carried out to the house; and

d.   not least, for him to have a holiday or other period of rest.

Support before assumption of appointment

14.47.1 A bishop-designate may need special secretarial and administrative support between when the announcement is made and when he takes up his appointment. This is particularly so where he has only limited administrative support in his existing office.

14.47.2 We recommend that as soon as an announcement is made, the Bishops' Resources Group of the diocese in which the bishop-designate will serve should endeavour to provide that support, no doubt in liaison with the Bishops' Resources Group of the diocese in which the bishop-designate is currently serving.

Removal costs

14.48.1 We have referred[23] to the present arrangements for the payment of removal costs and resettlement expenses within a combined overall limit of, at present, £8,000.[24]

14.48.2 This leads to the capricious result that the greater the distance between the new bishop's present house and his future house, and so the greater the removal cost, the less is the maximum amount of the resettlement grant.

14.49 We recommend that, as with clergy:

a. the removal expenses and the resettlement grant should be considered as separate matters;

b. the removal expenses should be paid as incurred; and

c. there should be a separate scale for the reimbursement of resettlement expenses.[25]

Retirement

14.50 We take the opportunity here of making a corresponding recommendation with regard to removal expenses incurred on retirement. We recommend that, on retirement, a bishop's removal expenses should be reimbursed.

Hand over procedure

14.51 It has surprised us that, at present, there are no structured arrangements for one bishop to hand over to another. This will not always be possible, but where it is possible we think that it will be beneficial. We envisage that this will be so where one bishop hands over to another as the diocesan; and where one bishop hands over to another as an area bishop. We appreciate that it might not be so appropriate where a suffragan without specific geographical responsibility is to hand over to another, particularly if the successor will have a materially different job description. At a recent enthronement service, the outgoing diocesan handed his pastoral staff to his successor. It was a simple ceremony of immense significance and profound meaning to all those present.

14.52 Accordingly, we **recommend** that wherever possible there should be a structured hand over, and that in that process account should be taken of any material changes in the role which is to be performed.

chapter 15

Local provision of resources

Introduction

15.1 We have recommended[1] placing block-granted funds under the control of the diocesan bishop to be used for the provision of resources for all bishops in the diocese. In this chapter, we consider some aspects of the application of those funds.

DBFs and regional co-operation

15.2 We have not envisaged that each diocesan and his Resources Group should necessarily make independent arrangements for the procurement of services and facilities. In many cases these will be provided most effectively by the DBF and, in one important case which we note later (para. 15.13.1), we think that they should be.

15.3 However, we **recommend** that representatives of all Resources Groups within a region should consider whether resources might best be provided on a collective basis. We are aware that at present some DBFs combine in making arrangements for bulk purchases, and we recommend that that approach should be pursued in the provision of resources for bishops.

Pro bono support

15.4 We have little doubt that, as much in some quarters outside the Church as within it, there is a considerable potential pool of goodwill which can be used to support episcopal ministry.[2] In some circumstances, it can be difficult for bishops personally to seek such support, but there should be no difficulty in their Resources Group doing so. Secondment of a member of staff and provision of IT equipment or IT training for staff or IT technical support are all examples. Engagement of persons of ability who have retired early to help with administration and research, perhaps on payment of an honorarium, is another example.

15.5 We take the view that there is nothing unacceptable in such an approach, but, rather, we **recommend** that it should be actively pursued. Indeed, if financial constraints on the Church become much tighter, we could envisage *pro bono* support being an essential element in the provision of future support at the level which is now regarded as adequate.

15.6   *Pro bono* support of a bishop has wider benefits. The discussions leading to it, and consideration of feedback from it, are one means of making known more widely what the bishop does; and obtaining *pro bono* support is a possible means of involving others in the affairs of the Church.

Support staff generally

15.7   A diocesan will usually have a senior secretary or personal assistant, a part-time assistant secretary, and a chaplain or a lay assistant. A suffragan will have a secretary or personal assistant. In addition, a diocesan may have a driver and a gardener: in most cases they will be engaged on a part-time basis.

15.8   We have received much evidence of the skill and loyalty of many of those in all of these capacities: their work may involve many hours of unpaid overtime and their working conditions may be very far from ideal.

15.9   The pressures on bishops are, in our view, likely to increase even further. We therefore take the view that a bishop should have personal support staff of a size and calibre which would free him to the maximum extent from all non-essential administrative and related work, and, as a corollary, that he should to the maximum extent be able to delegate such work.

15.10   A bishop needs to have a relaxed relationship with each member of his personal support staff. Accordingly, we **recommend** that, so far as possible,[3] a newly appointed bishop should be able to change staff already in post. Technological advances can mean that a member of staff who was highly suitable in one era is less so in another. Furthermore, developments in the style of a bishop's ministry can lead to a change in his support requirements, such as a greater need for research assistance. And, if personal chemistry is wrong, that is not necessarily a criticism of either party.

15.11 We consider that staff training will become even more important than in the past.

Secretarial staff

15.12.1 We recommend that in ordinary circumstances:

    a. a diocesan should have a full-time senior secretary and a part-time secretary; and

    b. a suffragan should have a full-time senior secretary.

15.12.2 The senior secretary should be of sufficient calibre to enable the bishop effectively to delegate to him or her.

15.13.1 Although, in general, we think that the diocesan, with his Resources Group, should be able to obtain resources from whatever source he thinks best, we **recommend** that:

    a. all secretaries should be employed by the DBF; and

    b. there should be specific recognition on DBF salary scales of 'bishop's principal secretary'.

15.13.2 We also **recommend** that although the secretaries would be employed by the DBF, the bishop should be involved in their selection to the same extent as at present.

15.13.3 We hope that these arrangements:

    a. would avoid a bishop having to deal directly with increasingly complex employment law issues;

    b. would be part of a wider arrangement under which the DBF would, from a pool of staff experienced in Church administration, provide cover on a temporary basis as required; and

    c. would facilitate a movement of staff between the diocesan office and the bishop's office.[4]

15.14.1 We see this recommendation as having two other advantages. First, at present there can be anomalies in the terms and conditions of service between the bishop's staff and senior staff employed in the diocesan office or elsewhere in the diocese. Pension entitlements have been mentioned to us as an example. We hope that, by this means, these anomalies would be progressively eliminated.

15.14.2 Second, no system can be expected to work perfectly, and if any difficulties do arise between a bishop and his secretary, this arrangement would provide the member of staff with the opportunity for discussion, without disloyalty, with the officer within the DBF who is responsible for personnel and other human resources issues.

Chaplains and lay assistants

15.15   We have examined at some length the support which is given to a diocesan either by an (ordained) chaplain or by a lay assistant.

15.16.1 At present:

a.   where the diocesan has a chaplain:

   i.   the Commissioners pay:

      aa. his or her stipend (usually at the diocesan minimum stipend level); and

      bb. national insurance and pension contributions; and

   ii.   although the practice varies, often the DBF provides accommodation (either from its own housing stock or, if part of the see house is used, by renting from the Commissioners);[5] and

b.   where the diocesan has a lay assistant:

   i.   the Commissioners pay:

      aa. a contribution to his or her salary cost (the salary being calculated at civil service higher executive officer or senior executive officer grades); and

      bb. the total national insurance and pension contributions;

   ii.   the DBF usually pays any excess salary costs; but

   iii. neither the Commissioners nor the DBF provide accommodation.

15.16.2 There are differences in individual cases, but broadly, the economic cost is the same in either case.

15.16.3 There is, therefore, no case for making the choice on economic grounds.

15.17.1 Our views are that:

    a.   the most important factor is the maturity and depth of experience of the individual, whether or not he or she is ordained;

    b.   we have seen examples where both models work well; and

    c.   there is no overwhelming advantage, in general circumstances, in either model over the other.

15.17.2 If a bishop appoints a lay assistant, he should be able to ascribe to the post whatever title he thinks appropriate in local circumstances. The expression 'lay assistant' may be appropriate, but the other possibilities include 'lay chaplain', 'lay administrator', and 'bishop's staff officer'. What are important are a clear job description, and a clear understanding of the person to whom each member of the bishop's personal staff reports.

Travelling: generally

15.18   In outline, the present position is that:

    a.   both a diocesan and suffragan are entitled either:

        i.   to have a car provided; or

        ii.   to be paid a mileage allowance if they use their own car for official travel;

    b.   although in general diocesans and suffragans are entitled to choose a car from the same list, a diocesan is entitled to a larger car than a suffragan as the diocesan may be driven;[6]

    c.   a diocesan, but not a suffragan, is entitled to a driver, often part-time; and

    d.   where public transport is used for official travel, the bishop is entitled to reimbursement of the cost. A bishop is expected to take advantage of special fares where they are available, and if he is aged 60 or over, he is expected to take advantage of a senior citizen's railcard, but in all cases it is for him to decide whether, when travelling by train, first class or standard class is appropriate.

Travel by car

15.19 In relation to travel by car, there are three questions:

a. should a diocesan be provided with a car and a (part-time) driver?;

b. should both diocesans and suffragans be provided with a car for their own sole use?; and

c. should the facilities provided for a diocesan to travel by car differ from those provided for a suffragan?

15.20.1 On the first question, we have no doubt that there are many occasions on which it is an efficient use of time for a bishop to be driven, and that this facility should be made available to him when appropriate. Furthermore, in some parts of the country there may not be good connections when travelling by public transport.

15.20.2 We recognize that if the driver is employed by the bishop (or by the DBF) and is specially selected for the purpose, it may well be easier for the bishop to deal in the back of the car with work which may be confidential while he is being driven.

15.20.3 We also note, however, that very widely in the commercial and professional world, a separate car and driver is not now provided, but that there is a contract with a car hire or similar firm to provide a car and driver as and when required.

15.20.4 It may well not be possible to make satisfactory arrangements of this nature in some parts of the country, but we **recommend** that the Resources Group should seriously explore the possibility.

15.20.5 We further note that in a number of instances both diocesans and suffragans are from time to time driven by their wives, and that the wives provide a hidden subvention to the Church when doing so.

15.21.1 Generally, we **recommend** that the Resources Group should explore the most appropriate and cost-effective provision of travel by car.

15.21.2 It may be that it is more effective for a car without a driver to be provided on a contract basis as and when required.[7]

15.21.3 Furthermore, both diocesans and suffragans, after demanding days, can be required to travel long distances late in the evening. If only for safety reasons,[8] it may well be appropriate for both to be driven. On other occasions, even where safety or exhaustion are not issues, bishops' time might most productively be used by being driven.

15.21.4 These issues are all best decided locally.

Train travel

15.22.1 No convincing evidence has been adduced to us which would indicate that there is any abuse with regard to the class of travel. Where concentrated and confidential work is to be done on a train, on some occasions there may be no realistic alternative to travelling first class, but that will by no means always be so.

15.22.2 We **recommend**, however, that there should be established the guidelines that:

    a. in general, travel by train should be standard class;[9] but

    b. first-class travel is fully acceptable where this is the only way in which the travelling time can be used effectively, especially during rush hours.

Air and sea travel

15.23 Some bishops travel regularly outside England[10] in the ordinary course of their diocesan work. No suggestions have been made to us that the present arrangements[11] are not working satisfactorily, and we make no recommendations with regard to them, save that such costs should be specially reflected in the calculation of the formula amounts.[12]

Incidence of travelling costs

15.24.1 We make at this stage a further recommendation about travelling and associated costs. It reflects our views that to a very large extent, the true cost of Church activities should be identified, and that in general costs incurred in relation to other bodies should be paid by those bodies where they can afford to do so.

15.24.2 Accordingly, we **recommend** that where a bishop travels outside his diocese to a meeting of a church body, his travelling and subsistence costs should normally be paid by that body, and not be borne by his local account. This would apply, for example, to meetings of the House of Bishops, the General Synod, the Archbishops' Council, committees of those bodies, and national church-related charities. This already happens when diocesans who are members of the House of Lords attend for duty in that House.

15.24.3 We also **recommend** that where a bishop accepts an invitation from a non-Church body which is of financial substance to speak at an event, the presumption should be that the costs would be charged to that body. There will be a natural reluctance to do this, and in some cases it would be clearly inappropriate.[13] But, in other cases, there seems to be no reason why the Church should be, in effect, subsidizing such bodies.

15.25 We recognize that regularly bishops will incur expenses when travelling from their dioceses to attend consecrations, and that these costs will continue to be borne by the bishop's local account.

Information technology
15.26.1 Dioceses have differed in their commitment to the use of information technology, although we have noted that there is rapidly becoming greater consistency between them.

15.26.2 We are also conscious of the pace of IT development and the increasing use of the Internet. Some bishops have told us that as recently as about 1990, they would have been regarded as remarkably bold had they predicted that by the year 2000 there would be a computer in every bishop's office.

15.26.3 This is not an issue which is peculiar to bishops. It affects diocesan offices, and the Church as a whole. We have no doubt that nationwide protocols for both hardware and software and for the use of the Internet need to be prescribed by the Archbishops' Council.

15.26.4

We do, however, think that there is scope for obtaining at a local level equipment to the specification of the national protocol, as well as training and technical support and we **recommend** that the Resources Group should actively explore this possibility.

Hospitality

15.27 Bishops must have the facility with which to provide hospitality, in the sense of welcome.[14] Hospitality is often provided in the house, but this is not necessarily the case.

15.28 There are many in business, professional and other walks of life who welcome others, and provide hospitality for them. To a greater or lesser extent, this is usually (but not always) an activity which is ancillary to their main role. We observe that in the case of bishops, the exercise of the ministry of welcome or the provision of hospitality is not an ancillary, but is indeed an integral, part of their role.[15]

15.29 We recommend that the Resources Group should reflect on how hospitality can best be provided, and we return to the subject in the context of bishops' houses.[16]

Warning

15.30 If, following consultation, there is broad agreement on our recommendation for block-grants and the local provision of resources, then before implementation of the proposals there would need to be specific consideration of the VAT implications[17] and, possibly, a special agreement[18] reached with Customs.[19] There are VAT issues, but we would not expect them to be insuperable.

chapter 16

Suffragans

Introduction

16.1 In this chapter, we consider:

a. certain issues affecting suffragans generally; and

b. specific issues affecting Provincial Episcopal Visitors (PEVs).

Theology

16.2 We have referred previously to:

a. there being one order of bishops, which embraces diocesans and suffragans without distinction;[1]

b. by virtue of that fact, our view that for resourcing purposes the same *principles* should apply to all bishops, including the principle that resources should be provided according to need not status;[2] and

c. there being differences in function[3] which result in there being differing resourcing needs.

The recent history

16.3 Before commenting on specific resourcing issues, it may be helpful for us to outline the history of the support given to suffragans in modern times.

16.4.1 We regard the modern era as having begun in 1870, with the consecration of two additional suffragans.[4]

16.4.2 Since then the number of suffragans has steadily grown. The figures are:

1901	9
1921	21
1941	38
1961	44
1966	49
1974	59
2001	65[5]

Stipends

16.5.1 Until the 1950s, the stipends of suffragans were paid from diocesan, not central, funds.

16.5.2 The Commissioners began to pay the stipends in the early 1950s, on fixed national scales,[6] and have continued to do so until the present time. We have shown[7] that this is not because the Commissioners are under a legal obligation to pay the stipends, but that they do so in the exercise of their discretion.

Houses

16.6.1 Dioceses have always been responsible for the provision of houses for suffragans. These houses are usually owned by the DBF, but in exceptional circumstances, they may be rented by them.[8]

16.6.2 Although the responsibility for the provision of the houses has always been that of the dioceses, the Commissioners used to make grants to DBFs towards the cost of acquisition, improvement or replacement of these houses. In general, the grant was up to two-thirds of the cost, with the remainder of the cost being met by the diocese. If the house was sold without being replaced, the grant was repayable to the Commissioners from the proceeds of sale. In the more usual case where the house was sold, and a replacement house was acquired, the Commissioners' grant towards the cost of the first house was, in effect, rolled over into the replacement house. If not all the proceeds of sale of the first house were required for the purchase of the replacement house, the grant was repayable to the extent that this could be done from the surplus proceeds of sale.

16.6.3 The Commissioners have not provided any new money for this purpose since 1994. However, where grants made before 1995 are repaid, the Commissioners have been willing to reapply the amount repaid for similar purposes.

Outgoings

16.7.1 The main outgoings in respect of suffragans' houses are or have been rent (if the DBF holds the house under a lease); the cost of maintenance, repairs and insurance; as applicable at the point of time being considered, general rates, community charge or council tax; and water rates or water charges.

16.7.2 Prior to 1967, in some cases the suffragans paid out of their stipend some or all of the outgoings on their houses, and in other cases the outgoings were paid by the DBF. In order to take account of this, there were two rates of stipend, a higher rate when the suffragan was obliged to pay the outgoings and a lower rate when they were paid by the DBF.

16.7.3 Between mid-1967, when standard rates of stipend were introduced, and 1990, the Commissioners paid one-half of the outgoings and the DBF paid the other half.

16.7.4 Since April 1990, as part of the revised arrangement in respect of working costs which is noted below, the DBF has paid all outgoings.

Working costs
16.8.1 Prior to 1962 the working costs of suffragans were paid by DBFs.

16.8.2 The Commissioners began to make grants towards suffragans' working costs in 1962, initially on a variable basis. From 1978, the Commissioners made grants of fixed amounts to be applied towards these costs, with the excess of the actual cost over the amount of the grant being borne equally by the Commissioners and by the DBF.

16.8.3 From April 1990, the Commissioners have paid the working costs in full. As in the case of working costs of diocesans, the Commissioners pay these costs on a discretionary basis.[9]

Observations
16.9 We observe that:

a. for well over half of the modern era, suffragans' stipends were funded locally, not centrally; and

b. with the important exception of housing, the broad trend has been for the Commissioners progressively to assume more of the costs of supporting suffragans, and so equating them to this extent with diocesans.

Allocation by dioceses
16.10 We list[10] the numbers of suffragans in each diocese: there are notable differences in these numbers. The circumstances, particularly

the size of the population and the geographical area, vary greatly, but it is noteworthy that in a few dioceses there is no suffragan.[11]

16.11 The relationship between the number of bishops in a diocese and the size and apparent demands of the diocese is often loose. This subject generally is outside our remit and we commend it for further study by the appropriate bodies. We observe, however, that where there is a mismatch it causes financial tension because the stipend and working costs of the bishop are paid by the Commissioners whereas support by others is paid for by the DBF.

The selection of suffragans

16.12 Although there is only one order of bishops, embracing both diocesans and suffragans, the appointment process differs greatly as between diocesans and suffragans. We have previously[12] outlined that process. In the case of diocesans, there is widespread consultation. In the case of a suffragan, although there is consultation, in practice a suffragan is to a large extent appointed by decision of the diocesan.

16.13 This issue of selection has also been raised with us, on the ground that it is perceived that suffragans are appointed having regard very much to local requirements, whereas they are the natural pool from which diocesans are appointed. There are many exceptions, but as a broad generalization, most of the work of suffragans is based in the dioceses, whereas a material part of the work of diocesans is wider.

16.14.1 We do not wish to propose any alteration to the decision-making powers of the diocesan, and, in any event, it is not for us to do so.

16.14.2 We do, however, **recommend** that the provisions for consultation in the existing code should be fully followed so that the longer term potential of the candidate, as well as the particular needs of the diocese, are taken into account.

Job descriptions and appraisals

16.15 We repeat here our **recommendation**[13] that every suffragan should have a job description, and that it should be clear from that description what is expected of the suffragan and what support will be given to him by the diocesan.

16.16 It follows that we **recommend** that, as in the case of the clergy, there should be regular structured appraisals. We think that the form of those appraisals should be left for local decision and we do not, therefore, make any recommendation as to how they should be conducted.

16.17 This is not a *resourcing* issue – apart from the very fact that a suffragan is a major resource to his diocesan and his diocese – but the appraisal is a *need* of the suffragan.

Differences in scale of resources

16.18.1 We have commented on the differences between the scale of the resources[14] provided for a diocesan and those for a suffragan. Apart from living and working accommodation, the main differences are with regard to:

> a.   personal support staff: whereas a diocesan usually has two full-time and one part-time members of his personal support staff, a suffragan usually has only one member of staff;[15]
>
> b.   a diocesan can have a driver (often part-time), whereas there is no provision for a suffragan to do so;[16] and
>
> c.   a diocesan can have a gardener (usually part-time), whereas a suffragan has more modest gardening assistance.[17]

16.18.2 There are other less significant differences, such as with regard to the amount of the resettlement grant on appointment or translation.[18]

16.18.3 We comment later in this chapter[19] on the difference of treatment with regard to the housekeeper's allowance.

16.19.1 We repeat here our **recommendations** that:

> a.   the same *principles* should apply to suffragans as they do to diocesans, and, in particular, that all resources should be provided according to the needs of the individual bishop to enable him to do the job, and not according to the fact of whether he is a diocesan or a suffragan; and
>
> b.   the proposed Bishops' Resources Group[20] should be concerned with the needs of *all* bishops in the diocese.

16.19.2 We hope that these measures will eliminate inappropriate distinctions, while recognizing that different workloads[21] and responsibilities will lead to different resourcing requirements.

16.20.1 We have also referred to the differences in the provision of living and working accommodation, both as regards the minimum size[22] and as to the provider.[23]

16.20.2 It may be that, in due course, differences in the extent of accommodation will be reduced as part of the diocesan review of accommodation which we propose.[24] With regard to the provider of the accommodation, implementation of our longer term proposals with regard to the ownership of see houses[25] would result in all bishops' houses in the diocese being owned by the same body.

16.21.1 Our approach that distinctions in the scale of resources should be eliminated except where they follow from the actual job which is being done is born of the theological view which we take.

16.21.2 It is, however, reinforced by a practical consideration. The evidence which we have received shows that in at least some cases, the diocesan is regarded as 'the' bishop, and that a suffragan is regarded as 'only' an assistant to or deputy of the diocesan. Suffragans will be even more valuable to their diocesans and their dioceses if the fact that they are substantive bishops in the fullest sense is more widely perceived. The method and scale of the provision of resources can aid that perception.

Suffragans and archdeacons

16.22 The resourcing of archdeacons lies outside our remit, and beyond recognizing that archdeacons also are a significant resource to the bishops and the diocese, we generally do not comment on them in this report.

16.23 One specific issue, relating to archdeacons, has, however, been put to us. This is that some diocesans have told us that they would find it helpful for there to be the ability in certain circumstances to appoint an archdeacon instead of a suffragan, or the reverse. We refer to this as interchangeability of posts.

16.24.1 The relevant financial background is as follows.

16.24.2 As we have shown:

a. the Commissioners pay the stipend and working costs of a suffragan;[26] and

b. the DBF provides the living and working accommodation.

16.24.3 In the case of an archdeacon, the DBF pays the stipend and working costs, as well as providing the accommodation.

16.24.4 The amount of an archdeacon's stipend is very nearly the same as that of a suffragan.[27]

16.24.5 If one considers the matter from the viewpoint of the Church as a whole, therefore, broadly, the cost of a suffragan is the same as that of an archdeacon.

16.24.6 However, the incidence of that cost is materially different. As the Commissioners pay the stipend and working costs of a suffragan, but the DBF pays the stipend and working costs of an archdeacon, an archdeacon costs the DBF significantly more than a suffragan.

16.25   In our view:

a. the decision whether there should be a suffragan or an archdeacon should not be taken on financial grounds; and

b. as interchangeability of posts could be effected at no material difference in cost to the Church as a whole, a means should be found of transferring funds to make it possible if it is desirable for non-financial reasons.

16.26.1 The Turnbull Commission[28] recommended that DBFs should assume the responsibility for paying the stipends and working costs of suffragans, as well as of archdeacons. They recommended[29] this course, not as a means of achieving interchangeability, but as a way of encouraging a partnership between the Church centrally and the dioceses in the sharing of the overall costs of episcopal ministry.

16.26.2 We fully agree with the Turnbull Commission that the notion of such a partnership should be encouraged,[30] but we do not think that this is the most helpful way of doing so.

16.26.3 First, it would cause a shift in the financial burden which we do not think realistic at the present time.

16.26.4 Second, and more important in our view, it would recreate a distinction between diocesans and suffragans which we think would be unhelpful.

16.27.1 We recommend, however, that consideration should be given to introducing a special provision which should apply where (a) a suffragan see is left unfilled and (b) a new archdeaconry is established and (c) that archdeaconry is filled. The provision would be that, while the suffragan see remains vacant, the Commissioners would pay the stipend and the working costs of the archdeacon; or, under the block-granting system which we have proposed,[31] the Bishops' Resources Group should also be responsible for resourcing that archdeacon.

16.27.2 This would not involve the Commissioners in any additional expense.

16.27.3 It would achieve partial interchangeability of posts, but would not in itself cater for the position where an established archdeaconry was left vacant and there was a local wish to appoint a suffragan.[32] It is, however, the case that at present if a new suffragan see is created, the Commissioners will pay the stipend and working costs of the bishop; and our block-granting proposal envisages that the formula will automatically take account of the number of bishops for whom there are established posts in the diocese.

16.27.4 We also recognize that our proposal would lead to a distinction between a few archdeacons who were funded from the centre and the majority who were not, but we would not expect significant problems to ensue from that distinction.

Single bishops
16.28.1 One of the differences in the resourcing scales between diocesans and suffragans relates to those bishops who are single (whether they have never married or are widowers who have not remarried).

16.28.2 A single diocesan can claim for 50% of the cost of employing a housekeeper, up to a maximum of £1,500 annually. There is no corresponding provision for a single suffragan.

16.29   We surmise that the reasons for this distinction are that, in general, a see house is larger than a suffragan's house, so that the degree of housekeeping which is required is greater; and that a diocesan, but not a suffragan, is expected to receive overnight official guests.

16.30.1 We are unenthusiastic about the concept of a housekeeper's allowance, whether for diocesans or suffragans.

16.30.2 It implies to us the assumption that a married bishop has a wife who is willing and able – without payment – to provide house-keeping support.

16.31   We readily understand that because of the nature of some houses which are provided, exceptional costs are incurred. It may be, however, that as a result of the review which we propose of bishops' accommodation in each diocese, at least some of these cases will be reduced.

16.32   We recommend that:

16.32.1 As a transitional measure, the housekeeping allowance should continue to be paid to those who are presently entitled to it, and to any currently serving diocesans who become widowers while they are in post;

16.32.2 Subject to that, the housekeeping allowance should be discontinued;

16.32.3 The Bishops' Resources Group should take account of any exceptional costs which are imposed on bishops – whether married or single – in consequence of their being required to live in the accommo-dation which is provided; and

16.32.4 No provision should be included in the allocation formula[33] for a housekeeping allowance.

16.33   In relation to single bishops, we mention separately:

    a.   the isolation of a single suffragan and his secretary where they work alone;[34] and

    b.   the provision of hospitality by single bishops.[35]

Provincial Episcopal Visitors

16.34.1 Provincial Episcopal Visitors have been appointed[36] since 1994. There are two in the Province of Canterbury and one in the Province of York.

16.34.2 The two in the southern province are, formally, suffragans in the Diocese of Canterbury, and the one in the northern province is formally a suffragan in the Diocese of York.

16.35.1 PEVs are appointed to minister to those within the province who do not accept the validity of the ordination of women as priests, and who do not otherwise receive episcopal care and oversight from a bishop who is himself opposed to the ordination of women to the priesthood. PEVs work with the diocesan in providing this extended pastoral care and sacramental ministry.[37]

16.35.2 They seek to respond to whatever requests are put to them, and therefore do not exercise their ministry within the usual diocesan context.

16.35.3 PEVs in no way displace the authority and responsibility of the diocesan of a diocese, and they are enjoined only to exercise their ministry if they are requested to do so by the diocesan.

16.36.1 The work of PEVs differs from that of other bishops, whether diocesan or suffragan. They do not have the responsibility of other bishops for the selection, appointment and deployment of clergy. They have, by comparison with other bishops, little administrative work, and they do not have the role of other bishops in relation to the ordinary activities in a diocese.

16.36.2 On the other hand, PEVs are able to spend a much greater proportion of their time than other bishops in exercising personal pastoral ministry and teaching; and in the course of their work they travel much more than most other bishops.

16.37.1 The Commissioners pay the stipends and working costs of PEVs, in the same way as those of other suffragans.

16.37.2 Special arrangements apply in relation to housing. In outline:

a.   the DBF of the diocese in which it has been decided by the archbishop that the PEV should reside is responsible, in liaison with the Commissioners, for the provision of a house for the PEV on behalf of all dioceses in the province;

b.   likewise, the DBF of the diocese in which the PEV resides is responsible for the management of the house on behalf of all dioceses in the Province;

c.   the acquisition of the house is funded by a value-linked interest bearing loan provided by the Commissioners; and

d.   one half of the interest payable on the loan, and one half of the maintenance costs, are borne by the dioceses in the province.[38] The other half is borne by the Commissioners.

16.38   We understand that the work of PEVs is largely responsive to requests made to them. If for no reason other than the exceptional workloads of the Archbishops of Canterbury and York, PEVs do not have the regular conversations and exchanges which are common between other suffragans and their diocesans. In practice, the relationship of the PEV to his archbishop is more akin to that of a bishop to his metropolitan than that of a suffragan to his diocesan.

16.39.1 We have proposed[39] a system of block-granting to the diocesan of a diocese, who would be assisted by a Bishops' Resources Group.

16.39.2 We think that, in general, the same system should be adapted to apply to PEVs, but separate from the Resources Groups either of the dioceses of which they are suffragans or of the dioceses in which they are resident. It is easy for PEVs and those to whom they minister to feel embattled, and if either course were adopted there would be too much scope for suspicions (however unfounded) to grow.

16.40   We therefore **recommend** that:

16.40.1 A separate Resources Group should be established for all three PEVs;

16.40.2 The archbishops jointly should appoint a chairman for that group. The chairman should be of independent stance who in the eyes both of PEVs and the wider Church could be seen to act fairly;

16.40.3 The role of the chairman of the PEVs Resources Group would be parallel to that of the diocesan as the chairman of the other Resources Groups. The chairman's tasks would include:

> a. recruiting appropriately qualified and sympathetic persons to become members of the Resources Group;
>
> b. assisted by the Resources Group, arranging for the resources to be provided for the PEVs; and
>
> c. making the appropriate banking arrangements to handle the block-granted funds, perhaps with a DBF.

16.41.1 The amount of the block-grant provided for the group of PEVs would be calculated separately from that for other bishops: the standard formula would not be appropriate.

16.41.2 The calculation would have regard to:

> a. the above-average travelling costs; and
>
> b. the below-average administrative and managerial costs.

16.42 The work of PEVs is often rather isolated. They do not have the regular contact with other bishops in a diocese that is normal, and, as we have indicated, they do not have the close relationship with a senior bishop that is usually enjoyed by the suffragans. Therefore, although this goes beyond our remit, we also **recommend** that if a suitable senior bishop, perhaps very recently retired, were willing to act as the chairman of the Resources Group, he should provide the same monitoring support and supervision as other suffragans receive from their diocesans.

chapter 17

Bishops' wives

Support

17.1   One cannot examine the ministry of bishops in the Church of England without encountering the generous and dedicated support given by wives to their husbands' ministry. This is often at considerable personal cost in terms of time, energy and the sacrifice of other opportunities. It is a support that is often hidden from view and unacknowledged. There is of course a continuity with the kind of support given by the spouses of clergy throughout the Church. But we wish to make the particular point that the Church of England owes an incalculable debt of gratitude to the wives of most bishops, which we believe should be publicly acknowledged.

17.2   The type of support varies greatly. It includes – in no order of priority – catering for, often, many hundreds of visitors to the bishop's house during the course of a year (including moving round the furniture beforehand and doing the washing up afterwards); cleaning and tidying up; receiving visitors; doing the laundry after visits of overnight official guests; attendance at numerous functions; sharing visits to parishes; taking out-of-hours messages; managing the house, including attending to minor repairs, and liaising with the agent[1] with regard to more major works; managing the garden, and often working in the garden. Many wives have their own professional skills which they deploy in support of their husbands. Many have a pastoral role, particularly in caring for the spouses of clergy and their families, and for the bishop's staff and their families. All this, which supports their husbands as bishops, is done in addition to the support of their husbands as husbands, and often amid the demands of bringing up a family.

17.3.1   We have been impressed by the repeated instances that we have encountered of the unstinting way in which this support is given. It is given with generosity and without the slightest hope or expectation of recognition or reward. But if, as must be done for the purposes of this report, we put this in bald resourcing terms, it will be seen that this is a resource of great value which the Church has had at no financial cost.

17.3.2 It has also become clear to us that, as well as supporting their husbands in their episcopal ministry in a variety of ways, some bishops' wives, like some spouses of clergy, have developed their own distinct ministries within the Church. We fully recognize this, but the terms of this review do not permit us to make recommendations about the resourcing of this contribution made by bishops' wives to the life of the Church.

The trends
17.4.1 There are clear trends that are bound to affect the nature of the support which will be given to their husbands by bishops' wives in future. As with the majority of clergy spouses now, bishops' wives, especially the wives of suffragans, increasingly follow their own careers or independent activities outside the home. From the evidence which we have received, it appears that wives of bishops, particularly diocesans, often find it more difficult to sustain full-time professional careers, even if they wish to do so, owing to the heavy demands of running the house[2] and participating in day-to-day episcopal life. Nevertheless, we expect that the trend for bishops' wives to have full-time external careers will progressively become the norm for most bishops' wives, as it is in most clergy households, not least because of the recognition of the place of women in society and their greater expectations of professional fulfilment.

17.4.2 The conclusion in relation to resources is that it can no longer be assumed that in most cases a bishop's wife will not have external employment and will be available and willing to perform a traditional role.

The present position
17.5 The present position can be briefly summarized as follows:

a. bishops' wives are increasingly engaged in paid employment or in other demanding activities, whether or not paid, outside the home;

b. some bishops' wives have a vocation to their own distinctive ministry in the Church; and

c.   some bishops' wives choose to have a more direct involvement in their husbands' ministries, and when they do so they often thereby make considerable financial sacrifices.[3]

The basic principle

17.6   We recommend that there should be clearly adopted the general principle that no wife of a bishop should be prevented from pursuing her career or from following other activities by the demands made on her by her husband's ministry, or by the house in which they are required to live. However, some wives will continue to wish to involve themselves directly in their husbands' ministry.

Accommodation

17.7   We deal with the general issues of living and working accommodation in the remaining chapters, but we make two points at this stage.

17.8.1   The first relates to the difficulties that can arise where the bishop's office, and so his personal support staff, are located in the house.

17.8.2   The difficulties can be pronounced where staff need to have access to the kitchen. There continue to be instances of this, despite the Commissioners' laudable moves towards effecting physical separation of the private and official parts of the house.

17.9.1   Problems can arise as a result of the bishop's wife and his personal support staff working in the same premises.

17.9.2   In times of personal stress (whether for the bishop, his wife, a member of their family, or a member of the staff), this proximity can exacerbate tension. More generally, there can be difficulties in the relationship between the bishop's wife and members of his staff. Can the wife have access to his secretary? Can the wife properly ask the gardener to carry out some task?

17.9.3

The evidence which we have received shows that these problems can be at their most acute in the early years of the bishop taking up his appointment. The wife may be forced to share the house – her home –

with someone for whom she does not have a natural sympathy. On the other hand, the staff, having developed a working relationship with the wife of one bishop, may not find it easy to adjust to the different approach of the new bishop's wife.

17.10   We do not wish to overstate the issues. In our visits to bishops' houses we have seen repeated examples of harmonious and congenial relationships. But we have also had specific evidence that there can be problems and that they can be significantly diminished where the house is primarily the family home and not the office.[4]

17.11   The other point on accommodation to which we refer at this stage follows from the fact that increasingly bishops' wives will be engaged in employment or other activities away from the house. It prompts the obvious question: if large see houses or suffragans' houses are to be retained, who will run the houses and who will run their gardens? If extra staff need to be engaged, what will be the cost and who will bear that cost?[5]

17.12   A further point, which is related to, but wider than, accommodation (and which goes well beyond the issue of resourcing) is that husbands may increasingly be less willing to accept appointments which adversely affect their wives' careers, or which would involve living in a house which is less than easy to run. These are real issues in an increasing number of clergy appointments.

Resources for wives

17.13.1 We turn now to the separate issue of the provision of 'resources for wives.

17.13.2 We recommend acceptance of the principle that when a wife is acting directly in support of her husband in the exercise of his ministry as a bishop, then it is proper for the Church to provide her with the appropriate resources for the purpose.

17.13.3 For example, when the bishop's wife conducts correspondence in the running of the house, or where she is arranging official hospitality in the house or garden for the bishop, then it is right that she should have any necessary secretarial help; alternatively, she might be more appropriately assisted by being offered computer training for this and other aspects of running the official house. If a wife visits clergy and their families as an extension of her husband's pastoral ministry, her travelling expenses should be reimbursed.

17.13.4 Decisions about these matters should be taken locally. We **recommend** that the Bishops' Resources Group should make the appropriate provision for bishops' wives in the diocese.

Payment of wives

17.14.1 We have considered whether to recommend that bishops' wives generally should receive some form of remuneration. Almost all wives will make a substantial contribution, and we recognize that, where a wife does not have full-time external employment, she will often do things which in other circumstances would have to be done by a member of staff.

17.14.2 We have, however, concluded that any general allowance or honorarium would not be appropriate.

17.14.3 On the other hand, we do not see any objection to a bishop employing his wife to undertake specific duties for which she would be paid. We **recommend** that the following conditions should be satisfied, in all cases:[6]

a. there should be a written agreement (so that there can be no doubt as to the extent of the duties and the terms on which the duties are to be performed);

b. the wife should have the requisite skills and experience for the work proposed; and

c. if the bishop did not employ his wife he would need to employ someone else to perform those duties.

17.14.4 An example where this approach might be proper is the employment of the bishop's wife as a part-time secretary.

17.15.1 If only as a protection for the bishop, we **recommend** that if a bishop chooses to employ his wife, that decision should never be taken by him alone.[7]

17.15.2 If the bishop wishes to employ his wife as a part-time secretary, then acceptance of our proposals with regard to secretaries would result in her becoming an employee of the DBF, and so the DBF would be involved in the process.

17.15.3 In other cases, we think that the bishop should only employ his wife after consultation with the Resources Group.

Catering

17.16.1 On a more specific point, we **recommend** that there should be further clarification of the charges which can be made for catering in the bishop's house.

17.16.2 We have ourselves attempted to clarify this in our description of the present arrangements.[8] The same principles should continue to apply if our block-grant proposals are implemented.

17.16.3 Our formulation of these principles is that:

   a.   caterers may be employed for an official function;[9]

   b.   if the bishop's wife caters, she may make a charge which can be calculated in three ways:

   i.   she may make a charge, inclusive of the cost of the food,[10] according to the Commissioners' tariff. If there is some excess of the tariff figure over the actual cost of the food, then the bishop's wife can retain that for herself as some recompense for its preparation;

   ii.   she may make a charge on the same basis, but according to any other reasonable tariff adopted by the bishop, rather than according to the Commissioners' tariff; or

   iii.   she may charge the actual cost of the food, and in addition, a reasonable fee for catering. The reasonable fee would be measured by the amount which would be charged by a third party.

17.16.4 We recognize that this is a difficult area to prescribe and quantify and that decisions about it need to be taken at a local level. Many wives are willing to do the catering, which can be substantial, as a voluntary contribution to their husband's ministry. However, following the criteria that we have set out above, we think that the principle of a payment to the wife for the work involved in catering that she carries out for official occasions is proper.

17.17   Our general proposals with regard to the employment by a bishop of his wife do not apply to arrangements for catering (and we do not suggest that these arrangements would need to be reflected in writing), unless perhaps there was to be repeated large-scale catering for which the wife wished to charge at up to full commercial rates. In any case of doubt, the bishop could always consult with the Resources Group.

Further points

17.18   We have been concerned to make recommendations on the principles of payment. Any payment would need to be made either under the present budgetary arrangements or, under the future system that we have proposed, from the block-grant, administered through the Resources Group.

17.19   It is axiomatic that any amount, less allowable expenses, that the bishop's wife does receive (except in the case of catering, by way of reimbursement of the cost of food) would constitute income for income tax purposes.[11]

Bishops' husbands

17.20   The Church of England has not yet made a decision about the ordination of women to the episcopate. If there are women bishops, we think that the principles set out in this chapter should apply to all bishops' spouses.

17.21   In practice, we regard it as unlikely that the husbands of women bishops would provide the support in the house that has traditionally been provided by many bishops' wives. That fact reinforces the need for the review which we have proposed of bishops' accommodation.[12]

Part III

chapter 18

Living and working accommodation

Introduction

18.1   In the next chapter, we propose that there should be a separate reappraisal within each diocese of the requirements for see and suffragans' houses, and that in the course of that appraisal there should be considered:

a.   the style of the houses;

b.   the size of the houses;

c.   the gardens and grounds of the houses; and

d.   whether the bishops' offices should be located in their houses or elsewhere.

18.2   In this chapter:

18.2.1   After examining the use and costs of maintenance of bishops' houses, we propose a strategy for:

a.   introducing a new approach to the central funding of maintenance costs; and

b.   ultimately transferring the ownership of see houses to DBFs.

18.2.2   We also make a number of more detailed recommendations in relation to the present arrangements for accommodation.

Accommodation

18.3.1   There are many variations, but in the typical case a see house will comprise:

a.   a part which is used exclusively for working purposes: in this category we put, for example, the bishop's study; his secretary's office; and the bishop's chaplain's or lay assistant's office;

b.   the chapel;

c.   a bedroom, which is usually referred to as the 'official' bedroom, for the overnight accommodation of visitors;

d.   a part, which we describe in paragraph 18.6, and which is used for both private and working purposes; and

e.   a part which is the bishop's private living accommodation.

18.3.2   Contrary to the impression which might be gained from the external appearance of the house, the private accommodation is often modest.

18.4   In addition to these parts, it is not unusual for a substantial part of a see house which is a heritage property to be used for income-generating purposes which are not directly connected with the bishop's ministry. This may take the form of offices let either to the DBF or to a commercial organization, conference facilities, or facilities for receptions or other private social events.

18.5   Where a suffragan's office is in the house,[1] there will typically be the same broad divisions of use, but with the important differences that:

a.   because the number of his personal staff is smaller – a suffragan usually has only one secretary – the office accommodation is much smaller;

b.   a suffragan does not usually have a chapel in the house; and

c.   there is usually no separate bedroom provided for official guests.

18.6.1   In both see houses and suffragans' houses, that part of the accommodation which is used for both private and working purposes is typically a dining room, with its associated kitchen, a reception room – the two may be divided by a movable partition – and a cloak-room.

18.6.2   These rooms are provided in the expectation that they will be used for official purposes such as meetings and hospitality. The bishop may also use them for his personal purposes and in many cases the bishop (and his family if he has one) will consider these rooms to be part of their home.[2]

18.6.3 A bishop will welcome visitors to this part of the house with the same warmth as he would in welcoming guests into his private accommodation. The visitor will usually feel that they are being welcomed by the bishop into his home – and it is important that they should do.

18.6.4 The balance between official and private use of this part of a bishop's house varies from house to house and bishop to bishop. In some cases it is predominantly used for official purposes, and in most cases the giving of hospitality is a very significant element in a bishop's ministry.

18.6.5 While the nature and scale of the hospitality offered by a suffragan may differ from that of a diocesan, these general observations concerning the use of the bishop's house apply to both.

18.6.6 In the typical case of a see house, if one takes (a) the parts of the building which are used exclusively for working or official purposes and (b) the approximate proportion of the mixed user part which is used for official purposes, it is seen that well over half the total building is used for working rather than private living purposes.[3]

18.6.7 In the case of heritage properties, especially where part of the house is used for income-generating purposes, as described in paragraph 18.4, the proportion of the house used solely for private purposes will be even smaller.

Cost

18.7.1 We have seen that in 1999:

a. the expenditure of a recurrent nature by the Commissioners on see houses, described as 'bishops' housing', was £3.3 million;[4] and

b. the costs incurred by the Commissioners in administering see houses were nearly £700,000.[5]

18.7.2 The expenditure by DBFs of a recurrent nature on suffragans' houses was in the region of £320,000.

18.8   We have also seen[6] that, in 1999, the Commissioners spent somewhat in excess of £350,000 on capital improvements to see houses.[7]

Strategy

18.9   In subsequent sections of this chapter, we propose a new strategy in relation to see houses, involving a diminishing role on the part of the Commissioners. Our suggested strategy involves:

a.   redefining the approximate size for a see house;

b.   introducing a revised system of the central funding of requisite maintenance and repairs; and

c.   ultimately transferring the ownership of see houses to DBFs.

18.10   It follows that if that strategy were followed, the only main continuing role of the Commissioners in relation to living and working accommodation would be, through the Episcopal Committee,[8] to pre-scribe the standards. The Commissioners might also have a continuing long-term role in relation to heritage properties.[9]

18.11   Although we have observations on matters of detail, we do not propose any fundamental alterations to the present arrangements in relation to suffragans' houses.

Size of see houses

18.12   Three main factors which affect the requisite size of a see house are:

a.   whether it is also to accommodate the bishop's personal staff and their offices;

b.   whether it is to have accommodation for the provision of hospitality and for overnight official visitors; and

c.   the number of bedrooms which should be provided.

18.13   We deal with the first of these factors in the next chapter, and we consider here the other two factors.

Hospitality

18.14   The giving of hospitality[10] is not an ancillary part of a bishop's role, but an essential part of his ministry.[11]

18.15   In our view, the fundamental element of a bishop's hospitality – and, indeed, of a bishop's wife's hospitality – is not the offering of food or drink, but the warmth with which they receive and welcome visitors. The provision of refreshment is what flows naturally from that welcome.

18.16.1 Hospitality in this sense does not lend itself to easy categorization, but there are three major aspects:

a.   the reception and welcome of visitors where refreshment is ancillary to the main purpose of the visit;

b.   the reception and welcome of visitors where the provision of refreshment is the context in which the visit takes place; and

c.   the accommodation of overnight visitors.

18.16.2 In any particular case, one of these aspects can, and often does, merge with another.

Ancillary provision

18.17.1 The common case of the giving of hospitality where the provision of refreshment is ancillary to the main purpose of the visit is that of someone who comes to a meeting with the bishop, and who is given a cup of coffee or tea and a biscuit.

18.17.2 Whether or not a bishop's office is in his house,[12] in all but the most exceptional circumstances, visits of this nature will be entirely usual, and facilities for receiving the visitor and offering this type of refreshment will be necessary.

18.17.3 Accordingly, we consider that this facility should always be provided.

Lunch, supper and dinner

18.18.1 The second aspect of hospitality is where the bishop invites others to lunch, supper or dinner so that, in that context, he can get to know them, or discuss issues with them, or so that he can reciprocate hospitality which has been shown to him.

18.18.2 We have no doubt that a bishop should have the ability to provide hospitality in this way – although we are not in any way suggesting that the scale of the provision should be lavish.

18.19.1 However, the question is whether these facilities should be provided *in the house*.

18.19.2 It is not essential. In a few cases, bishops regularly offer hospitality elsewhere, but the great majority of bishops, in common with parochial clergy, prefer to exercise their ministry of hospitality in the house.

18.20 If a house is to have a dining room, reception room, kitchen and cloakroom for the provision of this type of hospitality, that will have a material effect on the size of the house.

18.21.1 We recommend that if such rooms are to be multi-purpose, and, in particular, if they are to be used frequently as meeting rooms, then they should continue to be provided.

18.21.2 On the other hand, if meetings are held elsewhere, so that there is little opportunity for multi-use, we are doubtful whether the expense of having a see house with that capability would be justified. However, if a see house is no longer to have that capability, it would involve a change of culture which could be thought to detract from the tradition of episcopal hospitality.

Overnight visitors

18.22.1 Most people invite into their houses, particularly to stay overnight, only their friends or relations.[13]

18.22.2 Bishops and their wives are different: they are *expected* to provide overnight accommodation for 'official' guests. In this context an 'official' guest is one who is calling upon the bishop in his capacity as such, as contrasted with a friend who stays with the bishop in his private capacity.

18.22.3 In taking evidence and making our enquiries we have encountered no reluctance on the part of bishops and their wives to receive such guests. This is so, notwithstanding that the so-called 'official' bedroom may be intermingled[14] with the private accommodation. We observe that this arrangement can be an intrusion – although they would not use that expression – into the private living space of the bishop and his wife.

18.23.1 If this practice is to continue, it follows that the see house needs to be large enough for there to be an official bedroom.

18.23.2 We have considered whether the bishop should no longer be expected to entertain official overnight guests, but that such guests should be accommodated in a local inn or hotel. Were this to be done, the requisite number of bedrooms in the house would be reduced, so that the existing house might be replaced with a smaller house. Excess capital value might be realized and, more importantly, ongoing maintenance costs reduced. The money thereby saved might well be more than sufficient to meet the local inn or hotel expenses of accommodating the visitors.

18.23.3 On solely financial grounds, we do think that a disposal of an existing see house and the purchase of an alternative one having a slightly reduced number of bedrooms would be justified, but that this issue should be considered in the context of any proposal to replace the existing see house primarily for other reasons.[15]

Private accommodation

18.24.1 We have described[16] the guidelines for the private accommodation which is to be provided for the bishop and his family.

18.24.2 In general, we regard these as modest.

18.24.3 However, we regard the guideline of five bedrooms for private purposes (in addition to the official bedroom) as being excessive. In our view, four bedrooms for private use should be the norm.[17]

Reappraisal

18.25 We recommend that:

18.25.1 the Commissioners should reappraise the guidelines for a see house.[18] Although in the next chapter we recommend a review of the location of the bishop's office, we record at this stage that we have not seen a case where we regard the present scale of working accommodation as being excessive; and

18.25.2 that reappraisal should establish, on a local basis, the recurrent costs which could be expected to be incurred, taking one year with another, in providing living and working accommodation to the revised standards. We deal with the significance of this later (para. 18.32.3).

Accommodation in suffragans' houses

18.26 We do not propose any alteration to the general guidelines for suffragans' houses.[19]

Heating, lighting and cleaning

18.27.1 We turn now to the separate subject of heating, lighting and cleaning see and suffragan houses.

18.27.2 As we have shown:[20]

a. in the case of a see house the Commissioners pay part of the cost, and the diocesan can claim income tax relief on part of the balance of the cost which he pays; but

b. in the case of a suffragan's house, the suffragan pays the whole of the cost, but is able to claim income tax relief on part of what he pays.

18.28.1 Where the suffragan's office is not in the house, so that the use of the house is very largely that of the bishop's residence, we regard this arrangement as being satisfactory.

18.28.2 Where, however, the suffragan's office is in the house, we regard the distinction between see houses and suffragans' houses as wrong. Accordingly, we **recommend** that where the suffragan's office is in the house, the same arrangement for the Commissioners to meet the direct expenses which applies to see houses should also apply to suffragans' houses. We would take the same view in relation to clergy houses, although that is outside our remit.

Maintenance and repairs

18.29.1 At present:

a. the cost of the maintenance and repair of see houses is paid by the Commissioners; and

b. the cost of the maintenance and repair of suffragans' houses is paid by the DBF.

18.29.2 We **recommend** that these arrangements should continue for the time being.

18.30 We also commend the Commissioners for having introduced, with effect from 1 January 1999, a rolling programme for the repair and maintenance of see houses based on a quinquennial survey.

18.31.1 There are great variations in the cost of maintaining see houses.[21] To some extent this is inevitable, in view of the different sizes, ages, natures and maintenance cycles of the houses, and the peak expenditure is almost always incurred when renovations are carried out during a vacancy.

18.31.2 However, this arrangement can involve inequity as between one diocese and another, and we do not think that it should continue indefinitely.

18.32 Accordingly, we **recommend** that:

18.32.1 In the course of the diocese-by-diocese reappraisal which we propose in the next chapter, it should be determined whether the recurrent maintenance costs being incurred in relation to the see house exceed those which would be the standard as established by the Commissioners' review, which we have proposed in paragraph 18.25.1;[22]

18.32.2 If the diocese, acting by the bishop's council, the diocesan synod and the DBF, so wishes, the use of the existing house as a see house should cease and the Commissioners should purchase a replacement house which accords with the revised guidelines;

18.32.3 Whether or not the house is changed, the Commissioners should thereafter only fund the maintenance and repair costs to the extent of the regional norm; so that

18.32.4 The balance of the costs of maintenance and repair should be paid by the DBF or from other local sources. This would be particularly significant if the existing property is retained.

18.33.1 Our concern is that ongoing recurrent maintenance costs borne by central funds should be reduced to the minimum required for the proper maintenance of a *standard* building meeting necessary requirements.

18.33.2 We refer in the next chapter to the use of properties which cease to be see houses and the need for a careful consultation programme.

Maintenance and repairs: heritage properties

18.34.1 Although we recommend in the next chapter that, as part of the appraisal, special attention should be paid to those see houses which are heritage properties, we do not propose that there should necessarily be a disposal of them.

18.34.2 We do, however, think that costs incurred by the Church of England in preserving the national heritage should be identified.

18.35.1 Accordingly, we **recommend** that where the cost of maintaining and repairing a see house which is a heritage property is greater than it otherwise would be, then that cost should be accounted for separately.

18.35.2 That would not in itself reduce the cost to the Church, but in our view it is misleading to regard *additional* costs which are incurred in the preservation of heritage properties as being part of the costs of bishops.

Prospective transfers of ownership

18.36.1 There are wide variations in the estimated values of see houses. The average of the indications of the values of see houses is about £550,000, but with one exception,[23] the values range from £350,000 at one end to several at or above £1 million at the other end. (These are the values of the entire properties, and not merely of those parts of them which are used for the bishops' private accommodation.)

18.36.2 To some extent these differences are due to the property values in different parts of the country, but they cannot be explained by that fact alone, and there is no general correlation between the value of the see house and the affluence or otherwise of the area.

18.36.3 We think that this arrangement leads to inequity between dioceses.

18.37   We therefore **recommend** that:

18.37.1 As a result of the reappraisal within the dioceses, where a see house does not accord with a new specification, then if the diocese[24] so wishes, there should be the opportunity to change it;

18.37.2 Any such change should be at the expense of the Commissioners;

18.37.3 The Commissioners should then transfer, without payment, the ownership of the existing see house (if it is to be retained) or the replacement house to the DBF; and

18.37.4 Thereafter, the DBF should be solely responsible for its upkeep.

18.38   In making these recommendations, we have in mind that:

a.   in our view, the maintenance of all bishops' houses and (if separate) offices is better dealt with locally;

b.   in many DBFs, there are established property departments, with experience in the maintenance of parsonage and other houses;

c.   for so long as the Commissioners own the see houses, there is bound to be a substantial central cost in their supervision; and

d.   where heritage properties are retained as see houses, specialist professional skills can be bought in by DBFs.

18.39.1 Although we think that, in principle, a DBF should be responsible for the cost of maintaining a see house which is in its ownership, we **recommend** that for a transitional period of five years the

Commissioners should pay a decreasing subvention to the DBF to meet part of that cost.

18.39.2 In accordance with our general recommendations,[25] the amount which is distributed to dioceses by way of Selective Allocations should be increased by the amount which the Commissioners save on the maintenance of see houses.

Sale and lease-back of see houses

18.40.1 We have considered, but not examined in depth, the possibility of selling the estate of see houses, and taking back a lease, on terms that the purchaser is responsible for their on-going maintenance.

18.40.2 This is a course which is analogous to that adopted by some others.[26]

18.41.1 We are not persuaded by the merits of such a course in respect of see houses, partly because of their different nature and widespread geographical locations. Accordingly, we make no recommendation that the estate of see houses should be sold and leased back.

18.41.2 We could, however, envisage the possibility that at some (probably remote) time in the future that approach might be adopted in respect of *all* houses, including bishops' houses, in a diocese or in a region.

Suffragans' houses

18.42   We make two observations with regard to suffragans' houses. The first is with regard to a chapel.

18.43.1 The guidelines provide that there is to be a chapel in a see house, but there is no corresponding provision for a chapel in a suffragan's house.

18.43.2 We consider that all bishops, whether diocesan or suffragan, need a place in which to worship, but in many cases that can (and does) take the form of a bedroom or other room or space which is adapted for that purpose, rather than being a chapel as such.

18.43.3 In our view, a chapel is essential only if it is required for purposes which go beyond those for private worship by the bishop, his immediate family and his staff. An example of such wider purposes might be the case of an area bishop who undertakes frequent licensings and who does not have ready access to a nearby church.

18.43.4 Accordingly, notwithstanding the difference in treatment between diocesans and suffragans, we **recommend** that:

a.   all suffragans' houses should have, at the minimum, a room or other space for worship; but

b.   there should be a requirement to provide a chapel as such only where there is a demonstrable need.[27]

18.44.1 We have stated[28] that the same *principles* should apply to the resourcing of diocesans and suffragans, although the application of one of those principles, namely that resources should be provided according to need, may lead to different actual resources being provided.

18.44.2 We are conscious that, at present, there is the marked difference that see houses are provided by the Commissioners, but suffragans' houses are provided by the DBF.

18.44.3 We observe that if our long-term recommendation[29] about the transfer of see houses to DBFs is accepted, the present difference with regard to ownership will eventually be eliminated.

Terms of occupation

18.45.1 At present a bishop occupies his house by permission of the owner, namely the Commissioners in the case of the see house and the DBF in the case of a suffragan's house. See houses are unencumbered assets of the Commissioners and are not part of the temporalities[30] of the see which vest in the diocesan.

18.45.2 However, there appears to be no document generally used to record the respective rights and duties of the owner and the occupier.[31] This can lead to uncertainty.

18.45.3 We **recommend** that there should be a written licence. We regard this as being consistent with the bishop having greater involvement in the preparation of the premises budget.[32]

18.46   We have recommended previously[33] that every effort should be made to coordinate the availability and suitability of the house, which should be in a good state of maintenance, with the appointment of a bishop.

chapter 19

Review of bishops' accommodation within dioceses

Introduction

19.1   In this chapter, we **recommend** that there should be within each diocese a review of the living and working accommodation which is appropriate for the bishops of that diocese. For the present, we exclude from this recommendation the dioceses of Canterbury and York, pending our further report with regard to Lambeth Palace and Bishopthorpe.

The proposal

19.2.1   This review would, in many cases for the first time, look comprehensively at the living and working accommodation requirements of all bishops in the diocese.[1]

19.2.2   The review would be concerned not so much with the present position, although that would necessarily be the starting point, but with what those requirements are likely to be in the medium and longer term. It follows that bishops currently in post would be unlikely to be affected by whatever plan emerges from the review process.

19.3.1   We make the recommendation for this review because we consider that there are issues which need to be addressed, but that the solutions should be governed to a material extent by local conditions and local wishes. These may vary widely from one part of the country to another.

19.3.2   Although we have proposed an overall review within the diocese of bishops' accommodation, we consider that the issues which we deal with in this chapter would warrant structured central consideration, even if no such comprehensive review were to take place.

19.4.1   There are four important background factors to the proposed reviews.

19.4.2   First, the Episcopal Committee[2] would prescribe minimum accommodation standards for diocesans and suffragans.

19.4.3   Second, there would be the introduction, on a local basis, of a regime for making a standard provision from central funds for the maintenance of see houses.[3]

19.4.4   Third, if as a result of the review a different type of see house were seen to be appropriate, then that change would be effected by the Commissioners. In other words, the Commissioners would bear the restructuring costs.[4]

19.4.5   Fourth, after any necessary restructuring has been effected the ownership of see houses would be transferred to the DBF, who would then have the ongoing maintenance responsibility.[5]

19.5   In making this proposal, we are not suggesting that change is necessary in all cases. We are, however, suggesting that the issues need to be considered seriously in all cases.

19.6   The specific issues on which we now comment are:

a.   image;

b.   the garden and grounds;

c.   the location of the bishop's office; and

d.   the special considerations which apply when the see house is a heritage property.

Image of the house

19.7   In the course of our review, we have visited a number of see and suffragans' houses in various parts of the country. In doing so, we have applied the 'gate test': we have stood at the gate or the beginning of the drive to the house and we have asked ourselves the question: 'What image does this property convey?'[6] It has been salutary.

19.8   We do not consider the fact that a bishop's house may be comparatively large in itself indicates that the house is inappropriate. The essential point is that the bishop and, where he is married, his wife share their house generously and selflessly with others. Our experience is that they do so.

19.9.1   There may be, however, an acute tension between the impression which is given of a large house and its grounds, and the reality of what goes on within it.

19.9.2   First, we have shown[7] that much of the house is given over to working or official use rather than private residential use.

19.9.3   Second, in our experience, most bishops have a modest personal standard of living.

19.9.4   Third, and most important, Christians, and especially bishops and other clergy as the most public representatives of the Church, are to bear witness to the simplicity, as well as the generosity, of the Christian lifestyle. The appearance of the house may run contrary to that witness.

19.10   We found no evidence to suggest that bishops and their families live in a grand manner or that they occupy their houses in a possessive or ostentatious fashion. However, it seems that for many people in society – many of whom have little real knowledge of the Church – the fact that a number of bishops live in large houses creates a feeling of distance and separation. For so long as this continues, we see no end to misrepresentation, and we cannot believe that it assists the bishop in the exercise of his ministry.

19.11   The issue arises particularly in relation to heritage properties, but it is not confined to them. Indeed, it seems to us that in one respect there is a greater danger with non-heritage properties: it is easier for the man who stands at the gate, but who has never passed through it, to assume that in some undefined sense the bishop owns the house than if the bishop lives in a palace or a castle. Furthermore, there is in one sense an aspect of perceived class-neutrality to a historic see house, as to a historic rectory, which would not be replicated in a move to a more modern, but still substantial, detached property. This might be particularly so if the replacement house were in an area largely occupied by professional people and other members of what some might regard as the comfortable middle classes.

19.12   We do not suggest that there should be any attempt to prescribe a national blueprint: what is appropriate may be much conditioned by local circumstances, and the issue should be decided locally.

We know that this is a subject which is on the minds of many bishops and we hope that in the course of the local reviews there will be careful reflections on the gospel imperatives in deciding the future housing needs of bishops within the local context.

Gardens and grounds

19.13.1 We turn now to the gardens and grounds of bishops' houses. We have described the resources which are provided in respect of gardens.[8]

19.13.2 Particularly in the case of see houses, the gardens can be large, extending to well over an acre. Gardens and grounds need management and maintenance. At present, all diocesans employ a gardener. Fourteen[9] employ full-time gardeners: the remainder have part-time gardeners or engage contractors. In 16 cases,[10] a cottage or other living accommodation is provided for the gardener free of charge. This has given us some anxiety, although the provision of this accommodation is to be seen in the context of modest salaries.

19.13.3 Although the point arises most frequently in relation to the gardens and grounds of see houses, it can also apply to suffragans' houses. Some suffragans have told us of the problems which comparatively large gardens bring, particularly as gardening assistance for suffragans is much more modest.[11]

19.14 There is no doubt that a large garden can be a useful resource not only to the bishop, but also to the local community. The bishop is able to use the garden for receiving a large numbers of visitors. Furthermore, local charities and other community organizations appreciate the opportunity to hold events in the garden.

19.15 On the other hand:

19.15.1 Only a relatively small proportion of either church members or the population at large would use the garden, and only at certain times of the year;

19.15.2 A large garden may well contribute to a (false) image of episcopal grandeur;

19.15.3 The management of the garden can impose a significant burden on the bishop's wife – and we have stated earlier[12] that her willingness and availability to undertake this should not be assumed; and

19.15.4 Some bishops' wives expressed to us a sense of guilt that there are large, and under-utilized, gardens attached to their houses.

19.16 In the course of the diocese-by-diocese review which we propose, we recommend that there should be an expert analysis of the cost of the maintenance of the garden; the possible use of contract gardeners or others instead of employed gardeners; and also of the opportunities for disposal of part of the grounds and for maximizing their use should the house itself be retained.

The location of the bishops' offices: general

19.17 We recommend that in the review there should be considered the location of the bishops' offices.

19.18.1 The issue is material for two principal reasons.

19.18.2 First, there is a common interest to ensure that there is in operation the arrangement which is most supportive to the bishop and which is operationally most cost-effective.

19.18.3 Second, if the bishop's working accommodation is in his house, that inevitably affects the requisite size of the house. Although it is not inevitably so, the size of the house usually also affects the size of the garden or grounds. It, therefore, has a direct effect on maintenance costs, as well as the cost of the capital represented by the house. On the other hand, if the working accommodation is elsewhere, the cost of the acquisition and maintenance of that alternative accommodation needs to be taken fully into account.

19.19 We consider first the current models and then make some observations.

Location of the bishop's office: the models

19.20 There are some variations, but at present there are four basic models for diocesans:

a.   where the living and working accommodation is in the same building, but where there is no clear demarcation between the two;

b.   where the living and working accommodation is in the same building, but where there is a clear physical demarcation, at least between the working offices and the remaining accommodation;

c.   where the working offices and perhaps a meeting room are located in a building which is separate from, but very close to, the house, and separate from the diocesan office; and

d.   where the working offices are away from the house and are in the same building as the diocesan office or in a building very near to it.

19.21   Where the see house is a large heritage property, some or all of this accommodation may be in only one wing of the building.

19.22   The basic models in the case of suffragans are:

a.   the most usual case, where the living and working accommodation is in the same house;

b.   where the office is in a commercially rented and serviced office building;

c.   where the office is in the diocesan office; or

d.   where the office is in an area office.

19.23.1   We refer briefly at this stage to the diocesan office and then to the area office.

19.23.2   The diocesan office is the building, or the principal building, in which the DBF carries on its operations.[13]

19.23.3   As we have stated,[14] the diocesan is in no sense the manager of the diocesan office, and in that capacity has no *legal* responsibility for its affairs, although he does have a great moral responsibility to act if something goes seriously wrong.

19.23.4 All DBFs discharge the same statutory functions, but beyond those functions, in practice, the role of the diocesan office within the diocese varies.

19.23.5 At the risk of oversimplification, at one extreme the diocesan office is the central support-base for the diocese.

19.23.6 At the other extreme, it is that and also one of the focal points of the diocese. This is so in practice where at least one of the bishops and, in some cases, one of the archdeacons uses it as his working-base, and where the bishop's senior staff and other significant meetings take place there.

19.24 Area offices are a newer concept. They are established where there is a formal or informal area scheme, and provide the working-base for, at the minimum, the suffragan and one archdeacon.

19.25.1 The issue is as to the location of the *office*, that is where the bishop will deal with most of his administrative work and where his support staff will be based. It will usually include facilities for meetings and often facilities for the provision of simple hospitality.

19.25.2 We envisage that save, perhaps, in the most extraordinary circumstances, if the bishop's office is not in the house, the bishop will have in the house a place for worship[15] and a study; and that the study will be large enough for the bishop to be able to see a few people in it.

Location of the bishop's office: observations

19.26.1 We make two general observations.

19.26.2 First, the attitude of an individual bishop is very largely affected by the arrangement which he inherited on appointment. The majority of bishops who are currently serving are working in the accommodation which was provided for them when they were appointed and have had no choice in the nature of these arrangements. Yet 87% of bishops have told us that they think that the current arrangement, whatever it is, is best suited to their needs.

19.26.3 Second, there is a small but significant trend to be observed. Some recently appointed suffragans have more experience than most diocesans of having working accommodation away from their houses, whether in parish offices, the diocesan office, area office, or commercially rented premises. Parish clergy are becoming increasingly used to working in parish or other offices. This may well affect the expectations of future generations of diocesans.

19.27 As a background to the aspect of the review which we have proposed which relates to the location of the bishop's office, we rehearse some of the issues. In favour of the diocesan bishop's office being in, or very close to, the diocesan office, it can be said that:

19.27.1 The diocesan has thereby immediate and recurrent access to key officers and specialists who are based in the diocesan office;

19.27.2 The diocesan office can supply back-up assistance in peak times of the bishop's workload, or absences on the part of the bishop's support staff;

19.27.3 Some cost-effectiveness can be gained by the use of shared resources (such as the services of receptionists, telephonists and IT support staff);

19.27.4 There is increased understanding on the part of staff of what is happening and, therefore, an easier working relationship between the bishop's staff and the staff in the diocesan office; and

19.27.5 A small number of bishops' wives (significantly mostly younger wives) have stated their personal preference for the location of the office away from the house.

19.28 Against co-location, it can be said that:

19.28.1 If a bishop spends a significant part of his time working in the diocesan office, there is a risk that this would convey the false impression that the bishop runs the diocesan office;

19.28.2 Key officers in the diocesan office may seek too much of the bishop's attention;

19.28.3 If the house is not conveniently located, considerable time can be spent by the bishop and his staff on travelling between the two;

19.28.4 If the bishop is to receive visitors in the diocesan office, there may be some loss of privacy and some loss of the warmth of hospitality, although much will depend on the reception arrangements and internal configuration of the diocesan office;[16] and

19.28.5 If the bishop's office is in the house, he is not involved in travel to it, and so can make the optimum use of his time.

19.29.1 We have also considered the matter from the viewpoint of the bishop's wife.

19.29.2 If the bishop's office is located away from the house, it is more difficult for the bishop's secretary to provide his wife with the assistance which we consider proper.[17]

19.29.3 On the other hand, there is some, but again not conclusive, evidence that if the bishop's office is in the house, that constitutes a temptation for him to overwork, and that a bishop's home-life might be improved if there were a separation of home and office.

19.30.1 It has been said to us that one disadvantage of the bishop's office being in the diocesan office is that when he is at home he would not have ready access to his files.

19.30.2 We recognize the force of this in the present circumstances, but we are unimpressed by it in the longer term. We do not envisage a paperless office, but as more and more information will be stored electronically, the physical place of storage will become less important: what will matter will be access to that information, and, with the appropriate equipment, information which is stored electronically can be accessed from almost anywhere. We envisage that there would invariably be a computer terminal in the bishop's study, and that in future all bishops will be fully computer literate.

19.31 Our general conclusions on this subject are that:

19.31.1 No one model is clearly appropriate in all cases, and we are aware of examples of all models which appear to be satisfactory;

19.31.2 Local circumstances should in each case be taken fully into account;

19.31.3 If there is a local move to separate home and office, we would not discourage it; but

19.31.4 The decision should be taken on wider than solely financial grounds.

19.32.1 There are, however, stronger arguments for a suffragan's office to be separate from his house. Although this is beyond our remit, these are the same as in the case of an archdeacon. We are concerned at the sense of isolation which can be experienced by the suffragan, and the lack of a ready opportunity for easy face-to-face exchange of views with other senior members within the diocese. We are equally concerned with the isolation of the suffragan's secretary, particularly in view of the fact that the bishop's work will often take him away from the house; that the secretary will usually be the only member of the bishop's support staff; and that in our view it will be increasingly unlikely that the bishop's wife, if the bishop is married, will be at home for much of the day.

19.32.2 Furthermore, in the usual case where the suffragan's secretary is the only member of his personal support staff, if he or she is working alone there can be difficulties if he or she is ill or on holiday. The bishop may find himself having to deal with numerous telephone calls and other routine matters which should not be taking up his time.

19.33 Our fundamental approach is that the location of the bishops' offices should be determined according to local circumstances. However, subject to that, we encourage the move towards the establishment of area offices and where geography makes this appropriate for suffragans to work in the diocesan office.

Heritage properties

19.34 Special considerations apply in relation to the see houses which are national heritage properties.[18] In the course of the review of bishops' accommodation in the diocese, it might be concluded that the properties should continue to be used for this purpose, but there will be national concern as to the future of the properties if they cease to be, or to include, see houses.

19.35 It is very unlikely that a heritage property would accord with the new guidelines[19] for episcopal housing. Nevertheless, our proposal is that, if the diocese[20] so wishes, it should be able to accept a transfer of the ownership of the house from the Commissioners for continued use as the see house, and meet at first part[21], and ultimately all, of the maintenance costs.[22]

19.36   If, however, the diocese did not wish to do so, then it would be for the Commissioners to provide a replacement see house, and transfer that to the DBF. It would then be for the Commissioners to deal with the future of the heritage property.

19.37.1 There are general policy issues regarding heritage properties which go well beyond our remit, and we recognize that see houses are only a very small proportion of the heritage properties which are owned by the Church.

19.37.2 Although we think that there are issues about the use of such properties as places of work and residence for bishops, we can readily understand that the Church might well wish to retain them for other reasons.

19.37.3 A code has been evolved by Government[23] for dealing with historic buildings which are no longer required for operational purposes. In such cases, the future of the building is not dictated solely by narrow financial considerations, but broader issues of the value and benefit of the building to the public are taken into account. A similar approach is followed by the Commissioners when they deal with redundant churches which are historic properties.[24] We recommend that the same general approach should be adopted with regard to historic properties which cease to be used as see houses.

19.38   Accordingly, we **recommend** that:

19.38.1 If a historic building ceases to be used as a see house, the Commissioners should in the first instance not seek to dispose of it, but should seek to manage it, as a net income-producing asset. In this respect the efforts which the Commissioners have made in recent years towards making large see houses financially self-supporting should assist;

19.38.2 If the Commissioners could not manage the property to derive net income, or if the value of the property let was materially less than the amount which it would fetch if sold on the open market, then the

Commissioners should take the advice of the Archbishops' Council on whether it was in the wider interests of the Church for the property to be retained, even if there was a recurrent cost in so doing, and the Commissioners should be entitled to act on that advice; and

19.38.3 If it was not thought to be in the wider interests of the Church for the property to be retained, then the Commissioners should be empowered to arrange for the property to be transferred, if appropriate without charge, to an existing or new heritage trust, together with, if essential, some endowment.

19.39 This would require a modification to the Commissioners' general obligation with regard to assets vested in them to seek the best financial return which can reasonably be obtained, and we **recommend** that such a change should be sought.

19.40 While recognizing that this is a subject which is much wider than historic see houses, in our view the retention of a property which does not produce a net income in the hands of a reliable body which would ensure its conservation is more important than who owns it.

Bishops' wives
19.41 We restate[25] here that, in conducting the review, it should not be assumed that the bishop will have a spouse who is able and willing to spend substantial amounts of time in managing the house and its garden. No doubt the factors relating to the future roles of bishops' wives which we have previously described[26] will be fully taken into account in the review.

Summary of objectives
19.42 In summary, the review should be concerned with the question: what is best for the diocese, taking into account matters episcopal, pastoral and financial?

The review process
19.43 We recommend that the review within each diocese should be conducted by a group established for the purpose under an independent chairman. It should include the diocesan, the chairman of the DBF and a representative of the Commissioners. The group should take evidence from, among others, the wives of all bishops in the diocese who are willing to participate.

19.44   We **recommend** that the review process should be initiated by the Commissioners, in view of their existing obligation to consider from time to time the suitability of see houses, but that it should be conducted locally.

19.45   We have considered whether the additional burden of participating in such a review should be imposed on the diocesan, but we have concluded that it is right to do so. We have no doubt that such a review will have the collateral advantage of contributing to the understanding of those in the diocese who become involved as to the work of its bishops.

appendix A

Methodology

A. Launch of the review

1.   The review was launched at a press conference which was held at Lambeth Palace on 21 May 1999. We issued a press release on the same day.

B. Phases of the review

2.   Our work has comprised:

    a. ascertaining the facts;

    b. inviting submissions;

    c. taking evidence and advice;

    d. devising principles and propositions, and discussing them with bishops and their wives;

    e. formulating recommendations; and

    f. writing this report.

3.   We have endeavoured to keep bishops and their wives, as well as other interested parties, generally informed as our work has progressed.

C. Ascertaining the facts

4.   We have sought to ascertain the facts:

    a. by seeking information from bishops and their wives;

    b. by seeking information from diocesan secretaries;

    c. by taking oral and written evidence; and

    d. by making our own enquiries, particularly of the Church Commissioners and members of the staff of their Bishoprics and Cathedrals Department, as well as of various members of staff of other central church bodies.

D. Inviting submissions

5.   We issued specific invitations to make submissions to:

    a.   all bishops;

    b.   all bishops' wives;

    c.   the Archbishops' Council;

    d.   the Church Commissioners;

    e.   all members of General Synod;

    f.   the Consultative Group of Chairmen and Secretaries of Diocesan Boards of Finance;

    g.   all diocesan secretaries; and

    h.   the four serving Members of Parliament who since 1 January 1997 had asked Parliamentary Questions on matters germane to the review, namely:

        i.   Mr Norman Baker, MP;

        ii   Mr Ben Bradshaw, MP;

        iii   The Hon Mrs Gwyneth Dunwoody, MP; and

        iv.   Mr Simon Hughes, MP.

6.   We also issued specific invitations to those who are listed in Appendix B to give evidence.

7.   By letter published in *The Church of England Newspaper* and a corresponding news item in *The Church Times*, we invited all members of the wider Church and the public generally to make submissions.

E. Information from bishops and their wives

8.   We decided at an early stage to invite all bishops and their wives to complete detailed questionnaires.

9.   We devised pilot questionnaires, and various members of the Group held discussions to develop those questionnaires with:

    a.   four diocesan bishops and their wives;

    b.   three suffragan bishops and their wives; and

c.   one suffragan bishop who is not married.

10.   We sent the questionnaires in their final form to all bishops and their wives.

11.   We followed those questionnaires by asking those bishops and their wives (the majority) who expressed themselves willing to do so to complete detailed time-sheets for a three-week period.

12.   We also obtained much information by various members of the Group:

a.   attending certain regional meetings organized (for other purposes) by the Commissioners' Bishoprics and Cathedrals Department;

b.   visiting the bishops and their wives whom we list in Appendix B; and

c.   discussing the propositions to which we refer in paragraph 22 of this Appendix in regional meetings with bishops and their wives. It was not possible to make timely arrangements to meet with the bishops and their wives in one particular region, but we participated in meetings in all other regions.

13.   Apart from that one regional meeting, we have seen, or visited, every bishop and every bishop's wife who asked us to do so.

F. Information from Diocesan Boards of Finance

14.1   We also sent questionnaires to all diocesan secretaries. This was in part because of the absence of any centrally held or collated information about the cost of the support of episcopal ministry which is provided by dioceses.

14.2   We were grateful for the 100% return of completed questionnaires from diocesan secretaries, as well as for various items of further information which we subsequently requested.

G. Evidence

15.   We obtained much information in the course of taking evidence from those to whom we refer in Appendix B.

H. Enquiries

16.   We have made numerous enquiries, particularly of the staff of the Commissioners' Bishoprics and Cathedrals Department and of their finance department, as well as of the staff of various divisions of the Archbishops' Council.

17.   We have recorded in the Preface to this report our gratitude to all of the members of staff who have assisted us.

I. Other churches

18.   We have not sought to make a detailed study of the practice in churches of other denominations, although we have made enquiries of, and have taken account of the resourcing of leaders of, the Roman Catholic Church, the United Reformed Church, the Methodist Church and the Baptist Church in England, as well as of the Church of Scotland.

19.   We have not made a comparative study of the corresponding arrangements in other churches of the Anglican Communion, although we have taken evidence from two bishops of the Episcopal Church of the United States of America.

J. Principles and propositions

20.   At about the halfway stage in our work we issued two papers, one setting out principles for resourcing bishops and the other setting out certain propositions.

21.   The principles paper reflected much of our thinking on that aspect as it had been developed by then. It formed the basis of what became Chapter 9 of this report.

22.   The propositions paper set forth a number of issues which we thought warranted debate at that stage. These propositions were not proposals or provisional proposals, but the responses to them were very helpful to us in reaching our conclusions.

K. Meetings, visits and interviews

23.   The Group has had:

    a.   22 plenary meetings; and

b.   one plenary two-day residential meeting (at St George's House, Windsor).

24.   In addition, various members of the Group have:

a.   participated in 3 regional meetings arranged by the Commissioners;

b.   participated in 8 other regional meetings, particularly to discuss the principles and propositions papers;

c.   participated in 9 other visits to bishops or groups of bishops, usually also with their wives, and on some occasions also the diocesan officers; and

d.   conducted 19 interviews with those who gave evidence.

25.   In addition, the Chairman addressed the Bishops' Meeting on 7 June 2000.

Visits and evidence

A. Visits

1.   One or more members of the Group visited in connection with the pilot questionnaires:

    a.   four diocesan bishops and their wives, namely:

        i.   the Bishop of Bradford and Mrs Smith;

        ii.   the Bishop of Manchester and Mrs Mayfield;

        iii.   the Bishop of St Albans and Mrs Herbert; and

        iv.   the Bishop of Salisbury and Mrs Stancliffe;

    b.   three suffragan bishops and their wives, namely:

        i.   the Bishop of Exeter, then Bishop of Birkenhead, and Mrs Langrish;

        ii.   the Bishop of Ely, then Bishop of Dorchester, and Mrs Russell; and

        iii.   the Bishop of Dorking and Mrs Brackley; and

    c.   one suffragan bishop who is not married, namely the Bishop of Basingstoke.

2.   Members of the Group participated in the following regional meetings with bishops and their wives:

North West Region	Comprising bishops and their wives in the Dioceses of Blackburn, Carlisle, Chester, Liverpool, Manchester and Sodor and Man.
North East Region	Comprising bishops and their wives in the Dioceses of Durham, Newcastle, York and the Bishop of Beverley (PEV).
South and West Yorkshire Region	Comprising bishops and their wives in the Dioceses of Bradford, Ripon and Leeds, Sheffield and Wakefield

East Midlands Region	Comprising bishops and their wives in the Dioceses of Derby, Leicester, Lincoln, Southwell and Peterborough.
West Midlands Region	Comprising bishops and their wives in the Dioceses of Birmingham, Coventry, Hereford, Lichfield and Worcester.
Eastern Region	Comprising bishops and their wives in the Dioceses of Chelmsford, Ely, Norwich, St Edmundsbury and Ipswich, Peterborough, St Albans and the Bishop of Richborough (PEV).
South West Region	Comprising bishops and their wives in the Dioceses of Bath and Wells, Bristol, Exeter, Gloucester, Oxford, Salisbury, Truro and the Bishop of Ebbsfleet (PEV).
Southern Region	Comprising bishops and their wives in the Dioceses of Chichester, Guildford, Portsmouth, Salisbury and Winchester.

3. One or more members of the Group visited:

a. the Bishop of Derby, the chairman of Derby DBF and others;

b. the Bishop of Gibraltar in Europe, Mrs Hind and the suffragan Bishop of Europe;

c. the Bishop of Kingston;

d. the bishops of the Lichfield Diocese;

e. the Bishop of Liverpool and Mrs James;

f. the Bishop of London and Mrs Chartres;

g. the Bishop of Oxford, the chairman of the Oxford DBF, the diocesan secretary and others;

h. the Bishop of Portsmouth and Mrs Stevenson; and

i. the Bishop of Winchester and Mrs Scott-Joynt.

B. Oral evidence

Oral evidence has been given to one or more members of the Group by:

a. Mr Stephen Adam — Lay administrator, Diocese of Winchester

b. Canon Michael Austin — Formerly Archbishops' Adviser for Bishops' Ministry

c. Mr Norman Baker, MP

d. Captain David Brown, OBE, RN — Bishop's assistant to the Bishop of Lichfield

e. The Worshipful Sheila Cameron, QC — Vicar-general of the Province of Canterbury; Chancellor of the Dioceses of London and Chelmsford; Chairman of the Archbishops' Group on the Episcopate

f. Mr Keith Cawdron — Member of General Synod; Diocesan Secretary of the Diocese of Liverpool

g. Elizabeth Filkin — Parliamentary Commissioner for Standards

h. The Rt Revd Richard Grein — Bishop of New York, USA

i. Mr John Holroyd, CB, CVO, DL — Previously Prime Minister's Appointments Secretary

j. The Ven. Gordon Kuhrt — Director of Ministry, Archbishops' Council

k. Brigadier Peter Maggs — Ministry of Defence

l. The Revd Dr John Mantle — Archbishops' Adviser for Bishops' Ministry

m. The Very Revd Dr John Moses   Dean of St Paul's Cathedral

n. Mr Geoffrey Penzer   Management consultant (Penzer Allen)

o. The Rt Revd Andrew Radford   Bishop of Taunton

p. Mr Anthony Sadler   Archbishops' Appointments Secretary

q. The Rt Revd and Rt Hon The Lord Sheppard of Liverpool   Formerly Bishop of Liverpool

r. The Rt Revd William Swing   Bishop of California, USA

s. Mr John Truscott   Church consultant and trainer

4. Meetings with one or more members of the Group have been held with:

a. Mr William Chapman   Prime Minister's Appointments Secretary

b. The Rt Hon The Lord Hurd of Westwell, CH, CBE, PC   Chairman, Archbishops' Review of the See of Canterbury

C. Presentations
The Group received presentations from:

a. Mr Christopher Daws   Church Commissioners' Financial and Deputy Secretary

b. Mr Shaun Farrell   Financial Secretary of the Archbishops' Council

D. Written submissions
5. In addition to various letters from bishops and their wives throughout the process, the Group received and considered written submissions from:

a. The Revd J W Masding   Chairman,
                                   the English Clergy Association

b. Mr Ben Bradshaw, MP

c. Captain David Brown, OBE, RN   Bishop's assistant to the Bishop
                                   of Lichfield

d. Mr Keith Cawdron   Member of General Synod,
                                   Diocesan Secretary of the
                                   Diocese of Liverpool

e. Mr Simon Parton   Diocesan Secretary, Southwark
                                   DBF

f. Mr Stuart Emmason   Member of General Synod

g. Mr David Gurney   Chairman, Norwich DBF

h. Canon Christopher Hall   Member of General Synod

i. Mr John Holroyd, CB, CVO, DL   Previously Prime Minister's
                                   Appointments Secretary

j. Mr Paul Jefferson   Member of General Synod

k. Mr Harry Jeffery   Member of General Synod

l. Father Simon Killwick   Member of General Synod

m. The Ven. Gordon Kuhrt   Director of Ministry,
                                   Archbishops' Council

n. Mr P G H Law   Diocesan Secretary,
                                   Rochester DBF

o. Mr Brian McHenry   Member of General Synod
                                   and member of the
                                   Archbishops' Council

p. Mr Barry Moult
   (with the Bishop of
   Warrington)

Chairman, Liverpool DBF

q. Canon Gordon Oliver

Bishop's officer for ministry
and training, Diocese of
Rochester

r. Mr M D C Roberts

Member of the Church
Commissioners' audit
committee

s. Mr Anthony Sadler

Archbishops' Appointments
Secretary

t. Dr Stanley Shere

Consultant physician

u. The Very Revd H E C Stapleton

Formerly Dean of Carlisle

The number and disposition of bishops

The following table shows in relation to each diocese:

a. the numbers of established posts for bishops on 1 January 2001; and

b. in the case of suffragans, whether they are area bishops, suffragans without general area responsibilities, or PEVs.

(1)	Diocese, each with a diocesan (2)	Number of area bishops (3)	Number of suffragans without area responsibilities (a) (4)	Number of PEVs (5)	Assistant bishops (b) (6)	Remarks (7)
1	Bath & Wells		1			
2	Birmingham		1			
3	Blackburn		2			
4	Bradford		none		1	
5	Bristol		1			
6	Canterbury		2	2		Note c
7	Carlisle		1			
8	Chelmsford	3				F
9	Chester	2				I
10	Chichester	2				F
11	Coventry		1			
12	Derby		1			
13	Durham		1			
14	Ely		1			
15	Exeter	2				I
16	Gloucester		1			
17	Guildford		1			
18	Hereford		1			Note d
19	Leicester		none		1	Note b
20	Lichfield	3				
21	Lincoln	2				I

(1)	Diocese, each with a diocesan (2)	Number of area bishops (3)	Number of suffragans without area responsibilities (a) (4)	Number of PEVs (5)	Assistant bishops (b) (6)	Remarks (7)
22	Liverpool		1			
23	London	5				F and I
24	Manchester	3				I
25	Newcastle		1			Note e
26	Norwich		2			
27	Oxford	3				F
28	Peterborough		1			
29	Portsmouth		none			
30	Ripon & Leeds		1			
31	Rochester		1			
32	St Albans		2			
33	St Edmundsbury & Ipswich		1			
34	Salisbury	2				F
35	Sheffield		1			
36	Sodor & Man		none			
37	Southwark	3				F
38	Southwell		1			
39	Truro		1			
40	Wakefield		1			
41	Winchester	2				I
42	Worcester	1				F
43	York	3		1		I, Note f
44	Europe		1			
Total	44	36	30	3	2	

Grand Total of archbishops and diocesan and suffragan bishops	115	Note g

Key with regard to area schemes:

F   denotes a formal area scheme

I   denotes an informal area scheme

F and I   which applies only within the diocese of London, denotes that part of the diocese is the subject of a formal area scheme and another part is subject to an informal scheme.

Notes:

a.   In some instances, suffragans who are shown in column (4) have no overall area responsibilities, but have particular responsibilities within an area for specific purposes.

b.   Full-time or part-time serving assistant bishops who are acting under ad hoc local arrangements and who are not treated by the Commissioners as suffragans. We have not listed honorary assistant bishops.

c.   The Archbishop of Canterbury is the diocesan bishop of the diocese of Canterbury, but many of his duties are undertaken by the Bishop of Dover. For stipend and resourcing purposes, the Commissioners treat the Bishop of Dover as if he were the diocesan bishop. However, in this table we have adopted the formal position and have treated the Bishop of Dover as a suffragan.

d.   The suffragan bishop in the diocese of Hereford is concurrently the archdeacon of Ludlow and in the latter capacity has specific responsibilities in that archdeaconry.

e.   In the diocese of Newcastle, the post is that of a full-time assistant bishop. For stipend and resourcing purposes, the Commissioners treat the holder of that post as a suffragan.

f.   The Archbishop of York is the diocesan bishop of the diocese of York.

g.   In their published statistics, the Commissioners exclude the two assistant bishops to whom we have referred in column (6), but include the Bishop of Lambeth, who is head of staff at Lambeth Palace, to give a total of 114 archbishops and diocesan and suffragan bishops.

A theology of episcopacy

by The Rt Revd Professor Stephen Sykes

A. Introduction

1.   Do you believe, so far as you know your own heart, that God has called you to the office and work of a bishop in his Church?

   Answer: I believe that God has called me.

Before the ordination or consecration of a bishop can proceed, the bishop is required to confirm that he believes that *God* has called him to an *office* in *God's Church*.[1]

2.   The Church of England professes the belief that God has, by the Holy Spirit, 'appointed various orders of ministry in the Church'.[2] These orders are specified as those of bishops, priests and deacons. The Preface to the Ordinal attached to *The Book of Common Prayer* (BCP) claims that 'it is evident unto all men diligently reading holy Scripture and ancient authors, that from the Apostles' time there have been these Orders of Ministers in Christ's Church'.[3]

3.   It is God's Church into whose office or order the new bishop is to enter, by God's own call.[4] The office is not a human invention; nor merely an arrangement by the Church of England. It was simply assumed at the time of the Reformation that there would be many other countries with similar orders in similarly reformed churches.[5] This hope was largely confounded until the growth of the Anglican Communion and the so-called 'wider Episcopal Fellowship'[6] took place. But it was the explicit intention of the Ordinal to continue and reverently to use and esteem those orders which the Church of God had used from the apostles' time.[7] The Anglican claim is that these orders are shared with other churches retaining the practice of episcopal consecration, despite certain doctrinal disagreements and despite the absence of mutual recognition.

4. All bishops are also priests and deacons. Not every aspect, therefore, of a bishop's ministry is encompassed by specifically episcopal roles and responsibilities. It is, for example, a common experience of bishops that aspects of diaconal ministry, notably ambassadorial activities in public life, assume renewed prominence. *Diakonia* as service, of course, never ceases to be an indispensable attribute of all ordained ministry.[8]

5. What, then, is specific about the office and work of a bishop? That is expounded in outline in the archbishop's charge before the bishop-elect makes his declarations. There is the work of leadership in relation to God's people;[9] there is the maintenance with fellow bishops of the unity, discipline and faith of the Church; there is the mission of the Church;[10] there is oversight, prayer and teaching for the diocese; there is the duty of knowing and being known by the people of the diocese;[11] there is ordination and commissioning of clergy and church workers;[12] there is the celebration of baptisms and confirmations, and presidency at the Holy Communion;[13] there is the duty of care for the outcast and needy;[14] there is the absolution of penitents. The list is long and illustrative rather than systematic, though the ASB version shows signs of deliberate amplification on the tasks envisaged in the BCP.[15] It is assumed that the candidate for the office has been 'called, tried, examined, and known to have such qualities as are requisite for the same'.[16]

B. The Church of God in time and eternity

6. It is necessary briefly to consider the nature of the Church of God itself as framing, conditioning and shaping all ministerial offices. The Church has both a temporal and an eternal character; it both exists in time and also participates in God's eternal sovereignty.

7. It is the unique calling of the Church to carry out God's mission in the temporal order and to offer to God the worship of the whole creation.[17] This is both a 'ministry of reconciliation' (2 Corinthians 5.18-21) and a blessing of an indescribably generous God for his gracious gifts (2 Corinthians 9.8-15), a 'bringing of all things in heaven and earth together under one head, even Christ' (Ephesians 1.10). An ASB Embertide Collect addresses God as one who has entrusted to his Church 'a share in the ministry of your Son, our great High Priest'.[18]

8.   To carry out this mission the Church receives the gift of 'power from on high' (Acts 1.8). It is the power to preach 'good news to the poor, freedom for prisoners, recovery of sight for the blind, and release for the oppressed' (Luke 4.18). It is the power to offer prayer from the heart of creation (Romans 8.19-27), and to call on God as Father (Galatians 4.6). It is a life-giving power, like that power by which Jesus himself was raised from the dead (Ephesians 1.19, 20).

9.   But it is evident, in the exigencies of the life of the Church on earth, that the power is not the *possession* of members of the Church, who are subject to frailty and sin (2 Corinthians 4.7).[19] Paul knows that he must speak of his own weakness, as well as of his power (2 Corinthians 13); and those to whom he writes are prey to the temptations of doctrinal error (Galatians 1.6) and moral failings (2 Corinthians 12.20). The ministry of the gospel of the glory of Christ is through the medium of 'jars of clay' (2 Corinthians 4.7).

10.   There is an intrinsic relationship between the Church on earth, struggling to know and to do God's will with courage and persistence, and the Church of the heavenly Jerusalem, the city of God. There, angels and the spirits of the righteous join to praise God in the presence of Jesus, the mediator of the new covenant (Hebrews 12.22-24).[20] It is assumed that the sovereignty of God will embrace not merely the saints of the old covenant, a 'great cloud of witnesses' (Hebrews 12.1), but also 'many from east and west' (Matthew 8.11). In contemporary theology it is frequently asserted that the Church is sign, instrument and foretaste of God's sovereignty, but not the whole of it.[21] It is emphatically denied that the activity of the Holy Spirit is confined to the life of the Church.[22]

11.   The temporal character of the activity of the Church necessarily relates its life, including the office and work of those in holy orders, to both the primary and secondary environments. The primary environment is constituted by such elements as geography, climate and human biology; the secondary by the diverse and constantly changing patterns of human culture. The work of the Church is embedded in a particular time and place in a way analogous to the incarnation of the divine Word. Jesus, the Christ, the Son of God, was born a Jew at a particular time, in a particular place. In an analogous, but not an identical way, the Church's divine mission is lived in all the specific circumstances of particular primary and secondary environments.[23]

12. All aspects of the life of the Church should, therefore, carry a double character; to be at once fully immersed in the multiple contexts in which women and men live their lives, and also to point to God's own rule and sovereignty over all that is transient and not to be conformed to a merely mundane mind (Romans 12.2). This is no easy vocation. Nor is it easy, in all the exigencies of human culture, to distinguish which features of the life of the Church bear which character.

13. The relation of the old and new covenants provided classical theology with an instance of the need to distinguish (and the difficulty of distinguishing) between elements of truth which had merely temporary relevance, and those which are lasting.[24] Recent theology has emphasized the internal diversity of different parts of both Old and New Testaments, which provide evidence for a state of continuous adaptation and interpretation of past traditions.[25] The resulting picture is more complex and dynamic, and adds new difficulties to the arguments for and against change. But it is beyond doubt that, in the life of the Church, constant change has occurred and is bound to occur, as it seeks to embed its divinely given mission at particular times and in particular places.

C. The office and work of a bishop in the Church of God
14. Apart from the Ordinal, to which reference has been made above (para. 3), there exists no normative description for Anglicans of the office and work of a bishop.[26] Canon law speaks of the bishop as the 'principal minister' within his diocese, and ascribes to him various jurisdictional rights (see below para. 26).[27] The difficulty of distinguishing between what belongs essentially (as it were) to episcopal ministry and what might be ascribed to the accidents of history lies in the situation described in the previous paragraphs (7 and 8). The early history of the office in the Church is full of uncertainties and mystery; the later history contains massive developments (not excluding possibly serious deteriorations) and vast variety.[28]

15. Nonetheless there are certain structural considerations which persist in all accounts of the office and work of a bishop. First, an account must be given of the way a bishop's work fits in the context of God's mission to the world through the Church. Second, in carrying out this mission an account must be given of the relationships between a bishop and other members of the Church, both those holding public office and those not. Third, it will be necessary to describe different types of activity in which the bishop engages and those towards whom that activity is directed. Fourth, it will be possible to state the legal or jurisdictional powers of the bishop and to depict the less formal authority that accrues to the office. Finally, experience is likely to suggest the dangers, risks and abuses attendant upon the exercise of the office. It is at once obvious that the actual contents of the structure, not excluding the first feature, have varied in different times and places. Nonetheless the structure helps somewhat in locating the presence of major and minor variations over time, and will be adopted here.

D. The bishop and God's mission

16. It is natural and right to make the atoning and redemptive work of the incarnate Son the centre for understanding the life of the Church and its office-bearers. Specifically, in the light of the threefold office of the Son, as Prophet, Priest and King, so the bishop (as other office-bearers) participates in God's mission by proclamation, by priestly intercession, and by governance.[29] God's mission is one of love to the whole world; the bishop's work may not be reduced to that of a church-related functionary. Jesus came to seek and to save the lost (Luke 19.10); the bishop's task is both to point to that source of salvation, and to enable others to do the same. In the case of the bishop, the requirements of governance impinge also upon proclamation and intercession. The Ordinal of the BCP, substantially based upon the Pastoral Epistles, highlights the importance of 'guarding the deposit' of faith (1 Timothy 6.20). To teach from the Scriptures, to withstand and convince gainsayers, and to drive away 'all erroneous and strange doctrine', is the content of no less than three of the candidate's promises.[30] The ASB redressed the balance by reducing this emphasis to a single clause.[31]

17. The power of the Holy Spirit is specifically invoked at the moment of laying-on of hands, for the office and work of a bishop. Then follows a long prayer for 'the grace and power' given to the apostles to be sent upon the bishop to enable him to carry out his entire task. This is again summarized in a series of clauses. Significantly included in the specific practice of the bishop's ministry are confirmations and ordinations, means by which the Holy Spirit is given to 'increase the Church, renew its ministry, and unite its members in a holy fellowship of truth and love'.[32]

18. What, then, of the bishop's ministry in the light of the first article of the Creed, belief in God the creator and sustainer of all that is? It is tempting to succumb, and the Church has often succumbed, to a practical binitarianism so far as the life of the Church is concerned. To do so is to make certain parts of its life either unintelligible, or subject to forces of which it has little or no understanding. But the Church is plainly an organization, with goals, structures and processes not wholly dissimilar from those of other organizations. The bishop as a leader has powers of various kinds (including privileged access to information, and a capacity to administer rewards and sanctions) which cannot be denied or discounted without danger of self-deception. But it is part of the doctrine of creation that God is interested in good, human organizations. For the Church to admit that it was a voluntary human society would not entail denial that it was more. Richard Hooker (1554–1600), after all, identified the Church as 'both a societie and a societie supernatural'.[33] The Church is, for example, an employer, and it should aim to be a good one. A bishop's responsibilities for oversight of his diocese, or his task as a leader in a province, is bound to entail an understanding of good governance. Concentration on evangelism or sanctification has sometimes led to neglect of elementary duties.

E. The bishop's relationships
19. The relational character of episcopal ministry is established by its participation in God's mission shared by the whole people of God. Inside his diocese, the bishop is related to the whole population among and for whom God calls him to be a chief pastor and father-in-God (Canon 18.1), to those among that population who 'profess and call themselves Christians',[34] and to all those who have received the bishop's licence or commission, whether ordained or lay, to any office or ministry in the Church. The nature of these relationships differs with the specific tasks of particular persons or office. But it is notable that a very substantial sharing of responsibility for oversight takes place with archdeacons and other members of the bishop's immediate team (frequently including lay officers), with rural deans, and with the staff of the cathedral. With area, suffragan or assistant bishops, there may be specifically delegated episcopal responsibilities.[35] The act of sending a priest to a specific parish in the diocese similarly involves sharing in responsibilities. The act of consulting a synod on a major issue of diocesan policy is at heart a relational act. None of these relationships works well without a significant measure of trust. Trust

is nurtured by personal knowledge and concern, consistency, integrity and transparency.

20. Beyond the boundaries of the diocese the bishop has a unique relationship of obedience to the primate of his province.[36] He shares with other bishops in the Church of God a duty of care for the unity, holiness, catholicity and apostolicity of the Church. This should make of the bishop a naturally ecumenical person, in the literal sense of one concerned for the entire *oikumene*/world. The integrity and coherence of the Church's divinely bestowed mission should be a matter of consuming passion. The means, whether letters, or meetings, or mutual prayer, will follow from the intention. That the scope is not in principle restricted follows from the fact that the Church in question is the Church of God.

21. In order the better to serve the Church's mission in a particular context, such as a region or nation, any given bishop may be given the task of coordination of one aspect of that mission. In the recent past in the Church of England, we have been familiar with substantial responsibilities in relation to the Church's doctrinal or liturgical life, and of its involvement in education or public affairs. In each of these areas, and in many others, the Church has the opportunity to express a corporate view, or to promote serious and informed debate. The requirements for competence in these areas are formidable and not easily acquired, and to speak the common mind of the Church involves relationships both with relevant experts and discussion with other bishops and in synod.

F. The bishop's work
22. The work of the bishop is best presented by reference to the four (or five) marks of mission identified at the Lambeth Conference of 1988. These are:

- Evangelism: 'to proclaim the good news of the kingdom'
- Teaching: 'to teach, baptize and nurture new believers'
- Care for the needy: 'to respond to human need by loving service'
- Justice: 'to seek to transform unjust structures and society'.

A substantial portion of a modern bishop's life in the Church of England will be concerned with the appointment, support, encouragement and (very occasionally) the disciplining of the clergy of his diocese. All these activities may readily have the four marks of mission in view. It is vital, however, that these activities do not absorb the entire life of a bishop, who also has responsibilities towards those outside the Church. Many of the most formative liturgical and ecclesiological emphases of the Church of England have been in the past directed towards the instruction and sanctification of a baptized population. The Decade of Evangelism was necessary in England precisely because a balance had to be redressed in the context of a culture increasingly distant from the traditional message of the gospel. In the context of the Church of England baptizing fewer than 25% of babies, it is evident to all that England has become a mission field. A bishop is bound, therefore, to be a leader of that mission.[37]

23. Nor should the bishop's *teaching* activity be directed solely towards existing members of the Church. Or rather, there is no absolute distinction between matters of concern to the life of church members and those of the wider society – as the example of teaching concerning marriage and divorce demonstrates.[38] A range of major issues, concerning life and death, science and technology, entertainment, wealth and power impinge equally on professed members and those of indeterminate allegiance. One of the tasks of the bishop is to understand as best he may the complex and many-sided culture in which the gospel is currently taught to outsiders and insiders alike. He needs time, therefore, both to study and reflect on that culture.

24. *Care for the needy* embraces both the nature and causes of world poverty and also the distress which is absolutely local within the bishop's diocese. Precisely as bishop in the Church of God, there is no national boundary beyond which interest or responsibility fades out. Indeed in the light of the strongly prevailing political doctrines of national self-interest, a bishop has a duty to stimulate the conscience of people in his diocese to the reality and scale of preventable suffering in an interdependent world.

25. The addition of a fifth mark of mission, namely care for the environment, is an example of the fact that the marks of mission are themselves historically based. Again the bishop has no permission to draw the boundary of concern tightly around his diocese. But to understand the interconnections of the global economy by which the environment is being devastated is no small task. Again there is a clear task of encouraging both teaching and local action, to outsiders and insiders alike.

G. The bishop's powers and authority

26. The precise nature and extent of the bishop's jurisdictional powers are laid out in canon law, and have varied from time to time and place to place. Canon law empowers a bishop individually, or bishops collectively, to exercise judgments in matters of faith, morals or worship bearing directly on the unity, apostolicity, holiness and catholicity of the Church.[39] This law is the practical expression of the belief at the heart of the Church's prayer at a bishop's ordination. A bishop's authority so exercised is to be understood as a gift to the Church.

27. Whether a modern bishop likes it or not, he is also the inheritor of a tradition lodged in a culture which continues to create public expectations of his role. Part of the difficulty of the bishop's work consists, however, in the fact that though for some he may be a key player in the Establishment (a Lord Bishop!), for others he is a strangely dressed male in a purple shirt. Managing these expectations in a way consistent with God's own mission is an inevitable part of the task of a modern English bishop.

28. As already suggested above (para. 18), the fact is that within the Church, the bishop, by reason of his knowledge, articulacy, skilful personal relations, and presence on key committees, possesses significant powers. These powers are entirely comparable to those of leaders in other organizations, and include the capacity to award real or symbolic prizes, and to administer sanctions or disapproval with significantly negative consequences for particular individuals. These informal powers need to be seen in the context of what might loosely be called 'spiritual authority'. Again as a result of the prayer of the Church at his ordination and subsequently, it is recognized that the bishop stands in special need of God's grace and protection in the midst of all his responsibilities and opportunities, not merely those relating to precise jurisdictional matters. 'Spiritual authority' is recognizable as goodness, sincerity, holiness and humility; as such it is evident in the lives of many Christians. No one in holy orders has an automatic claim to these virtues; but it is a serious matter, entailing loss of 'spiritual authority', when they are absent.[40]

H. Dangers, risks and abuses of episcopacy

29.   The dangers, risks and abuses of leadership are documented from New Testament times. There is a shaming dispute among the apostles as to which of them would be greatest (Mark 10.41-45; Matthew 20.24-28; Luke 22.24-27); 'elders' are warned to tend God's flock without care for money and without tyrannizing over them (1 Peter 5.1-4). The prominence which episcopacy achieved even before Constantine carried with it amply documented dangers (Origen, *In Matth.* 16:8). Gregory the Great held the view that monastic training in humility was essential for those who held high office in the Church. The list of 'snares' of the 'calling' are constant and predictable: inaccessibility, tyrannous behaviour, pride, financial corruption, sexual abuses, favouritism, and injustice.[41] In the Lutheran Confession of Augsburg, the way in which bishops had exceeded the limits of legitimate authority is denounced.[42] At the English Reformation a conscious effort was made to reconfigure the tasks of episcopacy in accordance with the Pastoral Epistles, especially in respect of exemplary character and the public teaching of the faith.[43] In practice this did not wholly succeed, but the attempt left its mark on the Church of England Ordinal and remained a significant influence in the life of the Church. Consciousness of the potential for abuse in the powers of the bishop is evident in the ASB sentence, which opens the archbishop's account of the tasks of a bishop, 'a bishop is called to lead in serving and caring for the people of God and to work with them in the oversight of the Church'. Leadership is thus combined with service, care and co-operation. The sentence also reflects the legal requirement that the bishop consult the diocesan synod on major matters of policy within his diocese, and the jurisdictional rights and responsibilities of priests and laity on the General Synod.

The legal role of bishops

by Peter Beesley

A. Introductory
1. What is a bishop?

1.1   The Church of England recognizes three orders of ministry: bishop, priest and deacon.[1] In one sense, therefore, a bishop is simply a minister in bishop's orders. However, in the Church of England, bishops are not consecrated except to serve in a particular office.[2] A bishop without an office is in a similar position to a priest who has no benefice, licence or permission to officiate. He has the spiritual authority to perform episcopal acts, but lacks the legal authority to exercise his ministry.

1.2   Much of this chapter is concerned with the position of diocesan bishops because, within his diocese, the diocesan has full legal and episcopal authority and ordinary jurisdiction under the Sovereign. Area bishops, suffragan bishops, Provincial Episcopal Visitors (PEVs) and assistant bishops all exercise an episcopal ministry but, as will be seen, do so in the name of or under the authority of the diocesan.

2. The office of diocesan bishop

2.1   The popular perception of a diocesan bishop is of the individual who holds the see at a particular time. However, a diocesan bishop is also a corporation sole (as are archdeacons and incumbents), which means that the office has a legal personality distinct from the individual who happens to hold the office. An act by the bishop under his episcopal seal is an act of the bishop as a corporation and, in general, will bind the bishop's successors in office. Thus, for example, ministers licensed under seal[3] such as public preachers, priests in charge and assistant curates do not need to seek a renewal of their licences simply because the identity of the diocesan changes.

2.2   In the office of the diocesan bishop there are vested the temporalities and the spiritualities. The temporalities can be seen as the material assets of the see. In the past they would have included the episcopal estates and revenues and the see house, but from the mid-nineteenth century onwards these assets have been transferred to the Ecclesiastical Commissioners and, since their creation in 1947, the Church Commissioners. Probably the only temporality generally remaining is rights of patronage where the diocesan bishop is the registered patron of certain benefices within his diocese.[4] The spiritualities are those rights that attach to the bishop by virtue of his ordinary jurisdiction (the fact that he holds the cure of souls of the whole diocese by virtue of his position as its Chief Pastor and Father in God) and so would include the right to ordain priests and deacons, to admit and to institute to benefices, to license clergy or grant permission to officiate and to issue marriage licences dispensing with the requirement for publication of banns.

3. The appointment of diocesan bishops

3.1   During a vacancy in the see, the temporalities of the see revert to the Crown. The spiritualities are the responsibility of the guardian of the spiritualities. In most cases this is the archbishop of the province, but in certain cases it may be the dean and chapter of the cathedral of the diocese.[5]

3.2   Bishops must be at least 30 years old[6] and, at present, they must be male.[7] They are appointed by the Sovereign on the advice of the Prime Minster. Although in theory the Crown has an unfettered discretion in the appointment of diocesan bishops, in practice, since 1976, the appointment is made from names put forward by the Crown Appointments Commission. The Commission comprises the two archbishops, members elected by General Synod and from the vacant diocese and the Prime Minister's and the Archbishop's Appointments Secretaries.[8]

3.3   The new bishop is nominally elected by the college of canons of the cathedral of the diocese (until new statutes have been adopted pursuant to the Cathedrals Measure 1999, this function is exercised by the dean and chapter), but since the Reformation the reality has been that election is no more than confirmation of the Sovereign's nominee. The Crown sends a *congé d'élire* to the college of canons giving them leave to elect a bishop. The *congé d'élire* is accompanied by a letter missive directing the college to elect a particular person. This procedure is contained in the Appointment of Bishops Act 1533. King Henry VIII applied to himself the role of representative of the founders of English bishoprics, and therefore in one sense, the patron of the see. The college may not elect a person whom the Sovereign has not nominated, and if they then decline to elect the Sovereign's nominee the Crown may appoint by letters patent.

3.4   Following the election there is the quasi-judicial process of confirmation presided over by the vicar-general of the province. There are only two valid grounds on which the election may be opposed: that there has been a defect in the method of election or that the person before the court is not the person of the Crown's choice. Once the vicar-general confirms the election, the bishop-elect takes the oath of allegiance to the Crown and the oath of obedience to the archbishop and thereupon becomes in law the bishop of the diocese, and the spiritualities vest in him.[9] If he is not already in bishop's orders he may not perform the sacramental acts of a bishop until he has been consecrated.

3.5   Consecration requires at least three bishops one of whom is normally the archbishop[10] and is performed pursuant to a mandate from the Crown. After consecration (if it is required) the new bishop pays homage to the Queen and thereupon receives the temporalities of the see. This is followed by enthronement in the cathedral church of the diocese. Although it follows from what is said above that legal and spiritual authority have been vested in the new bishop prior to his enthronement, enthronement normally marks the formal start of his ministry in the diocese.

4. Suffragan bishops

4.1   'Every bishop is, within his diocese, the principal minister, and to him belongs the right . . . of celebrating the rites of ordination and confirmation; of conducting, ordering, controlling and authorizing all services in churches, chapels, churchyards and consecrated burial grounds; of granting a faculty or licence for all alterations, additions, removals or repairs to the walls, fabrics, ornaments or furniture of the same; of consecrating new churches, churchyards and burial grounds; of instituting to all vacant benefices, whether of his own collation or of the presentation of others; of admitting by licence to all other vacant ecclesiastical offices; of holding visitations at times limited by law or custom . . .; of being president of the diocesan synod' (Canon C 18 'Of diocesan bishops', paragraph 4).

4.2   It follows that all episcopal jurisdiction and authority in the diocese reside with the diocesan bishop. The diocesan may, however, have the assistance of one or more suffragan bishops in the diocese. A suffragan bishop is a titular bishop[11] appointed[12] to assist the diocesan in the exercise of his spiritual functions.

4.3   If the diocesan bishop wishes to create a new suffragan bishopric or secure an appointment to a suffragan see that has been vacant for five years or more, before petitioning the Crown, the diocesan must secure the approval of the diocesan synod and General Synod.[13] Where, as is more common, an appointment is sought to fill a recent vacancy, no synodical approval is needed for the diocesan to petition the Crown.[14] If his petition is granted, two names are submitted to the Crown through the Prime Minister, but in practice the first name will be appointed and the Sovereign will direct the archbishop to consecrate the suffragan-designate (unless he is already a bishop) and will assign to him a titular see within the province.

4.4   A suffragan bishop has no jurisdiction of his own. He may perform such of the diocesan bishop's functions as the diocesan cares to delegate to him. In the absence of such delegation he has no power to operate as a bishop at all.

4.5   Delegation to a suffragan bishop is effected by an instrument of delegation made under the Dioceses Measure.[15] The diocesan synod must consent before the bishop makes an instrument of delegation. Accordingly, a newly consecrated suffragan bishop, despite the fact of his consecration, cannot perform any episcopal functions until the diocesan synod has met.[16] Practice varies from authorizing the suffragan to carry out certain episcopal functions such as confirmation or ordination at the diocesan's direction, to authorizing him to perform all of the diocesan's functions. However, whatever the suffragan does pursuant to his instrument of delegation, he does in the name of the diocesan bishop and it is the diocesan's authority that he is exercising.[17]

4.6   Where there is a vacancy in the diocese, an instrument of delegation will continue in force until two months after a new diocesan bishop takes office.[18] By this means suffragan bishops are able to perform episcopal functions in the diocese even when there is no diocesan bishop and without reference to the guardian of the spiritualities.

5. Area bishops

5.1   In some dioceses[19] there are area schemes made under the
Dioceses Measure.[20] These schemes may provide for the permanent
delegation to suffragan bishops of specified functions of the diocesan
within a particular area of the diocese and may give a suffragan
episcopal oversight of that area to the exclusion, save for reserved
matters, of the diocesan. The delegation may only be revoked through
the making of a further scheme. Schemes must be considered by the
Dioceses Commission, approved by the diocesan synod and laid before
General Synod.

5.2   Although in practice, therefore, an area bishop has greater
autonomy and a more settled range of functions than an ordinary
suffragan, the functions that he exercises are still those of the diocesan
bishop and he has in law no original jurisdiction.

5.3   In considering the needs and resources of bishops, it would be
correct to say that the needs of an area bishop in exercising those
functions given to him by an area scheme are as great as the needs of
a diocesan bishop exercising those same functions in a diocese with no
area scheme, and distinctly more that those of an ordinary suffragan.

6. Assistant bishops

6.1   A diocesan bishop has an unfettered discretion to appoint any
bishop as an assistant bishop in the diocese and to grant him a
commission to perform episcopal functions. In practice assistant
bishops are normally retired bishops who happen to live within the
diocese, and generally the functions given to them are of a limited
nature.

6.2   An assistant bishop's commission will lapse upon the see
becoming vacant. It could be renewed by a suffragan bishop exercising
delegated powers during the vacancy (see paragraph 4.6 above), but
would again lapse when the suffragan's instrument of delegation came
to an end following the appointment of a new diocesan.

6.3   However, under the Church of England (Miscellaneous
Provisions) Measure 1983,[21] there is a procedure for emergency delegation
to a person in episcopal orders who is a member of the Church of
England. Such delegation could be of any functions not already delegated
by instrument or area scheme under the Dioceses Measure.

7. Provincial Episcopal Visitors (PEVs)

7.1 There exist two suffragan bishops in the diocese of Canterbury (Ebbsfleet and Richborough) and one in the diocese of York (Beverley) appointed for the purposes of the Episcopal Ministry Act of Synod 1993.

7.2 Under the Act of Synod parishes opposed to the ordination of women may petition the diocesan bishop requesting him to make 'appropriate arrangements for episcopal duties to be carried out in the parish'. This expression is not defined, but in practice means that episcopal functions in the parish (including the pastoral care of the clergy) are carried out by a bishop who is opposed to the ordination of women to the priesthood. Those functions are primarily of a pastoral nature, but would normally include carrying out confirmations and in some cases ordinations.

7.3 In some dioceses, this extended episcopal oversight is provided by a suffragan or assistant bishop who holds the appropriate views. In others, use is made of the PEVs, sometimes called 'flying bishops'.

7.4 PEVs are not in law a special category of bishop. They are suffragan bishops of the dioceses of Canterbury or York, but they are commissioned to function throughout their respective provinces where requested to do so by diocesan bishops.

7.5 It is fundamental to the Episcopal Ministry Act of Synod that the diocesan bishop remains the ordinary in his diocese.[22] Thus, if the diocesan bishop is the patron of the benefice, his functions as patron do not pass to the PEV, and if the diocesan is not patron, it is still for him to approve the making of an offer by the patron[23] and to institute, induct or license all clergy within the benefice.

7.6 This is not always appreciated by parishes that have petitioned for extended episcopal oversight. There is a common misconception that by doing so they are opting out of the diocese. This inevitably creates tensions. The diocesan bishop retains his jurisdiction over a parish that does not regard itself as being in communion with him. The Act of Synod does not have the force of a measure or canon and it could be changed or revoked by General Synod. Its provisions are under review at present.

B. The bishop and the nation
8. The national responsibilities of bishops

8.1   Although the primary responsibilities of a bishop are in respect of his diocese, bishops (both diocesan and suffragan) do nevertheless have responsibilities at national level. These arise by law, practice and public perception.

8.2   It is an incident of the establishment of the Church of England that its bishops are appointed by the Crown. However, bishops are officers of the Church rather than officers of the Crown, and there is no procedure by which the Crown can remove them from office.[24]

8.3   Because of the nature of their office in the established Church, diocesan bishops will be regarded, in respect of certain of their powers and functions, as public authorities for the purposes of the Human Rights Act 1998. In consequence it will be unlawful for them to exercise such powers and functions in a way that is incompatible with rights under the European Convention on Human Rights.[25]

8.4   The two archbishops and the Bishop of London are, by custom, appointed to the Privy Council and bishops sometimes hold office in the royal household.[26] However, it is through the House of Lords that diocesan bishops have their most direct role in the secular constitution.

8.5   The bishops at present have 26 seats[27] in the House of Lords comprising the two archbishops and the Bishops of London, Winchester and Durham automatically and 21 diocesan bishops in order of seniority. In addition to spending two or three weeks a year as duty bishop, bishops would normally attend debates on matters where they have a particular interest or which touched on other responsibilities that they had undertaken (for example, the chairman of the Church of England Board of Education will be expected to attend the House during most of the Lords stages of a major education bill).[28]

8.6   Bishops also have responsibilities within the Church at national level. All diocesan bishops are members of the upper house of convocation in their province and, in consequence, of the House of Bishops of the General Synod. There are also nine elected suffragan or assistant bishops in the House (six from the Province of Canterbury and three from the Province of York).[29] In addition, the provincial episcopal visitors, the Bishop of Dover and the Bishop at Lambeth attend meetings of the House if they are not already elected members.

8.7 The House of Bishops normally meets three times a year. It considers all legislative and liturgical[30] business that is coming before General Synod and prepares statements on various issues of public concern.

8.8 All diocesan bishops are expected to be involved in the life of the national Church in some way, for example as chairman of one of the Church's boards or councils or as president or chairman of a major Church charity. Many suffragan bishops also take on extra-diocesan responsibilities.

8.9 As the Government moves towards devolution of functions to the English regions, new structures such as regional assemblies are emerging. A number of bishops have become closely involved with these structures as 'lead bishops' for their region. If these moves continue it can be expected that the involvement of bishops in the new structures will increase and be put on a formal footing.

8.10 By virtue of their public position, bishops are often asked to comment on and express their views in many different areas. In the light of this the Church is establishing a system whereby each diocesan bishop has a responsibility to maintain knowledge and expertise in a particular field and can be called upon to give a public response in this area when required.

C. The bishop and the diocese
9. Power or influence?

9.1 It might be assumed from the quotation from Canon C18 in paragraph 4.1 above that, within his diocese, the diocesan bishop is all-powerful. However, as will be seen in this part, although the bishop does have a number of specific powers and functions there are areas where he has no coercive powers and the smooth running of the diocese depends as much on personality and relationships as it does on legal powers and duties. Nevertheless, if there are problems it will be the bishop who is expected by the public to solve them.

9.2 The bishop is often said to have jurisdiction as Ordinary within his diocese.[31] This simply means that he has original jurisdiction and does not derive his authority from a higher (temporal) official (contrast a suffragan bishop whose authority is entirely derived through delegation from the diocesan).[32]

10. Senior staff

10.1   In many dioceses the forum through which the bishop functions episcopally (in the sense of discussing and seeking advice on the exercise of his episcopal functions) is the senior staff meeting. This generally comprises the suffragan bishop(s), the archdeacon(s), the dean or provost of the cathedral and often the diocesan secretary. In some dioceses other senior officers such as the diocesan director of ordinands and the diocesan director of education are included.

10.2   As has been seen above,[33] the appointment of suffragan bishops is, in practice, under the control of the diocesan. Similarly the bishop will normally appoint the archdeacons.[34] The dean in an old dean and chapter cathedral will be a Crown appointment and in most cases the provost/dean of an old parish church cathedral will be appointed by the bishop.[35] Whoever appoints these dignitaries, however, they are freehold appointments. If they do not perform as expected the bishop has no power to dismiss them (although they are subject to the disciplinary procedures that apply to all clergy in the Church of England).

11. Diocesan administration

11.1   As the principal salaried lay[36] official of the diocese, the diocesan secretary is vital to the smooth administration of the diocese. As has been observed[37] the post is non-statutory and so there are no rules for appointment to it. However, in most dioceses the bishop would be closely involved in the appointment.

11.2   Under the diocesan secretary there will be staff, usually lay, whose number will depend on the size and resources of the diocese. Their function will be to service the diocesan synod and the various diocesan boards and councils. Administration of the diocesan finances will be one of their most important tasks. They will normally be employed by the Diocesan Board of Finance (DBF).

11.3   The diocesan secretary and other salaried diocesan officials (both lay and ordained), if they prove unsatisfactory, may be dismissed like any other employee (subject to the terms of their contract of employment and any right not to be unfairly dismissed under secular employment legislation). However, as stated above, their employer will normally be the DBF. There can in this area be some uncertainties about who exercises the functions of the employer, including the ability to dismiss.

11.4 With many senior officers, the DBF is likely to be exercising a role of convenience as being the body corporate that is the nominal employer of diocesan staff. There is not always a clear distinction between a contract of employment and a bishop's licence. In some cases both run concurrently.

11.5 There are those who are licensed by the bishop to exercise an office known to ecclesiastical law, such as a priest in charge of a parish. The priest's status is purely that of ecclesiastical office holder and the rights, duties and security of tenure of the office holder are wholly matters of ecclesiastical law. On the other hand, to take an example, the office of diocesan director of education is not an ecclesiastical office. It is an office created by statute,[38] to which the bishop appoints and the holder may be ordained or lay. The office does not carry with it any automatic entitlement to remuneration. If the office holder is a cleric, that remuneration could be provided in the form of a benefice or a residentiary canonry. However, it may equally be in the form of a contract of employment with the DBF, and this would always be the case where the holder is a lay person. One, then, has the holder of a bishop's appointment whose appointment as diocesan director of education can only be brought to an end by the bishop, but who is also an employee of the DBF under a contract of employment. Because the office of diocesan director of education is not an ecclesiastical office, if the bishop licenses the director without more, but the director is actually paid a salary by the DBF, then the director would have a contract of employment even though the bishop might assume that the director was in no different position from any other licensed cleric.

12. Diocesan synod and organizations

12.1 The diocesan bishop is president of the diocesan synod and a member of its house of bishops along with his suffragan(s) and other persons in episcopal orders working in the diocese whom the bishop, with the concurrence of the archbishop may nominate.[39] The model of the bishop in synod is an important one ecclesiologically for the Church of England.

12.2   The functions of the diocesan synod are to consider matters concerning the Church of England and to regulate provision for such matters in relation to its own diocese. It is also to consider and express an opinion on matters of religious or public interest (although it may not declare the doctrine of the Church of England); to advise the bishop on any matter that he may choose to consult it about; and to consider those things referred to it by General Synod and also from any of the deanery synods in the diocese.[40]

12.3   Generally speaking the function of advising the bishop in the first instance will be undertaken by the bishop's council and standing committee of the synod. The establishment of the synod and its regulation are provided for by the Synodical Government Measure 1969 and the Church Representation Rules (as amended) for the time being in force. In order for the synod to assent to a decision it must pass all three component houses (bishops, clergy and laity). Accordingly where the assent of the bishop is required for the resolution to pass it must not be lightly nor without grave cause withheld.[41]

12.4   While the diocesan synod is still notionally the principal organ of representative government in a diocese, the manner in which it is used by the diocesan bishop and senior staff varies considerably from diocese to diocese. The concerns and frustrations of the system as it stands as well as the positive aspects of the working of synod were considered recently.[42] The Bridge Report has highlighted the difficulties and problems between the working of the synod, the bishop's council and the senior staff meeting. In general terms it can be asserted that it is in the staff meeting and the bishop's council that the real decisions affecting the diocese and the parishes are now taken and these bodies now generally oversee the work and functioning of other diocesan boards and councils. In certain cases the issues before staff meetings and the bishop's council will then be subject to debate, discussion and approval in the synod.

12.5   In effect the bishop's staff meeting has become the forum for consideration of episcopal issues and the bishop's council the forum for diocesan issues. This represents a trend towards focusing the diocese and the decisions made about it on its bishop rather than on an amorphous synod.

12.6 Many dioceses have used the review of the central church structures that was begun by the Turnbull Report and completed in the National Institutions Measure 1998 to look at diocesan structures. Consequently many dioceses have in the past few years restructured diocesan organizations to follow a central and uniform pattern rather than having a free-standing existence. Thus in some dioceses membership of the DBF is co-terminal with the membership of the diocesan synod and the management of the board is placed within an executive committee, which may also be the bishop's council. Similarly, independent parsonage boards have been made sub-committees of the DBF. This effective streamlining has centralized itself on the staff meeting and the bishop's council and has meant that many diocesan synods have now become more general forums for debate and discussion on issues facing the Church and the diocese rather than management bodies.

12.7 There remain some organizations where the statutory requirements for their constitution limits this exercise. The constitutions required for the pastoral committee[43] (which reviews the arrangements for pastoral supervision in the diocese) and the diocesan board of education[44] (which has responsibility for education work in the diocese including church schools) among others are such as to secure an independent existence for those bodies.

13. The clergy

13.1 As will be seen below, all clergy[45] operating within the diocese derive the authority to exercise their ministries from the bishop. He will have commissioned, appointed, instituted or collated or licensed them or given them permission to officiate. Those holding his licence or a benefice will have sworn an oath of canonical obedience to him.[46] But the legal control that he exercises over them may, in reality, be limited or non-existent.

13.2 Those holding freehold offices[47] have security of tenure until retirement[48] and those holding leasehold offices[49] have security during their term of office. They may only be removed from office after due process in legal or judicial proceedings[50] which, because of their complexity or expense or because of the adverse publicity which proceedings attract, are rarely used. The bishop may therefore have little choice but to watch with growing frustration as his cathedral or one of his parishes is torn apart as the result of a mistaken appointment. Everyone will look to him to do something, but despite all the airy statements in the Canons about his authority, he may be legally quite impotent.

13.3   The licensed clergy are easier to remove. Those holding indefinite licences may have their licences revoked on reasonable notice when no reasons need be given, or summarily for good and reasonable cause when there is a right of appeal to the archbishop.[51] Licences granted for a fixed term may be revoked for good and reasonable cause and subject to the right of appeal.

13.4   The Clergy Discipline Measure, which received final approval from General Synod in November 2000, will (if it passes through Parliament and receives Royal Assent) change the procedure for dealing with clergy discipline cases. In essence its aim is to make proceedings against beneficed clergy simpler and cheaper. However, it will require bishops to follow the new procedure in discipline cases even where the cleric concerned holds only a licence. The Measure will also oblige bishops to take action on the expiry of a fixed-term clergy licence, failing which the licence will become indefinite. It will be essential that bishops have an accurate and efficient diary system to keep track of clergy licences.

13.5   Section 1 of the Measure imposes a duty to have regard to the role of the bishop who 'by virtue of his office and consecration, is required to administer discipline'. Under the Measure all disciplinary complaints[52] against clergy in the diocese will go to the diocesan bishop. He will then have a number of options open to him[53] including deciding to take no further action.[54] A decision to take no further action is, however, subject to review by the Clergy Discipline Commission.[55]

13.6   Finally it should be noted that Section 23 of the Employment Rights Act 1999 enables the Secretary of State by order to extend certain categories of employment rights to individuals who do not currently enjoy them. It would therefore be possible for the government to override any system of clergy discipline that the Church created.

14. Child protection
14.1   One area of increasing concern to the Church in general and diocesan bishops in particular is child protection. This is no doubt attributable to a general raising of awareness about child abuse issues

and the suggestion that, in the past, there have been instances of abuse by clergy being covered up by their church.

14.2   Such is the concern that the House of Bishops has published and recently revised a policy and guidance on child protection.[56] The policy is intended to apply throughout a diocese wherever church personnel may come into contact with children. Thus it applies to clergy; accredited lay ministers; and paid staff and volunteers who work with or have unsupervised access to children (and whose appointment and deployment may be entirely a parish matter, not under the control of the bishop).

14.3   There is no explicit legal duty on a diocesan bishop to implement the policy or to act in a particular way where allegations are made against clergy or lay ministers. Clearly in relation to specific allegations, public opinion might demand that the bishop follows a course of action that is simply not open to him. The bishop's power to act may be particularly limited where the allegation of abuse is against a cleric holding a freehold or leasehold office.[57] The bishop may not be able simply to remove clergy from office or suspend them as soon as an allegation is made. And the bishop has a responsibility for the pastoral care of his clergy – both offenders and the falsely accused and their families.

14.4   A bishop would clearly be open to criticism and possible legal action if he gave a known offender a post where he or she would have contact with children, or if the response to allegations of child abuse was simply to move the cleric concerned to another parish.

14.5   Issues of child protection have placed a very considerable extra responsibility and workload on the administrative staff of bishops in recent years.

D. The bishop and the cathedral
15. History of cathedrals
15.1   Prior to the Reformation in England there were nine cathedrals[58] in the charge of secular priests, governed according to a prebendal model and having statutes. The remaining eight[59] were monastic foundations. Of these, all but one[60] were Benedictine where the bishop was also the abbot of the community. At the Reformation the monastic cathedrals were refounded with statutes basically

following the prebendal model. In addition, King Henry VIII created five cathedrals[61] *de novo*. Even under the prebendal model the cathedral community enjoyed a considerable degree of independence from the bishop of the diocese in which it was situated.

15.2 In the middle of the nineteenth century as with the bishoprics so with the cathedrals many of their estates and revenues were transferred to the Ecclesiastical Commissioners so that many, but not all, of the cathedrals now own only a few properties, being those immediately contiguous to the cathedral or occupied by their clergy.

15.3 With the advent of the Church Assembly the cathedrals were gradually brought within the ambit of Measures under which fresh statutes were made.

15.4 The implementation of the Cathedrals Measure 1999[62] completes the transformation of the cathedrals into the modern context of being the mother church of and fully part of the diocese. Section 1 of the Cathedrals Measure 1999 specifies that 'any person or body on whom functions are conferred by or under the Measure shall, in exercising those functions, have due regard to the fact that the cathedral is the seat of the bishop and the centre of worship and mission'.

16. The position of the bishop in his cathedral

16.1 Section 6 of the 1999 Measure provides that 'the bishop shall have his principal seat and dignity in the cathedral. After consultation with the Chapter and subject to any provision in the statutes of the cathedral he may officiate in the cathedral and use it in his work of teaching and mission for ordinations and synods and for other diocesan occasions and purposes'.

16.2 The existing constitution and statutes of English cathedrals provide that the diocesan bishop is the visitor of his cathedral church, and that position continues under the 1999 Measure.

16.3 The bishop's visitorial role is now succinctly set out in the Cathedrals Measure 1999, where it is stated that he shall hear and determine any questions as to the construction of the constitution and statutes of the cathedral, which is a quasi-judicial role. In considering questions of construction he is subject to judicial review in the secular courts.

16.4   The Measure provides that a bishop may hold a visitation when he considers it desirable or necessary to do so or when requested by the council or the chapter of the cathedral. In the course of such a visitation he may give such directions to the chapter, to the holder of any office in the cathedral or to any person employed by the cathedral as will, in the opinion of the bishop, better serve the observance of the constitution and statutes. Furthermore he may at any time propose for consideration by the council of the cathedral, amendments to the constitution and statutes.

17. The cathedral clergy

17.1   The bishop's power to appoint the cathedral clergy is as limited as it is for the other clergy in his diocese. The dean or provost holds a freehold appointment and this will not be changed by the 1999 Measure (although provosts will be restyled 'deans'). In those cathedrals that had a dean and chapter prior to the 1999 Measure, the dean is appointed by the Crown. Although the appointment is made after consultation, there is no equivalent of the Crown Appointments Commission. In those cathedrals that were parish church cathedrals, the provost was (and the dean will be), in effect, appointed by the patron of the parochial living. In all but two cases[63] this is the diocesan bishop.

17.2   The residentiary canons of the cathedral have generally also held freehold appointments in most cathedrals. In some cases these appointments are also made by the Crown or others, but in many cases residentiary canons are appointed by the bishop. Under the 1999 Measure,[64] subject to the protection of existing office holders, the cathedral statutes may specify a leasehold term of office.

17.3   The honorary canons of a cathedral have generally been appointed by the bishop to a freehold office. Sometimes, depending on the precise terms of the cathedral statutes, their tenure can be linked to their holding some other post in the diocese, sometimes there is simply an expectation that they will resign their canonry when they cease to hold a parish or sector ministry post in the diocese. Under the 1999 Measure the cathedral statutes may, as with residentiary canons, provide for honorary canons to hold either freehold or leasehold office.

17.4   The method by which a dean or residentiary or honorary canon can be removed from his post is much the same as with the other freehold clergy of the diocese.[65] The bishop has therefore never been in the position of being able to dismiss the cathedral's clerical staff. Nor will he be under the 1999 Measure.

18. The bishop and the cathedral's constitution

18.1 Under the Cathedrals Measure 1999 for each cathedral a body was established called the transitional council whose duty it was to frame, with the consent of the diocesan bishop, and bring into operation as soon as practical an instrument providing the constitution of the cathedral and an instrument providing the statutes of the cathedral.

18.2 Transitional councils consisted of the diocesan bishop, the dean or provost; two residentiary canons; one non-residentiary canon; and five lay persons appointed by the bishop after consultation. At the time of writing, many are still working, but some have now completed their task.

18.3 Once the transitional council has completed its task and ceased to exist the cathedral will be governed by a council, a chapter, and a college of canons. The bishop is not a member of any of these (it would not be appropriate for the visitor of the cathedral to be a member of any of these bodies).

18.4 The bishop will in future be entitled to be present and speak, but not to vote, at meetings of the council. He will be responsible for appointing a lay person as chairman of it. The chapter may from time to time consult with the bishop in respect of the general direction and mission of the cathedral and the bishop may at any time seek the advice of the chapter on any matter.

E. The bishop and the parishes of the diocese
19. Ministry

19.1 The bishop holds the original cure of souls for all the inhabitants of the parishes of his diocese. In a parish that has a beneficed incumbent, the bishop shares the cure with that incumbent; in a parish where there is a priest in charge, that priest acts as the delegate of the bishop.[66]

19.2 All ministry in the diocese is derived from that of the bishop who institutes (or collates) the beneficed clergy and licenses all other clergy in the diocese, whether engaged in parochial ministry or sector ministry. The bishop also authorizes the ministry of retired clergy (by way of a Permission to Officiate) and also licenses all lay readers and lay workers in the diocese. The only exceptions to this are chaplains to the forces who are licensed by the Archbishop of Canterbury, some cathedral clergy and the clergy of extra-diocesan places.

20. Choice and appointment of clergy

20.1   In the case of incumbents, the bishop may be the patron of a benefice himself, or the patronage may be held by the Crown or the Lord Chancellor, privately or by a corporate body such as a college or university or patronage trust. If the bishop is not himself the patron of a living, he has, as does the parish, a right of veto against the presentation of a candidate to a living whom he may consider to be unsuitable.[67] In cases where patronage of a living is held by the Crown, many of the provisions of the law governing presentation do not apply and there is no veto against presentation by the Crown. However, in practice the Crown consults carefully with both the parish and the diocese before suggesting a candidate.[68] Otherwise the choice of the clergy in a diocese is the responsibility of the bishop although this is normally shared with, and sometimes delegated to, a member of the senior staff, i.e. a suffragan bishop or an archdeacon.

20.2   The bishop will normally be asked to provide a reference on a 'bishop to bishop basis' for clergy moving to another diocese and the bishop maintains a confidential file on each member of the clergy in the diocese, which is usually passed on when the cleric concerned moves. There are guidelines issued by the House of Bishops concerning the passing of files from one diocese to another. These files have been subject to the Data Protection Act 1998 since March 2000.

20.3   Where a parish is, or is about to become, vacant the bishop will be responsible for initiating, or considering, proposals for pastoral reorganization with the Diocesan Pastoral Committee. This may lead, after consultation, to suspension of the right to present a new incumbent, in which event the bishop will make pastoral provision for the care of the parish by appointing a priest in charge (see above). He may also 'restrict' presentation for a limited period where proposals for reorganization are under active consideration.

21. The bishop in the parish

21.1   The bishop's responsibilities in the parishes are shared with, and often exercised by, the archdeacon and the rural dean. The rural dean in particular is expressly commissioned to act for the bishop in supporting the ministry of all the clergy in the deanery and when necessary to bring matters to the attention of the bishop or archdeacon.

21.2   The office of churchwarden is an ancient one and by Canon churchwardens are the bishop's officers in each parish.[69] Having been appointed by the minister and parishioners each year, they are then admitted to office by the bishop or his delegate. They are responsible to the bishop for all matters in the parish which are not the responsibility of the clergy. They have a particular role during a vacancy in the parish in ensuring the continued life of the Church under the leadership of the rural dean.

21.3   The bishop will visit the parishes of his diocese as regularly as possible and certainly when required to do so to institute a new incumbent, to license clergy or to administer confirmation. He may also conduct a formal visitation of the parish if required or requested by the incumbent.[70] The bishop will also visit if it is necessary to consecrate a church building or burial ground or to dedicate an additional place of worship in the parish.

21.4   A bishop only has a very limited role within the faculty jurisdiction as this is exercised on his behalf by the chancellor of the diocese in the consistory court. The bishop's consent is occasionally required for specific matters, e.g. demolition or partial demolition of a church building. The bishop's views may be sought by the chancellor where issues of theology, ecclesiology or doctrine arise in the course of proceedings.

F. The bishop and the community
22. The consequence of establishment

22.1   The declaration in the ASB order for the consecration of a bishop[71] among other things provides that '[The bishop] is to promote the mission [of the Church] throughout the world. It is his duty to watch over and pray for all those committed to his charge, and to teach and govern them after the example of the Apostles, speaking in the name of God and interpreting the gospel of Christ. He is to know his people and be known by them.'

22.2   The bishop elect is then asked to make various declarations by the archbishop, among them:

Archbishop: Will you promote unity, peace, and love among all Christian people, and especially among those whom you serve?

Answer: By the help of God, I will.

Archbishop: Will you then be a faithful witness to Christ to those among whom you live, and lead your people to obey the Saviour's command to make disciples of all nations?

Answer: By the help of God, I will.

22.3   By virtue of its position as the established Church of the land, the Church of England has a responsibility to all citizens of this country. Almost every inhabitant of England lives within a diocese and an ecclesiastical parish[72] and therefore has a parish priest and also a bishop to whom they can look for moral Christian leadership and the offices and sacraments of the Church. Because the diocesan bishop holds the cure of souls of all those who live within his diocese the above declarations and questions demonstrate that the bishop in particular has a responsibility to be known within the life of the community beyond the Church.

22.4   The assertions of the ordinal are also to be found in Canon C 18(1): 'every bishop is the chief pastor of all that are within his diocese, as well laity as clergy, and their father in God'.

23. The bishop and his relationships within the community

23.1   The bishop's role and obligation to make himself known to the wider community are often expressed in his attendance at local occasions of importance, which may not necessarily be Christian in character, and also by making pastoral visits within the various communities he serves. This is an important aspect of episcopal ministry, albeit a time-consuming one, as it provides the bishop with the opportunity to engage with members of the local community with whom he may not normally come into contact.

23.2   The bishop will also maintain cordial links with other leaders within the local communities including Members of Parliament, leaders of local government, other churches and faiths, the police and other civil defence bodies and Her Majesty's Lord-Lieutenants. The bishop's standing as a community leader himself will enable him to have access to such groups of people and represent the Church and those members of society whose voice is not often heard, especially the 'outcasts and needy'.[73]

23.3   The bishop, while being a teacher of the faith within his diocese, may often be more broadly involved in education, not only in church schools but perhaps by being a governor (or holding nominations to boards of governors) of independent schools, and through the membership of the governing bodies of higher education colleges or universities. He may be similarly involved with charitable trusts and organizations operating in the diocese. The bishop may also consent to be the patron of charities (sometimes with no connection to the Church) in which he has a particular interest.

24. The effect of the bishop in the local community

24.1   A diocesan bishop is often uniquely placed to offer comment on developments of a local nature and to give views on local issues. His opinion will be sought by the local press and will no doubt have an influence on local events.

24.2   His position also means that he is able to take the initiative in drawing together disparate groups within the local community in seeking to find common ground and to better enable those of differing social backgrounds and political views to come together. The bishop's ministry in these areas, while often hidden and time-consuming, can confer a vast benefit on the life of the local community.

24.3   Being essentially non-party political the bishop has the opportunity as a Christian leader to offer moral guidance within the diocese and his position will mean that he can offer respected leadership in situations that cross political divides. Bishops often have an important and valuable part to play in campaigns of a local and national nature as well as being well placed to coordinate local initiatives.

24.4   It will be seen that the role of the bishop within the local community springs not from any statutory duty or obligation but from the spiritual authority with which he is vested at his consecration and enthronement and also from the canonical statements about his ministry. The fact that there are no formal legal obligations to act in this way does not diminish or undermine this important aspect of the bishop's ministry. The bishop is often uniquely placed to set forth the example of Our Lord to the secular community.

G. Closing remarks
25. Conclusions

25.1   By definition this has had to be a reasonably brief survey of the legal role and responsibility that a bishop has. However, what can be said is that the law in some way touches most aspects of the life of the Church and the place of the bishop within that life. The legal and spiritual demands of episcopal ministry are such that a bishop inevitably needs to be supported by resources that enable him to exercise that ministry fully. If the life of the Church is to be an effective witness to the gospel, then bishops in their ministry of oversight need to be adequately resourced so as to meet those demands.

25.2   It will be appreciated that there is a vast web of primary legislation, both Acts of Parliament and Measures of the General Synod, that impose responsibilities and obligations on bishops or permit certain actions and prohibit others. With each Measure of the General Synod that is passed in some way the legal role of bishops alters. To use some topical examples: the Cathedrals Measure 1999 has changed the bishop's relationship with his cathedral while confirming his role as visitor and his position with regard to the revision of cathedral statutes. The Clergy Discipline Measure will recast and redefine the role of the bishop in respect of clergy discipline and the actions he may or may not take and will also provide for an appeal against those decisions.

25.3   As well as primary legislation there is also much secondary legislation that seeks to assist in the work of ecclesiastical regulation. There are also many other sets of guidelines, codes of practice, policy statements and circulars which it has not been possible to examine in detail. Such quasi-legislation assists in guiding bishops in the operation and exercise of their powers and responsibilities conferred by primary legislation.

25.4   It has been seen that as well as formal regulation, much of the legal role of the bishop also centres in less formal arrangements. Indeed this reflects a classic view of canonical jurisprudence as restated by Canon Eric Kemp (as he then was):

> The 'ancient inheritance of the Church's jurisprudence' embraces two views of canon law: one stressed its hard side – some canons are coercive and mandatory; the other its soft side – some canons are exhortatory, consisting of standards which 'the Church thought ought to be observed but was not prepared to enforce by action at law'.[74]

25.5   By virtue of his episcopal ministry of oversight the bishop has to sit at the centre of the legal framework that exists to order and regulate the life of the Church. The legal role of bishops is not straightforward or simple. It is not always clearly defined, being a mix of statute, Canon and inherent responsibility.

25.6   It is a consequence of establishment that the Church is so ordered and regulated, but it should be the aim of those who have responsibility for such things, not least the bishop themselves, always to ensure that the legal framework within which they operate liberates and enhances their ministry and episcopacy as set forth in the Ordinal. In a world which is becoming ever more conscious of rights and obligations it is perhaps inevitable that the Church will be faced with more regulation. But the Turnbull report has called for legislation that is less prescriptive and more open to flexible forms of regulation so as to meet individual local circumstances.[75]

25.7   Indeed the Archbishop of York has encouraged a view of ecclesiastical regulation which adopts the theology of gracious gift which underpins the work of Turnbull.[76] The archbishop set forward a view that the law was both for the edification and sanctification of the Church; that it is a gift of God's grace which has as its goal the building up of the whole body of the Church in humility and love. He asks:

> [W]hat will best serve and promote the needs of the local community as well as the wider community of the Church, not only towards the building up of the whole body and increasing its effectiveness but also and in my view more importantly towards its edification and sanctification?[77]

It seems that in looking at the future resources and demands of those who lead the Church this question has an importance not only for the legal role of bishops but also for their entire ministry.

25.8   It is salutary to remember that the Church is not led into all truth by the law; the regulation of the life of the Church and the role of bishops has to be grounded in a theology and ecclesiology that is based in the Christian revelation as the Church of England has received it and is open to the promptings of the Spirit.

Matters commended for further study

During the course of our consultations, various respondents asked us to consider a number of subjects which were outside our remit but which we recognize warrant further consideration. In addition to those noted in the text, these subjects are:

1.   The basis on which suffragans are allocated to dioceses;

2.   The resourcing of deans and other cathedral dignitaries, and the relationship with the resourcing of bishops;

3.   The possible grouping of dioceses into regions for purposes going beyond consultation, and the establishment of regional offices (to replace diocesan offices) together with the provision of resources on a regional basis.

We also record that some bishops have mentioned their unease at the difference between the amounts of clerical and episcopal stipends.

Notes

chapter 2

1 Acts 6.1-6.

2 The word 'presbyter' means 'elder'.

3 The word 'priest' is simply a contraction of 'presbyter', as 'bishop' is a contraction of 'episcopos' – in England they became known as 'piscops', hence 'bishops'.

4 Ignatius, *Letter to the Smyrnaeans* VIII.

5 Ignatius, *Letter to the Ephesians* VI – 'when someone sees the bishop keeping silent, so much the more should he revere him . . . it is plain that we should respect the bishop as the Lord'. See also his Letter to the Philadelphians I – 'I have much admired this bishop's modesty, which is more influential by his silence than people who talk uselessly'.

6 But, for the purposes of this report, we use the expression 'episcopal' to refer only to that part of the ministry which is exercised by bishops.

7 Service of Institution and Licensing.

8 Icon is a Greek word (εικων) meaning 'image' or 'likeness'. Icons are pictures painted on wood, formal representations of sacred subjects such as Our Lord and the Saints, which were first venerated in the Greek Church and believed to have the power to convey blessings. Their use in worship and prayer has extended to many churches in recent years.

9 The only quasi-official definition of ecclesiology is that of *The Oxford Dictionary of the Christian Church* (edited by F. L. Cross: OUP, first published in 1957). The definition speaks of ecclesiology as 'the science of building and decoration of churches', but that is not the meaning intended by our correspondents. The word 'ecclesiology' is in such common and varied use that it would be helpful if the Doctrine Commission provided an authoritative definition.

10 ASB Service for the Ordination or Consecration of a Bishop, para. 13. This is the version of the Ordinal currently in use, and is in the process of revision. There is also an Order for the Consecration of Bishops in the Book of Common Prayer, which remains authorized, but rarely used.

11 See Appendix E, para. 3.4.

12 'Training in prayer should be the main preoccupation and service given by the bishops and clergy to the adult members of the church' (Gerard Hughes, *God of Surprises*, Darton, Longman and Todd 1985).

13 See, for example, Romans 12.3-5; 1 Corinthians 12.12-27.

14 This delegation may be by the terms of a formal Area Scheme, or by an Instrument of Delegation, under Section 10 of the Dioceses Measure 1978.

15 Ely Cathedral, 25 November 2000.

chapter 3

1 And in most, but not all, other Churches in the Anglican Communion. Although dioceses are the basic unit of administration, they are to be seen as part of a broader picture. On the one hand, at the national level there are various strategic and administrative functions relating to clergy (such as recruitment, training, setting terms and conditions, setting and administering pensions, and providing retirement housing). On the other hand, the upkeep of church buildings and the provision of worship services within them is dealt with at the parish and cathedral levels. In 2000 the total church expenditure was £796 million, of which £316 million was handled by diocesan offices. (Of the £316 million, £253 million was applied for the training, stipends, pension contributions and housing of the clergy in dioceses and parishes.) In financial terms, therefore, about 40% of the activity is at the diocesan level.

2 Jersey and Guernsey are not geographically part of England and, being separate Crown Possessions, they are not constitutionally part of the United Kingdom. In relation to the Church of England, they are attached to, but are not formally part of, the Diocese of Winchester, but in practice they are integrated with the diocese and their representatives play a full part in the government of the diocese. They fall within the jurisdiction of the Bishop of Winchester.

3 The Diocese of Sodor and Man.

4 This diocese is an integral part of the Church of England. Its area includes parts of North Africa and Asia.

5 See para. 16.34.

6 Their stipend will be determined by their non-episcopal role.

7 Such as conducting confirmations.

8 One former suffragan is serving as the Bishop at Lambeth and two other bishops are serving as deans. Our theological consultant, now principal of a theological college, was previously a diocesan.

9 In this report, we use the expression 'clergy' as distinct from bishops acting in their capacity as bishops.

10 Since 1976, the normal retirement age for stipendiary clergy has been 70: Ecclesiastical Offices (Age Limit) Measure 1975.

11 A senior partner in Messrs Lee Bolton & Lee, solicitors, actively assisted by Mr Nicholas Richens, another partner in that firm.

12 The presidency of the diocesan harks back to the presidency of the bishop at the Eucharist in the earliest form of dioceses.

13 Synodical Government Measure 1969, s.4(2).

14 Dioceses Measure, s.10.

15 Dioceses Measure, s.4(3).

16 Canon Ecclesiastical C18.5.

17 Church Representation Rules 1969, as amended, R. 34(1)(k).

18 Church Representation Rules, R.34(1).

19 Synodical Government Measure 1969, s.4(4).

20 Including the former provosts of certain cathedrals who are now deans.

21 The Articles of Association are one of the two formal documents which usually comprise the constitution of a company.

22 In respect of service after 1997. This responsibility was imposed on DBFs by the Pensions Measure 1997.

23 The Commissioners meet their own costs, and dioceses do not contribute to them. Furthermore, at present the costs of the Pensions Board are not met by dioceses, although the part, about one third (or £0.8 million), which relates to the clergy pensions scheme will be included in the contribution rate from 2002.

24 The fact that the DBF is the employer of such officers can lead to confusion (see *Synodical Government in the Church of England: A Review* [The Bridge Report] GS 1252).

25 Parsonage houses are vested in the incumbent.

26 See the discussion in Appendix E.

27 Within the canonical responsibility, we include those which a bishop assumes at his consecration, of which some are set out in the Ordinal, see para. 2.6.

28 Legal responsibilities may arise either under church legislation which, by receiving the approval of both Houses of Parliament and the Royal Assent, has become part of the law of England, or under state law, by Act of Parliament as in the case of legislation on health and safety at work.

29 A bishop is widely regarded as being under a moral obligation to give effect to a resolution of the House of Bishops.

30 For example, a canonical provision may become embodied in legislation.

31 An outline of the procedure for the appointment of a bishop is given in Chapter 14. A person becomes the diocesan at the point of time when the Vicar-General confirms his election and he takes the Oath of Allegiance to the Crown and the Oath of Obedience to the Archbishop, but if he is not already in episcopal orders he cannot perform the sacramental acts of a bishop until he has been consecrated. Furthermore, a suffragan may only do those acts which he is expressly authorized to do: Canon Ecclesiastical C20.2.

32 See para. 3.16.

33 The suggestion was that resources necessary to enable a bishop to do the acts which he is empowered to do as a bishop should be funded by the Commissioners, and that the resources necessary to enable a bishop to do the acts for which he needs the concurrence of the diocesan synod should be funded by the DBF.

34 See, further, Appendix D, para. 19.

35 It may be fortunate that bishops are outside the Working Time Regulations 1998 (SI 1998/1833) which implement the Working Time Directive (93/104/EC).

36 Which for bishops includes weekends.

37 In most cases, it ranges from 6.30 a.m. to 8 a.m.

38 Or later, when there are extended evening engagements, or when there are correspondence, preparation or telephone calls to be made urgently.

chapter 4

1 By the Ecclesiastical Commissioners Act 1836.

2 The Ecclesiastical Commissioners.

3 By the Ecclesiastical Commissioners Acts 1840 and 1850.

4 By the Ecclesiastical Commissioners Act 1860. The ownership of see houses was transferred to the Commissioners following the Episcopal Endowments and Stipends Measure 1943.

5 By the Episcopal Endowments and Stipends Measure 1943.

6 The Ecclesiastical Commissioners.

7 Section 67 of the Ecclesiastical Commissioners Act 1840.

8 By Section 8 of the National Institutions Measure 1998.

9 Under the Clergy Pensions Measure 1961 and the Pensions Measure 1997.

10 Some, such as tracts of the Hyde Park Estate, were substantial.

11 These were transferred to the Ecclesiastical Commissioners between 1855 and 1870.

12 The Church Commissioners were formed in 1948 to take over the functions of the Ecclesiastical Commissioners and the Governors of Queen Anne's Bounty.

13 The assets of the Clergy Pension Fund were transferred to the Church Commissioners in 1954 and certain parochial endowments in the 1970s.

14 Section 5 of the Episcopal Endowments and Stipends Measure 1943.

15 Pension contributions for clergy are at the rate of 21.9% of national minimum stipend. Pension contributions for bishops are paid at the following rates:

    a.   the Archbishops of Canterbury and York :   2 times the clergy rate

    b.   the Bishop of London   :   1.8 times the clergy rate

    c.   other diocesans   :   1.5 times the clergy rate

    d.   suffragans   :   1.25 times the clergy rate.

16 The basic clergy pension is normally calculated at two-thirds of the national minimum stipend for the previous year, and is adjusted annually, broadly in line with increases in the national minimum stipend. In order to qualify for the full pension, the pensioner, whether bishop or clergy, must have served for 37 years. The rates of pension paid to retired bishops are:

    a.   the Archbishops of Canterbury and York :   2 times the basic pension

    b.   the Bishop of London   :   1.8 times the basic pension

    c.   other diocesans   :   1.5 times the basic pension

    d.   suffragans   :   1.25 times the basic pension.

17 Part of £86.9 million for total clergy pensions as stated in the Commissioners' accounts.

18 Including the archbishops.

19 In Note 13 to the accounts.

20 Including the archbishops.

21 The cost of furnishing, as contrasted with supplying equipment for, offices of diocesans is treated as a housing cost.

22 In Note 6 to the accounts.

23 Accommodation costs of PEVs are met partly by contributions from DBFs and partly by the Commissioners.

24 In Note 18 to the accounts.

25 This is included in the sum of £39.7 million stated in Note 18 to the accounts.

26 In the accounts for 1999 the figure for capital expenditure on see houses is combined with the figure relating to the Commissioners' administrative offices (£1.4 million: see Note 18 to those accounts).

27 If inflation is ignored.

28 If inflation is ignored. If inflation, as measured by the Retail Prices Index, is taken into account, the increase is about 14%.

29 See Church statistics 1998, GS Misc 611.

30 The short-term prospect is that, taking all dioceses together, there will be a deficit of about £10 million on current account.

31 These figures include funds which have been raised for specific projects and are, therefore, restricted.

32 By sections 39 and 40 of the Finance Act 2000.

chapter 5

1 £8,000 is the tax-free limit for 2000/01: para. 24(g) of Schedule 11A to the Income and Corporation Taxes Act 1988.

2 There are two long-standing exceptional cases where the suffragan has a full-time secretary and a chaplain. In these cases the DBF pays the chaplain's stipend and pension contributions and the Commissioners pay the chaplain's working costs.

3 This is based on an examination which the Inland Revenue conducted into the actual costs incurred for official purposes in a number of clergy homes.

4 These figures applied on 1 January 2001.

5 See para. 6.5.1.

6 See para. 17.16.3.

chapter 6

1 These are items which are shown in paragraphs 5.7, 5.14, 5.18 and 5.21 as being payable from the local account.

2 See para. 7.7.3.

3 Each see house is managed on behalf of the Commissioners either by a member of the Commissioners' staff or by a member of a professional firm. The latter applies in most cases.

4 By the Bishoprics and Cathedrals Committee and the Board of Governors of the Commissioners.

5 See Chapter 13.

chapter 7

1 In reply to our questionnaire, 64% of bishops expressed themselves as broadly content.

2 By the Legal Officers (Annual Fees) Orders, made under the Ecclesiastical Fees Measure 1986.

3 Under the Legal Officers (Annual Fees) Order 2000.

4 Retainers payable by DBFs will amount to £839,591, by the Commissioners in respect of bishops' legal officers will amount to £608,625 and retainers payable to provincial registrars will amount to £100,552. Certain fees are payable in addition to these retainers. VAT is often payable in addition, and in some cases because the bishop's legal officer is the holder of an office, the Commissioners are required to pay employers' national insurance contributions on the retainers.

5 General Synod paper GS 1349X/1350X, dated June 1999, indicated that retainers paid were slightly under 60% of the estimated value of the work done for those retainers.

6 An example of state legislation is that on child protection. Our recommendations are concerned only with church legislation.

7 We do not doubt that the burden is increasing, but we have not checked the statistical validity of the proposition.

8 See para. 5.14.3.

chapter 8

1 See para. 1.1.

2 See para. 17.20.

3 As described in Chapters 2 and 3.

4 Although we do not propose any fundamental change in the scale of resources, in subsequent chapters we propose changes in the method of provision of those resources.

5 This is not necessarily confined to the diocese.

6 Some bishops expect continuing hostile attention in the national press, but generally supportive attention in the local press.

7 See Appendix D, para. 18.

8 We ourselves have indicated some of the changes which we think are likely.

9 Some bishops think that a reduction in their membership of the House of Lords may lead to a search for an alternative forum in which the views of the Church and of the regions can be heard nationally.

10 See Appendix D, para. 16: 'God's mission is one of love to the whole world: the bishop's work may not be reduced to that of a church-related functionary.'

11 See further Appendix D, para. 23: 'One of the tasks of the bishop is to understand as best he may the complex and many-sided culture in which the gospel is currently taught to outsiders and insiders alike. He needs time, therefore, both to study and reflect on that culture.'

12 See Professor Stephen Sykes' reflections in Appendix D, para. 18.

chapter 10

1 These percentages are based on the costs of housing and working costs in 1999. The calculation excludes the cost of stipends.

2 Apart from Associate Members, the committee has nine full members, of whom four are nominated by the Archbishops' Council.

3 We use the expression in the sense in which it is used in the Commissioners' accounts: see para. 4.26. The working costs which are at present paid for by DBFs are those referred to in para. 10.4.2, other than suffragans' housing.

4 See para. 4.11.

5 See page 22 in the 1999 accounts.

6 Corresponding to note 10, on page 32, of the 1999 accounts.

chapter 11

1 See para. 10.7.

2 See paras 10.17–10.19.

3 See para. 12.10.2.

4 See para. 13.13.

5 See para. 11.11.1.

6 This would involve giving an existing officer this responsibility, not creating a new post.

7 See para. 5.11. This function could also be similar to functions of the Bishoprics and Cathedrals Committee in circulating the Bishops' Notes which set out the rules and guidelines as to which working costs will be funded.

8 In particular, the committee would only have powers of persuasion in relation to a DBF. It would be able to make a block-grant to a diocesan conditional on his observing, so far as he was able, the guidelines, but we do not regard that as necessary, and would not wish to see that approach pursued.

9 Although in individual cases there have been difficulties in the provision of suffragans' houses, we have had no evidence that in general the accommodation standards are not being met.

10 An outline of the arrangements is given at para. 5.22.

11 See para 4.30.4.

12 See para. 10.8.1.

13 An example is the present widespread practice of bishops in dioceses in which cars are manufactured driving cars made locally.

14 See, for example, the booklet *Bishops' Learning* recently issued by the Archbishops' Adviser on Bishops' Ministry.

15 Broadly, in the professions, the individual does not lose his professional qualification, but cannot fully practise his profession. There is no equivalent provision in the Church.

16 Who is concerned primarily with induction and other training.

17 I.e. those who have not been retired for more than five years.

chapter 12

1 As that expression is currently used for the Commissioners' accounts: see para. 4.28.

2 See para. 5.14.

3 See paras 5.7, 5.14, 5.18 and 5.21.

4 The figures exclude those for the two archbishops, the Bishop of London and the three PEVs. The calculations exclude the costs of overseas travel, legal officers' fees and various block payments for the support of bishops generally.

5 See para. 5.19.1.

6 This only applies in relation to suffragans.

7 We understand that the Commissioners have attempted to correlate the present levels of costs with factors such as travel and hospitality without much success. However, in our view that should not dissuade further work being done.

8 See para. 16.40.

9 This is a system which governs the allocation to dioceses of Commissioners' funds for the support of parish ministry.

chapter 13

1 As to the nature and scope of working costs, see para. 4.28.

2   In the Commissioners' Annual Report and accounts. They are published annually, in advance, so that the accounts for the year which ended on 31 March 1999 published the stipends for the year from 1 April 1999 to 31 March 2000.

3   For the stipend year 2000/01, these were:

the archbishops	:	£55,660 (Canterbury) and £48,770 (York)
the Bishop of London	:	£45,480
other diocesans	:	£30,210
suffragans	:	£24,790

4   Pension contributions for clergy are paid at the rate of 21.9% of the national minimum stipend. This contribution rate may be called 'the clergy rate'. Pension contributions in respect of bishops are paid at the following rates:

a.	the Archbishops of Canterbury and York	:	2 times the clergy rate
b.	the Bishop of London	:	1.8 times the clergy rate
c.	other diocesans	:	1.5 times the clergy rate
d.	suffragans	:	1.25 times the clergy rate

5   Bishops are not employed by anyone. However, under the Social Security (Categorisation of Earners) Regulations 1978, they are treated as employees of the Commissioners for national insurance purposes and under s.19 of the Income and Corporation Taxes Act 1988 they are treated as employees for income tax purposes.

6   In particular, we recognize that the group comprising members of the House of Bishops and the Commissioners may come to different conclusions.

7   This is the account which the DBF conducts in its books for the block-granted funds: see para. 10.30.3.

chapter 14

1   The work of the Crown Appointments Commission is helpfully described in paper GS Misc 522A. A fuller account of the process will be found in the report of the review of the Crown Appointments Commission which is due to be published shortly before this report.

2   The Commission comprises the two archbishops; three clergy and three laity elected by the General Synod; and four members of the diocese elected by the Diocesan Vacancy in See Committee. The Commission is chaired by the archbishop of the province in which the vacancy has arisen. The Prime Minister's and the Archbishops' Appointments Secretaries attend as non-voting members.

3   Contrast the position in respect of suffragans: see para. 14.8.2.

4   The Sovereign is involved in relation to the Letters Patent and in giving a direction to the archbishop to consecrate the bishop-elect if he is not already in bishops' orders.

5   In an aide-memoire for diocesan bishops issued by the Archbishops' Appointments Secretary, February 1998.

6   The choice of consultees is a matter for the diocesan, but strong guidance is given in the Code of Practice for Senior Church Appointments (GS Misc 455, June 1995).

7   The responsibility is that of the diocesan to the Sovereign. Strictly, therefore, consultation with the archbishop is a matter of courtesy, but in practice it is substantive.

8   Under Section 10 of the Dioceses Measure 1978.

9   See para. 14.39.

10 The AABM is also concerned with bishops' continuing training.

11 Diocesans are accountable to the archbishop of the province, but this is generally understood to be canonically only.

12 It was introduced progressively and has been in full operation since 1998.

13 See para. 14.4.3.

14 A vacancy in see begins when the bishop announces his retirement: an interregnum begins when he actually retires.

15 With effect from 1 January 1999.

16 See para. 14.6.1. in the case of diocesans and para. 14.8.3. in the case of suffragans.

17 We have been told that the bill sent to one newly consecrated bishop was so large that he had to take out a personal loan to cover it; and that there was still an outstanding balance of that loan when he retired.

18 We are not suggesting that these should be new posts. In practice, this role is largely performed in the northern province by the Archbishop of York's senior secretary. In the southern province the Bishop at Lambeth has recently begun to coordinate the arrangements. The designated officer responsible for arranging the service and reception would be different from the officer whom we have recommended in para. 14.18.2. should be responsible for the overall coordination of the appointment process.

19 See para. 12.15.

20 We understand that this was generally the practice in the past, although more recently some consecrations have been of one bishop only. We recognize that on some occasions this is necessary in order to avoid vacancies which are too long.

21 For this purpose, we regard the date of enthronement as the date on which the diocesan takes up office.

22 See para. 14.38.

23 See para. 5.7.1.

24 This limit can be exceeded on application by the bishop, although the excess over the limit will be taxable.

25 As the reimbursement is of removal and resettlement expenses, we do not think that the differences between the amounts for diocesans and the amounts for suffragans are justified.

chapter 15

1   See para. 10.10.

2   It need not be said that all the members of the Review Group have been glad to provide their services *pro bono*!

3   Employment law imposes considerable constraints.

4   We consider in paras 19.29 *et seq* whether the diocesan office and the bishop's office should be in separate places.

5   In some cases the chaplain lives in the see house without any payments being made by the DBF to the Commissioners in respect of it.

6   Further details are given in para. 5.2.2.

7 One bishop, who uses the contract system, told us that it would be a serious impediment to his work in the poorer part of his diocese if he had, and was known to have, his own driver.

8 A suffragan told us that before his appointment, he had never had a motoring accident; within a short time afterwards, he had three. This does not prove our proposition, but it is consistent with it.

9 Or, perhaps, weekend first class, where it is available for a small supplement.

10 Examples are the Bishop of Winchester, in respect of travelling to the Channel Islands; the Bishop of Sodor and Man in respect of travelling from his diocese; and the Bishop in Europe.

11 Payment is made from the local account and, accordingly, the total cost is controlled by the budgetary allocation for local spending.

12 See para. 12.18.

13 For example, where the host body is poor.

14 See our definition at the outset of this report.

15 See 1 Timothy 3.2 and Titus 1.8.

16 See Chapter 18.

17 The basic point is that if, for example, the DBF employs the bishop's secretary, it may be regarded as making the supply of secretarial services to the bishop, and, therefore, be required to charge the bishop VAT.

18 We have seen that special statutory arrangements apply with regard to the income tax and national insurance treatment of bishops: see Chapter 13, footnote 5.

19 Value added tax is administered by HM Customs and Excise.

chapter 16

1 See para. 2.8.1.

2 See para. 9.9.

3 See para. 10.22.

4 With the appointment under the Suffragan Bishops Act 1534 of the suffragan bishops of Nottingham and Dover.

5 Excluding the suffragan sees held by the PEVs – see later in this chapter – and not including the posts held by the Bishop at Lambeth, the Assistant Bishop of Newcastle and the Assistant Bishop of Leicester: see Appendix C.

6 Originally there were two scales. The higher scale applied to suffragans who were required to meet outgoings from their stipend, and the lower to those who did not. In 1955, the higher scale was £1,750 p.a. and the lower was £1,650 p.a.

7 See para. 4.11.2.

8 There is a small number of instances where the house is not owned by the DBF or the Commissioners.

9 See paras 4.11.4, 4.11.5.

10 See Appendix C.

11 The creation of a suffragan see is a lengthy and formal process, within the purview of the Dioceses Commission.

12 See paras 14.4, 14.8.

13 See para. 14.20.

14 See paras 5.7, 5.11, 5.14, 5.18 and 5.21.

15 See para. 5.14.1.

16 In exceptional cases a suffragan might engage a driver on an ad hoc basis.

17 The Commissioners will pay up to one half of the gardener's costs incurred by a suffragan, up to a maximum payment by the Commissioners of £1,500 p.a.

18 See para. 5.7.1.

19 See para. 16.28.2.

20 See para. 10.22.

21 The geographical extent of the area of an area bishop can be greater than that of a diocesan, and within that area there can be a larger population than that of a diocese.

22 See para. 5.11.

23 A see house is provided by the Commissioners, a suffragan's house by the DBF.

24 In Chapter 15.

25 See para. 18.36.

26 See paras 4.11.2, 4.11.4.

27 The stipend of an archdeacon for 2000/01 is £24,630 compared with £24,790 for a suffragan.

28 The Archbishops' Commission on the Organisation of the Church of England.

29 The Report of the Archbishops' Commission *Working as One Body* paragraph 8.33.

30 See para. 10.4.

31 See para. 10.17.

32 Implementation of this suggestion would involve legislation.

33 See para. 12.15.

34 In practice, this applies only to suffragans because diocesans have a larger personal support staff.

35 See para. 18.19.2.

36 Under the Episcopal Ministry Act of Synod 1993. This is technically a resolution of the General Synod, not a Measure having legislative force.

37 Section 5(3) of the Act of Synod.

38 The Commissioners also make a subvention so that the dioceses in the northern province are not required to pay a larger contribution than those in the southern.

39 See para. 10.17.

chapter 17

1 The Commissioners appoint an agent for every see house: see para. 4.24.1. The equivalent for a suffragan's house is usually the diocesan surveyor.

2 The problem is more acute in the case of the wives of diocesans because, generally, a see house is larger than the house of a suffragan.

3 In one case known to us, the estimated cost of the loss of salary and loss of pension rights was in the region of £250,000.

4 The problems are also alleviated where there is good physical separation between the office and domestic areas.

5   Here we only pose the questions. We would expect the answers to emerge in the review which we recommend of bishops' living and working accommodation in each diocese: see Chapter 19.

6   Except catering, which we consider in para. 17.16.

7   The absence of allegations of impropriety should not discourage prudent precautions.

8   See para. 5.4.

9   In the case of catering which costs more than £400 after prior authorization.

10 The cost of wine is reimbursable as a separate item and is not included in the tariff.

11 If the wife does not have other taxable income, no income tax will be payable if the total of the net payments is less than the amount of the personal allowance: £4,535 for 2001/02.

12 See Chapter 19.

chapter 18

1   It will be seen (para. 19.26) that in a number of cases suffragans work from an area office or a diocesan office.

2   But some bishops use these rooms almost exclusively for official purposes.

3   An indication of this is provided by the heating, lighting and cleaning costs. The Commissioners pay a minimum of 50% of these costs (see para. 5.19) and the diocesan will receive income tax relief on a minimum of a further 12.5% of these costs (see para. 5.20).

4   See para. 4.19. The figure appears on page 22 of the Commissioners' accounts for 1999. It includes £28,700 in relation to suffragans' housing, and it also includes expenditure in relation to Lambeth Palace and Bishopthorpe.

5   See para. 4.30.4.

6   See para. 4.42.

7   This excludes expenditure on Lambeth Palace.

8   See para. 10.7.

9   See paras 19.39 and 19.40.

10 See the definition at the outset of this report.

11 See para. 15.28.

12 In Chapter 19 we recommend a review, according to the circumstances in each diocese, of whether the office should be in the house.

13 We make this statement from our own individual experiences. We have not sought to test its statistical validity.

14 This is notwithstanding the Commissioners' (proper) attempts to achieve separation: the internal configuration of a house by no means always makes this possible.

15 As discussed in Chapter 19.

16 See para. 5.11.

17 As it is for the houses of parochial clergy.

18 This recommendation is only a restatement of a legal duty: the Commissioners are under a duty from time to time to consider what residence they consider 'suitable': see para. 4.11.3.

19 We consider later in this chapter the provision of chapels in suffragans' houses: see para. 18.43.

20 See para. 5.20

21 In 1999, the average cost of maintaining and repairing see houses (other than Lambeth Palace, the Old Palace at Canterbury and Bishopthorpe) was £26,144. The lowest cost was £842 and the highest was £179,157.

22 See Chapter 19.

23 One see house is held under a short lease, and the estimated value of that lease is excluded from these figures.

24 Acting by the bodies mentioned in para. 18.32.2.

25 See para. 10.3.2.

26 For example, houses in England and Wales owned by the Ministry of Defence were sold in November 1996 to a purchaser, who was required to grant leases back of those properties which were required to accommodate military personnel and their families.

27 In many, if not all, cases such a need can be demonstrated in the case of see houses.

28 See para. 9.9.

29 See para. 18.37.

30 See Appendix E, para. 3.5.

31 A diocesan was previously asked to sign a licence, but that practice was discontinued in the 1980s.

32 See para. 6.19a.

33 See para. 14.36.1.

chapter 19

1 We are concerned only to propose a review of bishops' living and working accommodation, but it would be open to the diocese to extend the scope of the review if it thought fit. This might be the case, for example, if there were a wish to establish an area office, or if one or more of the bishops were to have working accommodation within it, or the diocesan office.

2 A new body which, in Chapter 10, we propose should be created: see para. 11.5.1.

3 See para. 18.25.2.

4 See para. 18.37.2.

5 See para. 18.37.4.

6 The same issues have arisen with large rectories or other clergy houses.

7 See para. 18.6.6.

8 See para. 5.14, 5.18.1.

9 This figure excludes those at Lambeth Palace and Bishopthorpe.

10 This figure also excludes those at Lambeth Palace and Bishopthorpe.

11 It is restricted to a payment by the Commissioners of one half of the costs incurred, subject to a maximum of £1,500 p.a.

12 See para. 17.14.2.

13 As to which, see para. 3.27.

14 Ibid.

15 This will usually be a room or area in the house which is set aside for the purpose, rather than a chapel: see para. 18.43.

16 We attach considerable importance to the reception arrangements, and the ability to receive suitably visitors who may be under stress.

17 See para. 17.13

18 We regard as national heritage properties the see houses in the dioceses of Bath and Wells, Canterbury, Carlisle, Chichester, Durham, Ely, Exeter, Hereford, Peterborough, Southwell, Winchester, Worcester and York. Lambeth Palace is a national heritage property, but is not a see house.

19 See para. 18.25.1.

20 Acting by the bishop's council, the diocesan synod and the DBF: see para. 18.32.2.

21 See para. 18.32.3.

22 See para. 18.37.4.

23 HM Treasury letter DAO (GEN) 13/92 of 23 July 1992 to accounting officers, as subsequently amplified.

24 Under the Pastoral Measure 1983 the Commissioners are responsible for the disposal of redundant churches. They have experience in the imposition on such sale of covenants governing the future use of the properties and the protection of the public interest.

25 See para. 17.4.

26 In Chapter 17.

appendix D

1 This of course presupposes the imperative for recognition of the office's magnitude and responsibility, cf. 1 Tim. 3.1. The following abbreviations are used: ANF = *The Ante-Nicene Fathers*, 10 vols., reprinted. (Eerdmans, 1994); CCSL = *Corpus Christianorum, Series Latina*; NPNF1 = *The Nicene and Post-Nicene Fathers, First Series*, 14 vols., reprinted. (Eerdmans, 1994); NPNF2 = *The Nicene and Post-Nicene Fathers, Second Series*, 14 vols., reprinted. (Eerdmans, 1994); SC = *Sources Chrétiennes*.

2 ASB, Ember Collect, p. 878; and see 1 Cor. 12.28.

3 There was a celebrated argument about this assertion arising out of a dissertation entitled *The Christian Ministry*, added by Professor J. B. Lightfoot to his 1868 commentary on Philippians. The Episcopal Church of the USA altered the statement in the Prayer Book of 1979 to read as follows: 'Holy Scriptures and ancient writers make it clear that from the apostles' time, there have been different ministries within the Church. In particular, since the time of the New Testament, three distinct orders of ministers have been characteristic of Christ's holy catholic church.' The evidence is briefly reviewed in *Episcopal Ministry: The Report of the Archbishops' Group on the Episcopate* (Church House Publishing, 1990), pp. 13–20. Cf., Preface to Ordinal (BCP); Tertullian, *On the Prescription of Heretics*, SC 46.130; John Chrysostom, *On the Priesthood*, NPNF1 3.4, SC 272.142; *Constitutions of the Holy Apostles*, ANF 7.421–2.

4 See the frequency of references to the call of God in the Ordinal (BCP).

5 Richard Hooker, *Of the Laws of Ecclesiastical Polity*, Preface 2.1–10; III.1.14; IV.13.5–6.

6 See 'Resolution 74' of the *Lambeth Conference of 1948*, and the Committee Report on 'Church Unity and the Universal Church', of the *Lambeth Conference of 1958* (SPCK, 1958) 2.24–5.

7 See Eusebius of Caesarea, *Ecclesiastical History*, NPNF2 1.1.; and also, Stephen Sykes, 'To the Intent that These Orders May be Continued: An Anglican Theology of Holy Orders', *Anglican Theological Review* LXXVIII, I (1996): pp. 48–63; R. W. Franklin, ed., *Anglican Orders* (Mowbrays, 1996) pp. 48–63.

8   For an excellent biblical, historical, and then contemporary overview see James I. McCord and T. L.
    Parker, eds., *Service in Christ: Essays Presented to Karl Barth on his 80th Birthday* (Epworth Press,
    1966). Also, J. N. Collins, *Diakonia: Re-interpreting the Ancient Sources* (Oxford University Press,
    1990); *The Diaconate as Ecumenical Opportunity*, Anglican-Lutheran International Commission
    (1996); Karl Barth, *Church Dogmatics*, vol. IV, part III, trans. G. W. Bromley (T & T Clark, 1962),
    pp. 889–90; Martin Bucer's *De Regno Christi*, in *Melanchthon and Bucer*, ed. Wilhelm Pauck (SCM
    Press, 1969), pp. 306–15.

9   Ignatius, *Epistle to the Smyrnaeans*, SC 10.162.

10 Cyprian, *On the Unity of the Church*, CCSL 3.5.252.

11 *Constitution of the Holy Apostles*, ANF 2.2.5.

12 Richard Hooker, *ibid.* 7.2.3.

13 Justin Martyr, *First Apology*, ANF 67.

14 Ibid.; Jerome, *Letter to Nepotian*, NPNF2 52.5.

15 The charge draws heavily on the proposed Anglican-Methodist Ordinal, drawn up as part of the
    unsuccessful scheme of union in England in 1968. The first two are new. Note the phrase, 'to lead
    in serving and caring for the people of God, and to work with them in the oversight of the Church', in
    R. C. D. Jasper and P. F. Bradshaw, eds., *A Companion to the Alternative Service Book* (SPCK, 1986),
    p. 440.

16 Jerome, ibid., 52.10; Chrysostom, ibid., 6.8.

17 'Man', said George Herbert (1593–1633), 'is the world's high priest: he doth present the sacrifice for
    all', in *Providence*. Cf. the ancient *Liturgy of St Mark*, ANF 3.17.

18 Ember Weeks Collect, for Vocations, ASB, p. 878.

19 See the late Russian Orthodox theologian, John Meyendorff, in *Catholicity and the Church* (St
    Vladimir's Seminary Press, 1983), pp. 26–9; and compare this with Constantine N. Tsirpanlis'
    statement, 'The Pneuma operates in all men and institutions . . .', in *Introduction to Eastern Patristic
    Thought and Orthodox Theology* (Liturgical Press, 1991), p. 86.

20 See also Rev. 5.

21 See, for example, Hans Küng, *The Church* (Burns and Oates, 1967), pp. 88–104.

22 Cf. ibid, pp. 162–179; Yves Congar, *The Word and the Spirit*, trans. David Smith (Geoffrey Chapman,
    1986); John Zizioulas, 'Communion and Otherness', *Sobornost, Incorporating Eastern Churches
    Review* 16:1 (1994): 7–19.

23 Cf. H. Richard Niebuhr, *Theology, History & Culture*, ed. William Stacy Johnson (Yale University Press,
    1996), pp. 63–73.

24 For example, the relationship between ceremonial and judicial law, the understanding and place of art
    in the Old and the New Testaments, gender roles, etc.

25 For an excellent overview of this very notion, see Gerhard von Rad, *Old Testament Theology*, 3 vols.,
    trans. D. M. G. Stalker (Oliver and Boyd, 1970), vol. 1, pp. 115–121, and especially n. 17.

26 Cf. 'The Decree on the Pastoral Office of Bishop in the Church of the Second Vatican Council, 1965', in
    N. P. Tanner, ed., *Decrees of the Ecumenical Councils, II* (Sheed and Ward, 1990), pp. 921–39.

27 Cf. the provision of Roman Catholic Canon Law in canons 375–411 of the Code of Canon Law,
    J. A. Coriden et al., eds., *The Code of Canon Law: A Text and Commentary* (Paulist Press, 1985)
    pp. 319–41.

28 On the early history, see Robin Lane Fox, *Pagans and Christians* (Penguin Books, 1986), chapter 10. Lane Fox argues that lifelong rule by a single bishop was a new phenomenon in the ancient world. The later history of the episcopacy is reviewed in *Episcopal Ministry*, pp. 39–77.

29 The connection between the term 'christos', anointed one, and the three-fold work of Christ as prophet, priest and king was made by Eusebius of Caesarea, *Ecclesiastical History*, NPNF2 1.3. It was developed by John Calvin in *Institutes of the Christian Religion*, trans. Henry Beveridge (Eerdmans, 1993), 2.15.1–2, and it entered Roman Catholic dogmatics in the nineteenth century through John Henry Newman, and is applied to the episcopal office in the *Dogmatic Constitutions of the Church: Second Vatican Council* (1964), sections 25–7. It is summarized in Canon 375: 'Through the Holy Spirit who has been given to them, bishops are the successors of the apostles by divine institution; they are constituted pastors within the Church so that they are teachers of doctrine, priests of sacred worship and ministers of governance.' See also, Geoffrey Wainwright, *For Our Salvation: Two Approaches to the Work of Christ* (Eerdmans, 1997).

30 The Ordinal, from the BCP. See also, Martin Bucer's *Censura*, in E. C. Whitaker, *Martin Bucer and the Book of Common Prayer* (Mayhew-McCrimmon Ltd., 1974) pp. 166–72.

31 The questions put to bishops are substantially the same as those asked of priests and deacons, with two variations on authority and evangelism. These bishops, priests and deacons agree to expound and teach the Christian Faith, 'as the Church of England has received it'.

32 From the Archbishop's prayer at the laying-on of hands, ASB, p. 394.

33 Hooker, ibid., I.15.2.

34 Note the BCP phrase in the 'Prayer for all conditions of men'; and the ASB requirement of the ordained that they promote the unity of all Christian people, ASB, p. 358.

35 To a 'college' of bishops in the context of the diocesan synod church law assigns a significant measure of responsibility for consent to major legislation. On suffragan bishops, see *Episcopal Ministry*, pp. 180–206.

36 There is an argument for saying that the oath of canonical obedience to the archbishop of the province, which is commonly taken before the service begins, should be publicly heard, as are the oaths of priests and deacons.

37 The bishop is to 'promote the mission of the Church throughout the world', ASB Ordinal, p. 388; see C. G. Brown, *The Death of Christian Britain* (Routledge, 2001), chapter 8.

38 See ARCIC, *The Gift of Authority* (CTS, 1999).

39 On the episcopate and canon law see especially N. Doe, *The Legal Framework of the Church of England* (Oxford: Oxford University Press, 1996).

40 The Jesuit theologian Henri de Lubac was especially robust in his denial that the ordination bestowed a higher dignity in participation in Christ, or a 'class of super-Christians', or made the ordained 'more of a Christian than the ordinary believer'. See *The Splendour of the Church* (Sheed and Ward, 1956), pp. 81–3. Compare with St Thomas Aquinas, *Summa Theologiae*, trans. Jordan Aumann O.P. (Blackfriars, 1973), 2a2ae.185.1–8.

41 The sardonic view of the lay theologian Origen (185–254) was that churches acquired the bishops they deserved; see his *Homily on Judges* 4:3; *Commentary on Matthew* 16:21-2; *Against Celsus*, 3.9; *Homily on Joshua* 7:6. See also R. Lane Fox, *Pagans and Christians*, p. 511, n. 58.

42 *Augsburg Confession*, Article 28.

43 See Bucer, *Censura*, pp. 168–70.

appendix E

1 Canon C1.

2 The Ordinal requires the reading of the Queen's mandate for the consecration and it is considered that the effect of the Suffragan Bishops Acts 1534 and 1898 is to prevent the consecration of a bishop other than to a specific see (see 'Senior Church Appointments' GS 1019, Appendix II).

3 Pursuant to Canon C12.

4 But the *ex officio* visitorships, trusteeships and governorships that are held by many diocesan bishops could probably be seen as temporalities.

5 This is certainly the case in the dioceses of the two archbishops and guardianship is claimed by the dean and chapter of Durham.

6 Canon C2.

7 Priests (Ordination of Women) Measure 1993, s.1(2).

8 For a fuller explanation of the procedure, see 'The role of the bishops in the second chamber' GS Misc 558, Annex C.

9 By the definite sentence, or act of confirmation, the vicar-general commits to the bishop-elect the care, governance and administration of the spiritualities. 'After election and confirmation, and not before, the bishop is fully invested to exercise all spiritual jurisdiction.' *The Ecclesiastical Law of the Church of England*, ed. W.G.F. Phillimore and C.F. Jemmett, second edition, p. 40.

10 Canon C2.

11 The names of the titular sees are contained in the Suffragan Bishops Act 1534 and are periodically added to or amended by Order in Council pursuant to the Suffragans Nomination Act 1888.

12 In accordance with the provisions of the Suffragan Bishops Act 1534.

13 Dioceses Measure 1978, s. 18.

14 'When a suffragan see is vacant the diocesan bishop has considerable freedom in choosing how to fill it. For instance he is not legally bound to consult or take advice before deciding on the two names to include in the petition to the Sovereign although in practice he will consult the Archbishop of the Province, who has the duty to consecrate the preferred candidate as required of him by the Sovereign. He is not required to consult people in his diocese, nor the Archbishops' Secretary for Appointments, although diocesan bishops invariably do both.' ('Senior Church Appointments' GS 1019, Appendix II, p. 6).

15 Dioceses Measure 1978, s. 10.

16 Although the giving of consent to an instrument of delegation may be a function that can be exercised under the standing orders of the synod by the bishop's council and standing committee (Church Representation Rules, rule 34(1)(k)).

17 The suffragan may, of course, be appointed chairman of various diocesan boards, committees and councils and he then has whatever authority the constitution of those boards and councils gives to the chairman.

18 Dioceses Measure 1978, s. 10(7).

19 Chelmsford, Chichester, Lichfield, London, Oxford, Salisbury, Southwark and Worcester.

20 Dioceses Measure 1978, s. 11.

21 Section 8.

22 Episcopal Ministry Act of Synod, recital (2).

23 Under s. 13(1)(b) of the Patronage (Benefices) Measure 1986.

24 A bishop who is physically or mentally incapacitated may be required by the archbishop to resign (Bishops (Retirement) Measure 1986); and a bishop guilty of an ecclesiastical offence may be subject to censure (including deprivation) under the Ecclesiastical Jurisdiction Measure 1963.

25 Human Rights Act 1998, s. 6(1).

26 Such as Dean of the Chapels Royal, Lord High Almoner and Clerk of the Closet.

27 This being the number of post-Reformation English and Welsh dioceses prior to the creation of new dioceses from the middle of the nineteenth century onwards.

28 See generally GS Misc 558.

29 Canon H3.

30 Any Measure, Canon or Act of Synod touching doctrinal formulae, the services or ceremonies of the Church or the administration of the Sacraments must be referred to the House before final approval by General Synod: Synodical Government Measure, Schedule 2, Article 7(1).

31 E.g. Canon C18, para. 2.

32 See para. 4.4 above.

33 Para. 4.3.

34 But if an archdeaconry becomes vacant because the holder has been appointed a diocesan bishop, the Crown will appoint his successor.

35 See para. 16.1 below.

36 There are diocesan secretaries who are in orders, but it is submitted that the post is lay in nature.

37 'Synodical Government in the Church of England' GS1252 at para. 6.38.

38 Diocesan Boards of Education Measure 1991, s. 1(4).

39 Church Representation Rules, Rule 30.

40 Synodical Government Measure 1969, s. 4.

41 Canon C18, para. 5.

42 See Synodical Government in the Church of England: A Review (The Bridge Report) GS1252, chapter 6.

43 Under Schedule 1 to the Pastoral Measure 1983.

44 Under the Schedule to the Diocesan Board of Education Measure 1991.

45 With the exception of those cathedral clergy not appointed by the bishop, at least to the extent of their ministry within the cathedral.

46 Under Canon C14. The oath is to 'pay true and canonical obedience . . . in all things lawful and honest'.

47 Such as suffragan bishops, deans and provosts, many residentiary canons, archdeacons and incumbents of benefices.

48 Or for life if their appointment pre-dated the retirement legislation.

49 Such as team vicars, many team rectors and some residentiary canons.

50 Under the Church Dignitaries Retirement Measure 1949 for incapacity in deans, provosts, residentiary canons and archdeacons; the Incumbents (Vacation of Benefices) Measure 1977 for incapacity in parochial incumbents or pastoral breakdown; and the Ecclesiastical Jurisdiction Measure 1963 where an ecclesiastical offence has been committed.

51 Canon C12, para. 5.

52 Other than those involving matters of doctrine, ritual or ceremonial.

53 Clergy Discipline Measure, s. 12.

54 The others are conditional deferment, conciliation, penalty by consent or formal investigation.

55 Clergy Discipline Measure, s. 13.

56 'Policy on Child Protection', Church House Publishing 1999.

57 See para. 13.2 above.

58 York, London, Hereford, Lincoln, Lichfield, Chichester, Exeter, Salisbury and Wells.

59 Canterbury, Winchester, Worcester, Ely, Carlisle, Durham, Rochester and Norwich.

60 Carlisle, which followed St Augustine's rule.

61 Chester, Peterborough, Oxford, Gloucester and Bristol.

62 Many of the provisions of this Measure do not apply to the cathedral church of Christ in Oxford – s. 37.

63 Sheffield and Bradford.

64 S. 9(1)(b) and s. 33.

65 See para. 13 above.

66 The authority for a bishop to appoint a priest in charge is contained in Canon C12. The present writers respectfully disagree with the assertion that a priest in charge has a cure of souls, contained in *Legal Opinions Concerning the Church of England* (Church House Publishing [1994], Supplement 1997), p. 214, para. 6.

67 Patronage (Benefices) Measure 1986, s. 13.

68 Patronage (Benefices) Measure 1986, ss 35 and 36.

69 Canon E1, para. 4.

70 See Canon C18, para. 4 and 'Points of Law and Practice Concerning Ecclesiastical Visitations' by Peter M Smith, 2 Ecc. LJ 189.

71 The Alternative Service Book 1980, page 382 (as amended by General Synod).

72 The exception being those who live within an extra-diocesan place such as a Royal peculiar and, possibly, some colleges in the Universities of Oxford and Cambridge.

73 The bishop is to have a special care for the outcast and needy: see declaration in the ASB Ordinal.

74 *English Canon Law*, ed. Norman Doe, Mark Hill and Robert Ombres (University of Wales Press 1998), p. 93, quoting E.W. Kemp, *Introduction to Canon Law in the Church of England* (London 1957).

75 See *Working as One Body: Report of Archbishops' Commission on the Organisation of the Church of England* (Church House Publishing 1995) esp. para. 6.40 quoting *English Canon Law*.

76 See 'The letter killeth, but the Spirit giveth life', an address to the Ecclesiastical Law Society's Conference at Manchester 14 March 1997 and reproduced 4 Ecc LJ p. 694.

77 4 Ecc. LJ 696.

Index

Index